THE INDEX TOWN WALLS

A Guide to Washington's Finest Crag

by Chris Kalman & Matty Van Biene

The Index Town Walls: A Guide to Washington's Finest Crag by Chris Kalman & Matty Van Biene

Published and distributed by:

Sharp End Publishing LLC

PO Box 1613

Boulder, CO 80306

t. 303-444-2698

www.sharpendbooks.com

ISBN: 978-1-892540-18-8

Cover Photos:

Graphic Designer: Sarah Nicholson

Proofreader: Melissa Lester

Publisher/Editor: Fred Knapp

Printed in Korea

WARNING

Climbing is a very dangerous activity. Take all precautions and evaluate your abili
carefully. Use judgment rather than the opinions represented in this book. The publisher and author assume no responsibility for injury or death resulting from the use of this book. This book is based on opinions. Do not rely on information, descriptions, or difficulty ratings as these are entirely subjective. If you are unwil
ing to assume complete responsibility for your safety, do not use this guidebook.

THE AUTHORS AND PUBLISHER EXPRESSLY DISCLAIM ALL REPRESENTATIONS AND WARRANTIES REGARDING THIS GUIDE, THE ACCURACY OF THE INFORM
TION HEREIN, AND THE RESULTS OF YOUR USE HEREOF, INCLUDING WITHOU
LIMITATION, IMPLIED WARRANTIES OF MERCHANTABILITY AND FITNESS FOR PARTICULAR PURPOSE. THE USER ASSUMES ALL RISK ASSOCIATED WITH THE USE OF THIS GUIDE.

It is your responsibility to take care of yourself while climbing. Seek a professiona
instructor or guide if you are unsure of your ability to handle any circumstances that may arise. This guide is not intended as an instructional manual.

ACKNOWLEDGMENTS

As is always true with a passion project, this one could not have been brought to fruition without an outpouring of support from the community, and our friends and loved ones. Without all the people who generously lent their time, energy, and emotional support along the way, this guidebook would have never happened.

The late Dave Pegg of Wolverine Publishing first lit the flame for this project when he expressed interest in it in 2013. Though he later sunk funds into other projects–without his support and confidence, this project would not have happened. RIP, Dave Pegg.

Before Dave stepped out of the picture, he put Chris and Matty in touch with Rob Price and Todd Kutzke–the brains behind Rakkup, who helped us to publish our digital guide in 2014. Their help with that process led directly to the creation of the book you hold in your hands. They also took Matt in an airplane (Rob's a pilot) to get aerial photos pro bono, and helped both us and Sharp End to bring the guide to print.

Of course, and this is not a shameless plug, Sharp End was absolutely unequivocally positively a dream to work with through the entire process. Fred Knapp is incredibly generous, kind, and easy to work with; and Sarah Nicholson is an absolute genius with all things graphic design-related. Without her, this guide would have taken three times as long to make, and would look one third as good.

The Washington Climber's Coalition deserves a special mention. Dave Haavik, Matt Perkins, Andy Salo, Darryl Cramer, Joe Sambataro, Eddie Espinoza, Truc Nguyen Allen, Jeremy Park–all these guys are incredibly important not just for their work at Index and for the part they played in purchasing and protecting the Lower Town Wall, but also for all they do for climbing in the great state of Washington. The entire board of the WCC encouraged us throughout the writing of this book, patiently walking us through the current state of access and land management. Darryl Cramer, in particular, deserves a big thank you. His guidebook, *Sky Valley Rock*, served as a template for this one, and an invaluable resource. Without his permission, we would never have taken the project on in the first place. Also, a big nod to Clint Cummins–for his incredible guidebook, available still (2017) at the Index General Store.

Many people lent a hand with thorough and helpful edits to the early proofs. Jon Nelson, Terry Lien, Greg Olsen, Blake Herrington, Ben Gilkison, Tom Ramier, Chris Henson, James Wyland, Michal Rynkiewicz, Ryan Hoover, Derek Pearson, Geoff Georges, Gabriel Cisneros, and Drew Philbin deserve a special thanks. Many of these folks, by the way, have put in countless hours establishing new routes, cleaning old ones, retrobolting, doing trail work, and performing other activities at Index.

Noted first ascentionists–past and present–deserve a huge thanks not just from us, but from everyone who climbs at Index. Darryl Cramer, Jon Nelson, Terry Lien, Greg Olsen, Greg Child, Greg Collum, Larry Kemp, Andy de Klerk, Dick Cilley, Max Dufford, Nicola Masciandaro, Erik Thixton, Cal Folsom (who was also instrumental in the construction of trails to UTW, Private Idaho and the Mid Walls), Karl Kaiyala, Justen Sjong, Mikey Schaefer, Mike Massey, Matt Kerns, Paul Boving, Debbie Brownstein, Jim Purdy, Fred Grafton, Chris Henson, Tom Ramier, James Wyland, Derek Pearson, Dave Repnik, Ben Gilkison, Blake Herrington, Steve Swenson, Michal Rynkiewicz, Ryan Hoover, Chandler Davis, and of course numerous others, worked their butts off to make Index what it is today.

Finally, the community is what makes Index the special place it is. We firmly believe that. Yes, the climbing is amazing. But if the people who frequented Index were not so endearing, it would not be such a wonderful place. In no particular order, and many other important people not withstanding, thank you to Brad Lignoski, Leah Zajac, Chris Tirrell, Mike and Ali Patz, Kevin Newell, Drew Philbin, Jens Holsten, Jess Campbell, Jenny Abegg, Doug Taylor, Sherri Lewis, Wayne Wallace, Sol Wertkin, Geoff Georges, Per Nesselquist, Kerwin Loukasa, Super Dave, Dirty Dave Elder, Grant Simmons, Dave Morrison, Jack Taylor, Rich Ellison, Kurt Hicks, Dave Burdick, Stamati Anagnostou, Abe Traven, Pat Sullivan, Mike Massey, Coach, Louie, Chuck.

A WORD FROM MATTY

Index. This is sacred ground. What you are holding in your hands, I hope, ends up being more than just a guide to rock climbs that you can go tick off willy-nilly (good luck with that by the way). It is my intention that this book serves as a lesson plan of sorts, for your own growth and learning. Learn about the area, its seasons, its inhabitants, the rivers, trees, and stone. Learn about the community. But mostly, learn about yourself. That is what I have experienced with Index as my teacher and what I most want to pass on to others.

I have encountered so much personal transformation within this forest and upon this stone that it's as if the whole arcana of Hindu deities is lurking throughout this corner of the Sky Valley, waiting for us to show up for our blessing. I have consulted Saraswati, the goddess of knowledge, in the midst of unlocking baffling cruxes. Ganesha has trumpeted forth through my growls and screams from within shallow corners and when scratching through barely-there crimpers. I've found myself dancing like Shiva, trying as gracefully as I can to land a foot on a distant knob. I've prayed to Lakshmi, for her luck, while standing on nothing slabs and channelled my inner Hanuman, the monkey god, to pull through the roofs of the upper wall. Durga, the Mother Goddess, represents inaccessibility which for me is always a common theme as I test myself at Index. It seems appropriate then that Kali, the dark mother and fiery goddess emerges from Durga's brow during battle, depicted holding a disembodied head that often represents the ego. It is indeed, in these moments, bloodied, beat, and battered where I've been able to submit to Index's rampage of difficulty, cast aside my expectations or fears, and humbly try again or call it a day and nurse my wounds in the healing waters of the North Fork of the Skykomish.

In either case, it is without fail that I have become wiser, tougher, more focused on the details, more nuanced in my action, and more grateful for the unique climbing experience that, as we like to say around here, Index provides. The specific medicine that climbing at Index bestows for you will likely be different than it is for me. Index will certainly dish out whatever it is that you need if you can allow yourself to leave your ego at the tracks, approach these walls with an open heart, and fall in love with this sacred place.

A WORD FROM CHRIS

I knew I wanted to help bring a modern guidebook to Index back in 2013 when I first heard that Sky Valley Rock was out of print. Of course, I didn't feel like I had any business authoring it. I was relatively new to the area, and hadn't even visited all the different walls yet. I queried some of my friends who I thought would be much better candidates, but none were interested. I asked Darryl Cramer if I could help him with an update to Sky Valley Rock, but he was too busy. Cramer's book was one of my most prized possessions! It seemed a shame to me that it was no longer available. And besides, a lot of new climbs had come along since he published his book. So I called Matty, asked if he would be interested in joining me in this crazy project, and before I knew it, we were getting to work.

That decision has not always been met with approbation and appreciation. Some people questioned my motives, others whether a guidebook would be a good thing for Index in the first place. Of course, I spent many long hours and sleepless nights agonizing over those very questions myself. I don't think there's one right answer; it depends upon your values and ethics. In the end, the ethic upon which I based my decision was one of conservation. I simply felt that–if done right–a new guidebook could help to conserve the incredible climbing resource that Index is. I have done my best throughout the past four years to keep that goal in mind, and to let it steer the ship.

Working on this book been a privilege, a pleasure, and a labor of love. I am grateful for the opportunity, and for everyone who has supported us in our efforts along the way. My parents, my sister, my friends (particularly Grant Simmons who repeatedly encouraged me to stick it out), and of course my loving girlfriend, Megan Kelly: thank you all for your unending support.

A new guidebook for this area can be a scary thing. But I firmly believe that the key to keeping Index spectacular is not in keeping it a secret (that ship has sailed, folks), but in sharing the love you have for the place with everyone who comes to climb here. Show them what makes this place so special, teach them about local ethics, demonstrate for them how to be a proper steward of the Index Town Walls. That is how you will foster community, and make sure that Index continues to provide for generations to come.

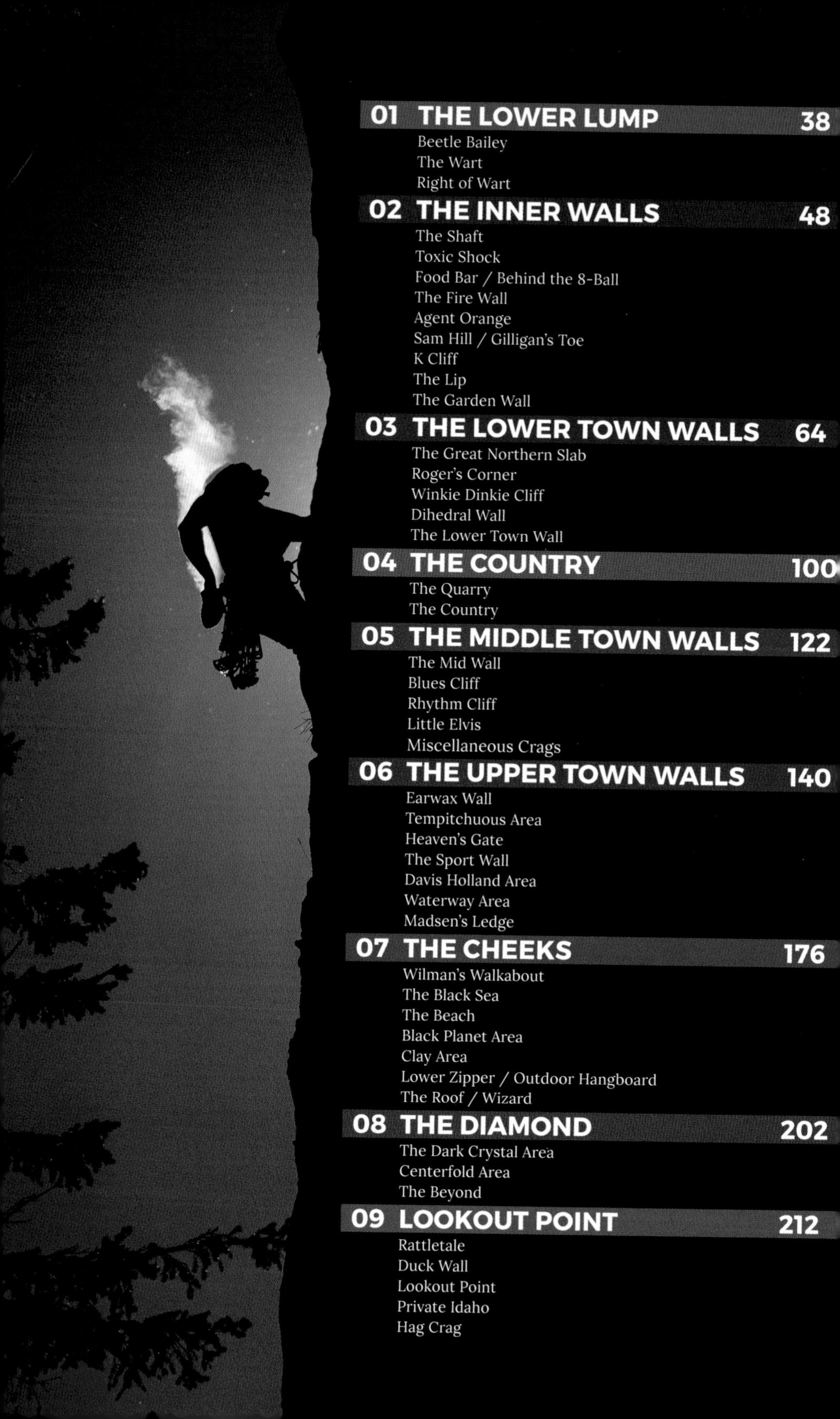

Andy de Klerk on Amandla, 1992 | Photo by Larry Kemp

REFACE

ıen we set out to make this book, our initial intention was to cover (and climb) every square inch of every gle route at Index. Our motivation was simple: to give back to the Index climbing community a guidebook t was accurate, informative, and beautiful. As we began to work on the book and delved deeper into the ries and history of Index climbing we began to realize that our initial goal was, given finite time and space, ıttainable. So we reformed it a little.

st of all, it is essential to understand that the Index Town Walls exist hin a temperate rainforest. It is both anomalous and wonderful that re is any dry, clean rock there at all. The sheer quantity of both at the ex Town Walls is, in and of itself, an argument for intelligent design. at said, the climate and forest act upon the rock in very predictable ways. ıtes that do not get climbed over and over again, year in and year out, reclaimed by the forest. Bolts, pins, and other fixed hardware that are stainless steel rust, corrode, and become unsafe. Moss swallows up ole faces. Dirt settles into cracks. Crimps get fuzzy. Spiders make their nes in fingerlocks, pods, and seams. For a guidebook to document every nbing route ever established at Index is possible—but to give reliable d current details on every such route at any given time is not. Some old nbs have been erased by rockfall, some are indistinguishable from the getation around them, and some are simply so out of vogue that they will ver see a second ascent.

lex has more neglected world-class routes than any other crag we can nk of. We surmise that this is largely due to two things: 1) a lack of motivation on the part of the community leave the comfy glory of the Lower Town Wall (LTW), and 2) a lack of reliable up-to-date information about other walls. The LTW is the closest wall to the parking lot, and it is where 90% of the climbing occurs at lex. Yet the quality of the rock and routes at Index stays consistently high throughout the whole area. As ffic continues to grow, and the community continues to expand, the LTW becomes more and more crowd-. Meanwhile, other area gems fade into obscurity.

we began plodding around the woods, exploring reclaimed and largely forgotten routes, our vision for the idebook began to shift. Our intention would not be to simply create a historically accurate document that s beautiful and informative. Our goal became to use this guidebook as a resource to help spread out the ckening traffic from the LTW to the other routes and crags that so deserve (and need) that traffic. With s book, we have attempted to create not only an accurate and comprehensive list, but also a weighted one. rough pictures, storytelling, and other tools, we have intentionally tried to draw the reader's (your) eye to mbs and crags you may not have seen before.

other words, we are trying to tantalize you to get out and explore. Spread out, find new areas, climb with rush, pull out weeds instead of just cursing them. When a climb is dirty, clean it up. When a wall has no ıtes, add some. Four star climbs were still being discovered in 2017. Chances are, they will be in 2018, and 19, and so on.

increasing traffic to other walls, and relieving traffic from the LTW, the Index climbing community can eate, maintain, and preserve this special place. If you are reading this, you are now a part of this proud com-ınity. Get out there, look around, and try your best to climb at all of Index's wonderful walls.

INTRODUCTION

* This entire book borrows heavily from Darryl Cramer's 2000 guidebook, *Sky Valley Rock*. The authors do not claim, or intend to claim, anything to the contrary. *Sky Valley Rock* was a primary resource for the writing of this book, and is often quoted, paraphrased, and emulated in the pages to follow.

What you hold in your hands is a climbing guidebook to what is generally accepted as the best crag in Washington, often touted as the best crag on the planet, and occasionally lauded with the high superlative of number one crag in the entire universe. While the weight of statistics lies against the latter assertion, the former two are likely true. For the authors of this book, it is certainly the best crag we have ever climbed at.

The Index Town Walls are a phenomenal collection of granite cliffs in the Skykomish Valley, just outside Seattle. The rock quality is incredible, and features a staggering array of climbing types. Everything from well-protected splitters, to multi-pitch sport and trad routes, to Grade IV aid climbs, to modern-style sport clip-ups can be found nestled in this scenic destination. The climbing style is unique. The weather is persnickety, but when it's good it's perfect. The surrounding views of some of the most jagged peaks in the Cascades are breathtaking; and the rock quality is out of this world. Imagine a hybrid of knobby Tuolumne faces, mixed with parallel-sided Yosemite Valley cracks, but with the texture of UK gritstone. The combination is astounding: knobs, pockets, crimps, jugs and slopers; seams, finger, hand, and offwidth cracks; stem corners, bomb-bay chimneys, friction arêtes, compression problems, and bouldery sequences; routes from 40 to 700 feet... and much more. Add to that a short approach, an abundance of four star routes from 5.6 to 5.13+, and a proclivity for safe falls, and you have all the makings of a crag so good that God, Yahweh, Allah, or whatever you want to call the great gig in the sky, would climb there him or herself.

Darryl Cramer's Sky Valley Rock

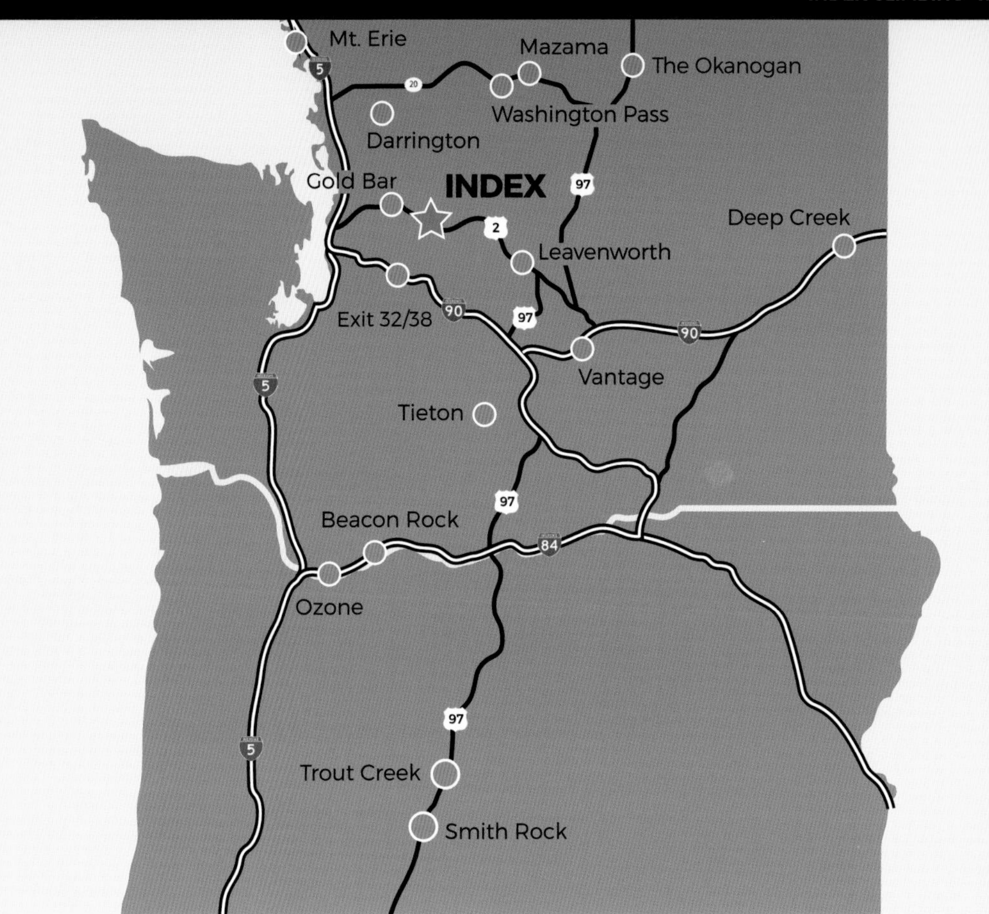

ɜETTING THERE

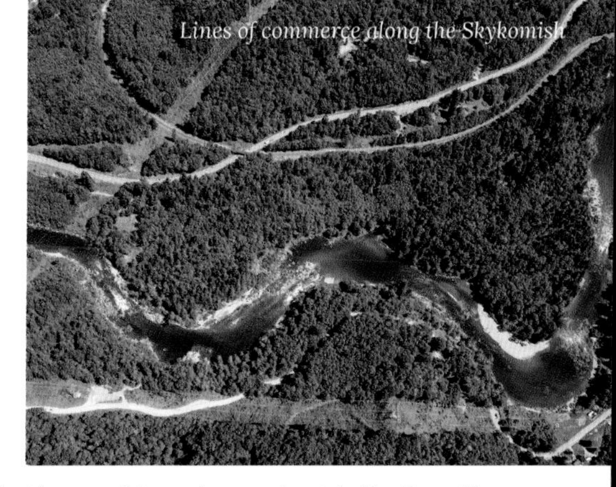
Lines of commerce along the Skykomish

ndex is located in northwest Washington state, along ighway 2. It is 54 miles northeast of Seattle, 60 miles est of Leavenworth, 120 miles northeast of Olympia, 50 miles southeast of Vancouver, B.C., 160 miles orthwest of Yakima, 220 miles northeast of Portland, regon, and 260 miles west of Spokane. The nearest ajor metropolitan area is Monroe–21 miles to the est.

herever you are coming from, you will access Index a Highway 2. If you are coming from the west, ontinue east along Highway 2 past Monroe, Sultan, tartup, and Goldbar. When you are 7.5 miles east of oldbar, turn left onto the Index Galena Road. If comg from the east, look for the Index Galena turnoff n your right 13.2 miles after the town of Skykomish. Continue on this road approximately ½ mile until you can rn left on 5th Street into the town of Index.

you are climbing at Lookout Point or The Diamond, park on 5th Street next to the city park and the post ffice. If you are climbing anywhere else at Index, continue on 5th Street one block until it dead-ends. Turn ft. Cross the train tracks, and continue another two blocks, around a 90 degree left hand turn, until the road ead-ends at a stop sign. Turn right (west). There is a large parking lot on your left after 100 yards (campound), and then another large lot on the right at 200 yards (Lower Wall lot). The last lot is the closest one to e Lower Town Walls, but can often be quite crowded and prone to car break-ins. No matter where you park, u're never more than half a mile from the Lower Town Wall.

BOULDERING
PROJECT

SEATTLE BOULDERING PROJECT
S·B·P

www.SEATTLEBOULDERINGPROJECT.com

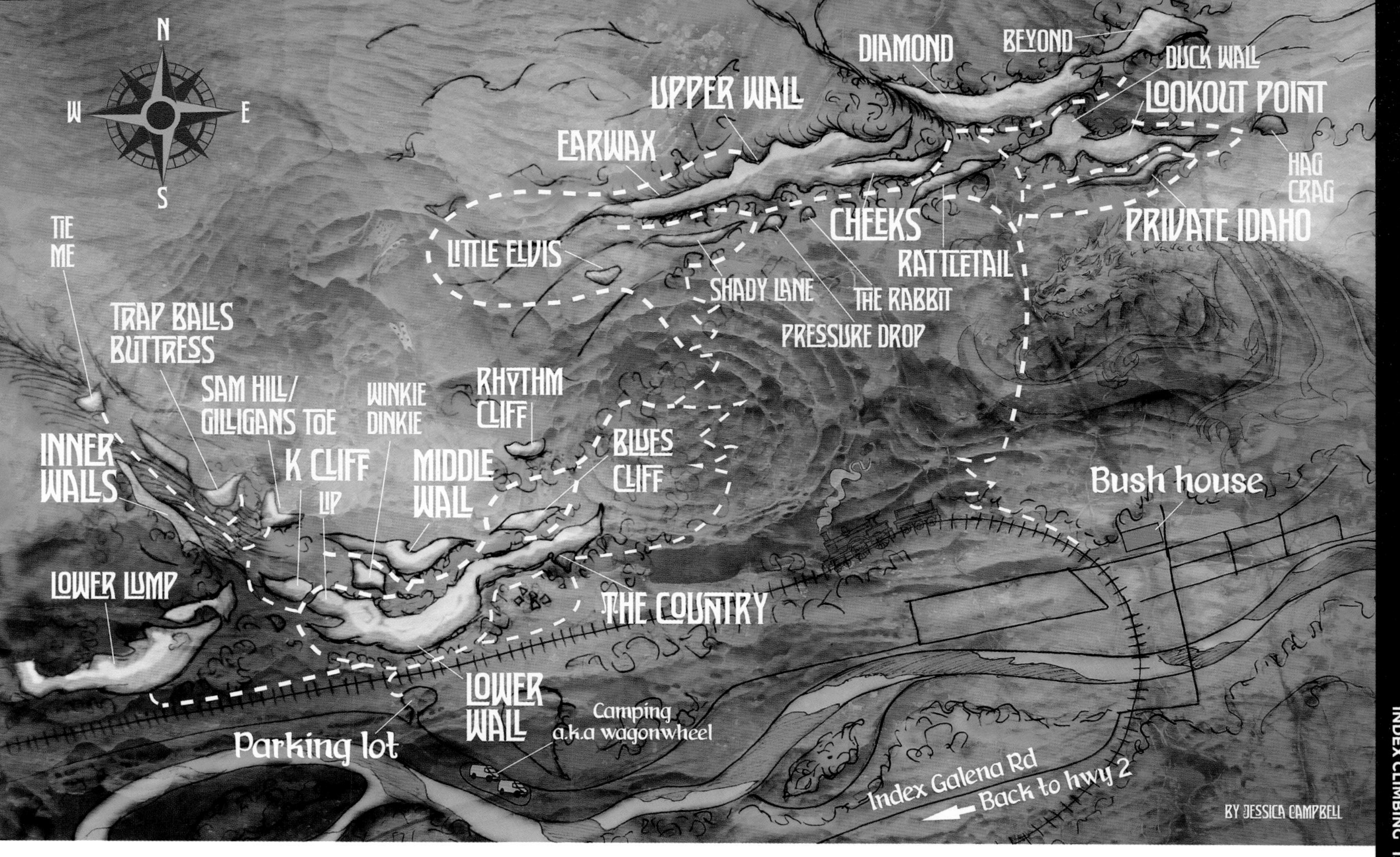
N
W
E
S
DIAMOND
BEYOND
DUCK WALL
UPPER WALL
LOOKOUT POINT
EARWAX
HAG CRAG
CHEEKS
PRIVATE IDAHO
LITTLE ELVIS
RATTLETAIL
TIE ME
SHADY LANE
THE RABBIT
PRESSURE DROP
TRAP BALLS BUTTRESS
RHYTHM CLIFF
SAM HILL/ GILLIGANS TOE
WINKIE DINKIE
INNER WALLS
K CLIFF
LIP
MIDDLE WALL
BLUES CLIFF
Bush house
LOWER LUMP
THE COUNTRY
LOWER WALL
Camping a.k.a wagonwheel
Parking lot
Index Galena Rd
Back to hwy 2
BY JESSICA CAMPBELL

We are excited to welcome Kai Lightner into the Bluewater Climbing family. Kai is an inspiring and kind person on and off the rock. We are honored to be keeping him safe with the softest catching, most durable climbing ropes in the world.
@kailightner
kailightner
ALWAYS BETWEEN YOU AND THE GROUND
BlueWater Ropes

Blake Herrington tackling the roof on Narrow Arrow Overhang (5.13a)

Bivying along the Skykomish.

ROOM AND BOARD

One of the joys of Index is how quaint and underdeveloped the tiny town is. Index itself is not an area for commerce, with the exception of the General Store and the Outdoor Adventure Center (commonly referred to as the River House). You can get beer and snacks at both but not much else. For most modern amenities, you'll need to head to Monroe or at least Gold Bar.

Currently, camping at Index is free, and a privilege. The main camping area is part of the Baker-Snoqualmie National Forest, and they enforce a two-week limit. Please respect the rules, and be friendly with the various FS personnel that come to maintain the place. Extended camping can be exchanged for volunteering, which is a good idea anyway and a great deal.

In the near future, the Outdoor Adventure Center plans to reopen the historic Bush House Inn and an established, paid campground nearby. For now, though, the best camping option is along the beautiful Skykomish River at the first gravel pullout on the left. This campground is enjoyed by a pretty diverse crowd: boaters, bikers, climbers, hikers, car-campers, and partying teenagers. Traditionally, it's also seen a strong presence from the methamphetamine and homeless communities—although major efforts were recently made by the county sheriff to enforce the camping limit and crack down on criminal activity.

Whoever your neighbor may be, do like your kindergarten teacher told you and follow the Golden Rule. There are many "atypical" looking individuals around Index who are not meth heads at all. That guy in flip flops, below-the-knee basketball shorts, and an oversized hoodie might just grab a few quickdraws and casually put a rope up on *Natural Log Cabin* for you, as you try to scrape your bottom jaw off the ground—so mind your manners.

A typical Friday night in Index.

he characters at Index are part of what makes the area special. They may look like they wandered out of an ld mineshaft somewhere deep within the hillside, and sound as if they've been smoking, drinking, and carous- ng for the better part of the last century. They may ask for beer, weed, carabiners, or all of the above–but they re neither thieves nor meth heads. They are harmless. Treat them, and everyone else you meet at Index, with espect and courtesy. People began loving (and living at) Index long before cams existed, rock climbing was in ogue, and the hipster revolution occurred. Be respectful of those who came before you, and those who will ome after you.

our options for nearby restaurants are mostly greasy, cheap, and filling. La Hacienda in Gold Bar is close, and as a great happy hour as well as $1 Taco Tuesdays. The Sultan Bakery has enormous portions at miniscule rices. Monroe has a Vietnamese restaurant, a Thai restaurant, and one of the best taco trucks around–La ichoacana. Located a block south of Highway 2 on Route 203 in Monroe in a gravel lot on the east side of the oad, La Michoacana has baby-sized burritos at an affordable price, and some of the best salsa options around.

our best bet for groceries is to get them before you arrive in Index. Monroe has an Albertsons, and a Grocery utlet. The Grocery Outlet sometimes has fantastic deals on Ben and Jerry's ice cream, and Clif Bars. In a inch, the General Store has you covered for beer, microwave burritos, canned food and the like. The best food the entire Sky Valley is almost certainly the little roadside cherry stands that pop up each summer along the ighway 2 corridor. These small shops have incredible cherries, apples, nectarines, salmon jerky, and other onderful foods at typically affordable prices. If you miss the Rainier cherries, you're missing out.

GEOLOGY

The Index Town Walls are part of the southern end of the geologic formation known as the Index batholith. Recent zircon and fission-track dating indicate that this chunk of stone is likely somewhere between 29 and 35 million years old. According to a research paper written in 2006 for the United States Geologic Survey, the Index batholith ranges from quartz diorite to rare granite, but it is predominantly tonalite and granodiorite. According to Darryl Cramer's *Sky Valley Rock*, however, the Index Town Walls themselves are a granite rich in biotite and hornblende—a rare rock within the Index batholith, which may explain why the rock here is so unique and special.

Greg Olsen on Preying Mantle back when it still existed. | Photo by Mike Mirande

ocal climber and geology student, Gabriel Cisneros, described batholiths thusly: "Imagine a batholith is a lava lamp and the blobs inside are the plutons. Not only is each pluton slightly different, a pluton can also have internal differences within their mineral assemblage and grain size due to different rates of cooling and changing pressures. As the pluton cools, it experiences a wide range of temperatures. Different minerals crystallize at different temperatures and the composition of the remaining magma changes. The result are plutons and batholiths with slight variations in mineral composition and grain size."

ust as other rocks of the Index batholith differ rom that found at Index, so too does the rock at ndex vary from wall to wall. Lower Town Wall rock s typically more grippy and rounded than Upper Town Wall rock. The Cheeks, The Diamond, Lookout Point, the Inner Walls—indeed, all the major ubregions of the Index Town Walls—have their wn unique and distinct feel.

ccording to Cramer, compression tests have shown Index granite to withstand pressures of 18,000 psi, naking it three to six times stronger than concrete. Yet, not every hold you touch is inherently solid. Index ock fractures in both horizontal and vertical lines, and can be subject to loose blocks, or even stacks of loose locks. Geologic time at Index is right now, and boulders the size of compact cars have been dislodged by limbers in the recent past. When placing protection behind flakes, always use caution. Even on popular LTW outes, loose blocks and flakes are still displaced from time to time (*Princely Ambitions* and *Shirley* provide two ecent examples).

ne of the wonderful things about Index rock is the regular presence of geologic intrusions and other anomlies. The ubiquitous Index knob is an example, as are crystal dikes. Both are found in abundance, and create xcellent face-climbing features. *Echolocation* is one of the most astounding knob climbs in Index, while *Heavn's Gate* follows a huge dike for almost all of its four pitches. Dikes and knobs make for some of Index's most nemorable and interesting climbs, and lend diversity to the area in a way few granite crags can emulate.

FLORA AND FAUNA

The Skykomish River Valley is incredibly wet—like 100 inches of precipitation per year wet. The area is part of a temperate rainforest, and you can certainly expect it to look, feel, and act like one. While many people complain about the rain, one should keep in mind (and close to heart) the important role it plays in creating and sustaining this spectacular ecosystem. The forests surrounding the perfect granite are intricate, robust, and vibrant habitats. Amazing things are happening in the forest all the time—just look around. Mosses and lichens cover almost every square inch of usable real estate (often to the chagrin of route developers). Dewdrops hang suspended from the slick tips of upshot mushrooms. Hermaphroditic banana slugs copulate—literally for hours—in nature's yin yang, each oozing away from the soiree, both father and mother of future slugs.

Oyster mushrooms: a proud bounty for a post-climb dinner!

Edible plants and fungi abound at Index. Black, salm-on, and huckle berries, salal, miner's lettuce, sorel, and wild mustards are just a few of the many tasty treats to be found in the area (the salmon berries in particular are a delicacy). Of course, in the Pacific Northwest, edible fungi are ubiquitous. Those with a good eye and a penchant for bushwhacking will find morels and lobster mushrooms in the spring, chante-relles and boletes in the fall, and oyster mushrooms year round.

The mighty Skykomish River.

The predominantly Douglas Fir forest (although it is in the Western Hemlock forest zone) is home to pine martens, black bears, foxes, coyotes, peregrine falcons, bald eagles, osprey, and (of course) bobcats. From time to time, there are closures on the upper town walls for peregrine falcon nesting. This has been the subject of hot debate in the past—and it is currently inconclusive whether raptor closures do anything at all for the birds. That said, staying away from peregrines—who can dive at speeds approaching 200 miles per hour—is almost certainly in the best interest of climbers. In any case, raptor closures are monitored and enforced, and we encourage you to respect them.

Fifty shades of green in the dense Index woods.

The Skykomish River is a wonderful spot to take a dip, cool your beers, or soak your forearms any time of year. Aside from its breathtaking beauty, it also hosts summer and winter runs of steelhead, and five distinct species of Pacific salmon (Pink, Silver, Chum, Sockeye and Chinook). In the fall, sea-run cutthroats spawn on the Skykomish, passing Index along the way. Their epic journey is incredible to watch as they bob, weave, and jockey for position. By the time they reach Index, many of the great fish are so beleaguered and decrepit that they simply eddy out near the shores, and die. The salmon spawn is one of the world's largest migrations of nutrients from one biome (ocean) to another (river valley), and is a vital part of the ecosystem.

Today, the Skykomish is part of one of the last "intact watersheds" (meaning composed of undammed rivers) in the lower 48. It is pristine, clean, and beautiful. That said, in 2012, American Rivers named it the 7th most endangered river in America, due to a proposed dam on the South Fork. While Index itself sits on the North Fork, a dam on the South Fork would set a dangerous precedent that could affect the entire area. As of 2017, it was still common to see signs and pickets along the Highway 2 corridor imploring, "Don't Dam the Sky!" Read up on the issue, and participate in the conservation, at http://www.savetheskyriver.org/.

HISTORY

As with just about anywhere in the United States the human history in Washington starts long before white folks came along. In the case of Index, the first people were the eponymous Skykomish. The name Skykomish comes from the Salish words skai ("inland") and mish ("people"). Until about the 1850s, these people lived in relative peace along the banks of the Skykomish River, mostly between present-day Monroe and Index. With the arrival of Euro-American settlers in the middle of the 19th century, the Skykomish—like many of the native tribes in the Puget Sound area and elsewhere—were ravaged by smallpox and other diseases. Early estimates at the number of Skykomish people prior to 1850 are variable, but by 1900, only a few hundred remained. In 1855 the Skykomish, along with a number of other tribes, signed the Point Elliot Treaty, and were assigned to the Tulalip reservation along the Puget Sound, nearly 50 miles northwest of Index. Of course, this reservation is by no means inland, and the geology, topography, climate, and ecology of that region differ greatly from the Skykomish River Valley. As late as 1900, a village of 240 Skykomish people was still in existence near Gold Bar. Today, though, the vast majority of Skykomish descendants continue to live on the Tulalip reservation, along with Snohomish, Snoqualmie, and people of other tribes.

Once the majority of the Skykomish people had been killed by disease or removed by treaty, the Skykomish Valley was declared by white settlers to be "open for business." Early timber operations existed along the riverbanks, and eventually, spread up the walls of the valley. Signs of timber operations, both past and present, are still ubiquitous throughout the Skykomish Valley, and much of the western portion of the state.

In 1892, the Great Northern Railroad was completed, cutting straight through the present day Highway 2 corridor. The arrival of the railroad to Index meant two things: first, easy transportation of people; second, easy transportation of very heavy materials, such as huge chunks of granite. And so, Index got its first big economic

break. By the turn of the century, the quarry at Index dominated the granite market in the Puget Sound. Many of the granite structures in Seattle, as well as the steps of the capitol building in Olympia, came from Index. You can (and should) visit the mining museum in town to learn much more about this era.

The most obvious and glaring remnant of the mining era is undoubtedly the enormous tunnel in the main wall at The Country, which was dug in 1984 by the Robbins Company (whose equipment helped to dig the Chunnel, between France and Great Britain). The Robbins Company signed a contract with the Department of Natural Resources (DNR) giving them access to test-mining at Index until 2003. In digging the 12' x 21' x 278' tunnel, the company's "Mobile Miner" removed nearly 2600 cubic yards of material from the wall. According to Darryl Cramer's introduction to *Sky Valley Rock*, "Due to the involvement of several people, the concerns of climbers were addressed and, instead of destroying the walls, the Robbins Company limited their activities and graded a parking lot and road now used almost exclusively by climbers." After the Robbins company gave up their rights to test-mining, the tunnel was used, for a time, by the University of Washington's Physics Department for experiments meant to prove the existence of the "Fifth Force."

During the U of W's tenure in the ndex tunnel, a large, padlocked vrought-iron door was installed at ts entrance. A clear, watery liquid vould perpetually ooze out from beneath the door, arousing suspicions and sparking imaginations of local limbers. In 2013, the door was emphatically sealed behind a concrete wall spanning the entire entrance. Yet he clear liquid continues to ooze from small pipes at the base of the wall. The obvious questions one needs to sk, in regards to the Index tunnel, are as follows: 1) Is it monsters or aliens that are sealed behind the wall; and) Is the clear ooze saliva from their rabid imaginings at the disembowelment of their human captors, or is it n endless stream of tears from their poor lonely souls? The scarier, and more plausible, idea that the door and vall were both installed in an attempt to protect visitors from harmful radiation left over from the Fifth Force xperiments is best unimagined.

owadays, the biggest fiscal draw of Index and the surrounding areas is, quite conspicuously, tourism. In 000, Cramer estimated that "over 15,000 people each year raft the Skykomish with commercial outfitters." oday, that number continues to rise steadily. Climbing, too, continues to grow in popularity. The number of limbing gyms in the Seatac area has more than doubled since the Cramer guide—a testament to the success f the industry. Furthermore, trad climbing is becoming more and more fashionable as major industry brands creasingly market the "adventure" aspect of climbing over the "sport" aspect. Car companies, banks, and even ollywood stars have caught on to the climbing craze. So we can expect climbing visitation to increase, at least r the foreseeable future.

CLIMBING HISTORY

Index's climbing history is typified by waves. Crests and troughs of activity have defined the area from time to time, decade to decade. At the time of the writing of this book, Index is experiencing another wave of exciting development, and a major outreach of support from the community. How long that will last is uncertain.

Like many crags in the United States, climbing at Index began as more of a training exercise than anything else. Washington is chock-full of incredible alpine peaks–many featuring excellent granite–and the Great Northern Slab (or the Free Area, as it was historically called) was a conspicuous training ground. The cracks and features of the LTW, and the tactics needed to climb the UTW, also bore an obvious resemblance to Yosemite. Being so close to Seattle, Index was for many years the perfect place for Washington climbers to hone their skills (although Leavenworth was then, and still remains, more popular).

1960s

While the majority of Index climbers today tend to stick to the Lower Town Wall crags, the 1960s were all about the Upper Town Wall. This should come as no surprise in the context of the "big objective" climbing of that era. The UTW is certainly the biggest, proudest, and most impressive wall at Index. If your eye was bent towards climbing mountains, you'd likely glance over the LTW entirely. In 1964, Dan Davis and John Holland rang in what "is generally regarded as the beginning of serious climbing at Index," according to Cramer, with a proud route through the tallest part of Index's tallest wall. The *Davis-Holland* is still a cherished classic, though it is now climbed almost solely as a free route. In 1966, *Town Crier* was established after several years of effort by nine different individuals, including (of course) the indomitable Fred Beckey. Though *Town Crier* was eventually freed (in 2007, by Justen Sjong) it is generally still aided, and is likely the most popular aid route on the UTW. *Waterway Left* and *Golden Arch* were two other notable routes of this epoch, both climbed in 1967. Sadly, one of the *Golden Arch*'s first ascentionists–Jim Madsen–perished, shortly after the FA, in the course of a rescue in Yosemite. The large ledge cutting across the right side of the Upper Town Wall was named in his honor. According to Royal Robbins, in an obituary in the 1969 edition of the *American Alpine Journal*, "Jim Madsen was one of the most shining of a brilliant new generation of young American climbers... He was the stuff of which heroes are made. And he loved the beauty of the mountains."

It wasn't all UTW in the 60s, though. The LTW had a small group of devotees busily ticking off some of the most obvious lines in the area. Doug Leen, Roger Johnson, Richard Mathies, and Greg Donaldson gave life to obvious classics such as *City Park*, *Iron Horse*, and *Roger's Corner* as well as many other variations–all using aid climbing tactics. Perhaps most impressively, Donaldson and Mathies climbed the full *Narrow Arrow Overhang* in 1968.

During this period, Index saw its first-ever climbing guide, a modest book penned by Donaldson. By the 70s the stage was set for a free climbing explosion.

Max Dufford demonstrating the "French blow" | Photo by Larry Kemp

70s

ing this era, free climbing at Index began to develop as climbers (most notably Mark Weigelt) began to "sys-
atically and extensively clean the routes [at Index]" as Cramer writes, in *Sky Valley Rock*. The result of this
ning was the development of The Free Area—now known as the Great Northern Slab (GNS). At the time,
ost all the free routes at Index were on the GNS. Meanwhile, aid climbers ticked off nearly every obvious
ck system on the LTW. Index climbers began to make a stir in the larger climbing community as well, with
first hammerless ascent of The Nose of El Capitan (Index local Bruce Carson, in 1974, with Yvon Chouinard),
the first hammerless ascent of a Grade VI (according to Cramer, though I can not find information to
roborate this report).

ou're imagining that everyone was weaning off aid climbing at this time by freeing lowly 5.6s and 5.7s on the
S, think again. Don Heller and Don Harder snagged the first free ascent of *Godzilla* (5.9+) in 1972. *The Da-
Holland* got its first free ascent in this decade—a combined effort by Al Givler, Tom Nephew, Mead Hargis,
Ossiander, and Pete Doorish. Perhaps most notably, Paul Boving freed *Thin Fingers* in 1977 (the tricky 5.11a
x still baffles many a strong climber today). Keep in mind that Wild Country did not start manufacturing Ray
dine's newly-invented cams until 1977. All of these routes were freed on pins, nuts and hexes.

ly, Boving fell and died attempting to repeat *Thin Fingers* in 1977, shortly after his groundbreaking first free
ent. Boving was an incredibly gifted climber, and well-known throughout the community. In spite of so
ny successes throughout the 70s, including early efforts at a new guidebook which were printed in *Summit*
gazine, Boving's death ushered in Index's first obvious lull—a period Cramer referred to as "The Doldrums."

980s

ile the early 80s saw Index's first real guidebook, and Peter Croft freed *Iron Horse* to the *Ringing Flake* (in
1!), progress came slowly for Index climbing. Leavenworth was still seen as the go-to area for Washington
nbers, and with the UTW climbed and freed, Index no longer had any "big objectives"—at least from a moun-
ieering perspective. Yet a dedicated cadre of devotees remained, and went quietly about their work, clean-
and even bolting on rappel. This decade marks the beginning of what might most appropriately be called
Cramer-Nelson-Olsen-Lien-Dufford-Folsom-Collum Era. During the next 20 years, those seven climbers
d a variety of others, to a lesser extent) would combine to establish the majority of the routes at Index.

hough bolting on rappel was the scourge of the time, and drew significant reproach from the climbing com-
nity when it became de rigueur at Smith Rock, few people
de a fuss when Greg Olsen and Jon Nelson (two of Index's
st prolific first ascentionists) rap bolted *Terminal Preppie*
starlight in 1982. At the time, such a move would have been
tright blasphemy nearly anywhere else in the country. But
Index, things were different. "Ground-up FAs at Index were
t of the question, so it didn't seem like any contradiction at
to prep routes on rappel," Olsen explained, in a *Climbing*
gazine article called The Index Club, which came out in
09. "At some point...I began to feel that bolting was simply
other cleaning task. Much less difference between brushing
d bolting once ground-up [ethics aren't] applicable. It all
t starts to feel like route prep after eight hours of scrub-
ng. Nobody would be climbing at Index today had it been
veloped as a collection of one-time moss epics."

cording to Greg Olsen, the roto-hammer did not hit Index
til much later. Virtually all of the LTW shield routes were
lted by hand. Even so, Terry Lien was a hand-drilling ma-
ine, and face climbing at Index was born. Incredible walls
ch as the Sport and Earwax walls (sadly, these have become
s and less popular over time, due in part to decaying bolts
ring the 80s) were heavily bolted almost overnight.

ce climbing became all the rage at Index, but good clean
ack climbing did not disappear entirely. A certain gentle-
an from Wyoming, the late Todd Skinner, set up camp along
e Skykomish River, and began rehearsing the moves on the
W's most obvious and aesthetic crack: *City Park*. He was

Greg Olsen on the FA of Leapin' Lizards (5.10c) | Photo by Russell Erickson

not a local, which was strike one. And in spite of the laissez-faire ethics of the era, his rehearsal of the move on toprope earned him (at least with some locals) strike two. Also, Skinner was a well-known and well-publicized climber, and he made sure to have photographers on hand to document his climb. Strike three. To thw his efforts, local climbers smeared grease from the nearby railroad all over the tiny crack. But Skinner was n to be deterred. He burned the crac clean with a blowtorch, and eventu fired *City Park's* first free ascent in 1986 on pre-placed gear.

A busy day at Index in the 80s | Photo by Larry Kemp

At the time, *City Park* (5.13+) was th hardest crack climb in the country. It may not hold the same distinctio now, but to this day it has still only seen a handful of free ascents. *City Park* saw its second free ascent the same year, when the double amput Hugh Herr, climbed it with custom made attachments for the end of hi prosthetic legs to fit into the tiny constrictions (RESPECT). It would not see another free ascent until 19 (Chris Schlotfeldt); and didn't reciev a proper redpoint until 2006 (Mikey Schaefer).

A new guidebook was printed in 198 and listed 142 routes.

1990s

In *Sky Valley Rock*, Cramer says surprisingly little about the 90s at Index. He notes the legendary Karl Kaiyala return and his ascent of *Sisu* in 1990, prompted by the advent of sport climbing. *Sisu* was the UTW's first rou established all free—and this ushered in an era of new possibilities. Within a year, three other full-height free routes graced the UTW. Cramer went on to add that aid climbing came back into vogue, and that The Quarry got a few routes, but that's about it. "All in all," he states, "the last half of the decade was reminiscent of the doldrums of the 70s."

If this is truly the case, it must be due to an absolute explosion of routes from 1986 to 1993. Between 1960 an 1986, the number of documented routes at Index grew from zero to 142. That's an average of 5.5 routes per year. Between the 1986 guidebook, and Clint Cummins' 1993 spiral-bound paper guidebook (still available in the Index store today!), that number of routes ballooned from 142 to 521. If we average that increase evenly over the seven years between guidebooks, we see a growth of a whopping 54.14 new routes per year. This wa almost certainly the most productive period of Index new-routing. Furthermore, since there is a finite amou of cliff space at Index, one would expect there to be a finite amount of routes. Hence, route establishment graphed against time would have to taper off eventually. If the latter part of the 90s were slow in terms of ne route production, perhaps it was only because there was comparatively little real estate, and because the ear part of the 90s was so productive.

At the same time as climbers were freeing ground-breaking lines (in 1992, Andy de Klerk freed *Amandla*, 5.13b/c), and breaking-in routes through cleaning and regular traffic, Darryl Cramer, Dave Haavik, and others were beginning to form what would become the Washington Climber's Coalition. Seattle's Vertical World (America's first climbing gym) transitioned from a club to a business, and even loaned Cramer use of their co puters while he was putting together Index's best guidebook to date, *Sky Valley Rock*.

While a historical vision of progress (new routing) may have slowed in the late 90s, a modern version of progress (conservation, crag and route maintenance, and community building) grew. Index started to become a bona fide home crag—and the interest started to go beyond merely scaling its walls. The timing couldn't have been more perfect. All over the country, land managers were taking notice of climbing, and trying to figure out what to do about it. Washington State Parks started tackling the issue of climbing in the 90s, creating a climbing management plan for Beacon Rock along the Columbia River. The isolation and separatism that Inde climbers enjoyed for the first 40 years of climbing there was poised to come to a head.

2000-PRESENT

The t-shirt that helped purchase the Lower Town Wall.

o much has happened in the past 17 ears, that it's hard to know where o start. Justen Sjong brought his osemite free climbing success back o the UTW aid routes on which he cut is teeth, and freed *Town Crier* and *reen Drag-on*. Mikey Schaefer freed asically all of the freeable (at the time) pper Town Wall routes, as well as ost of the hard LTW routes (including *ity Park*). Drew Philbin, Dave Moroles, en Gilkison, Mike Patz, and Blake Herington also continued the proud tra- ition of hard Index free climbing. The rst ascent torch was passed to Chris lenson, Tom Ramier, Mike Massey, ames Wyland, Derek Pearson, Ben ilkison, Dave Repnik, John Tetzlaff, Robert Rogoz, Doug Taylor, Geoff Georges, Michal Rynkiewicz, Chandler avis, Ryan Hoover, Brian Ebert, and many others (and Jon Nelson continues, to this day, to put up new routes). he focus of new routing has begun to shift towards retrofitting old aid lines for free climbing, cleaning old and rgotten lines, rebolting, and exploring. Areas like Lookout Point, The Cheeks, The Diamond, Earwax, and the ner Walls have all received major overhauls in the past five years.

nd, sadly, many great routes were reclaimed by the forest. Although climbers have become more ubiquitous, ey almost all flock to the LTW. A handful of routes: *Toxic Shock*, *Great Northern Slab*, *Princely Ambitions*, *Iron orse*, *Japanese Gardens*, *City Park*, *Godzilla*, *Thin Fingers*, *Tattoosh*, *S.S. Ultrabrutal*, *Cunning Stunt*, *Climax ontrol*, and *Davis Holland/Lovin' Arms* probably account for nearly half of the traffic at Index. As time goes n, the LTW and other walls at Index have actually gotten shadier, as the forest that was cut down by old gging and mining operations grows back. As a result, some walls get mossier, and mungier, while others get ore crowded.

he most notable thing to transpire in the past two decades is almost certainly the purchase of the Lower own Wall by the Washington Climber's Coalition in 2011 after two years of fundraising (you can read all about e purchase of the LTW on p.99). The purchase was a landmark achievement for the WCC, and permanently stablished the LTW as a "Climbing Reserve." The WCC plans to transition control of the land easement to the ate parks in the near future, on a number of conditions favorable to both climbers and route developers. It ill be the very first Washington State Park to have a Climbing Management Plan written by CLIMBERS!

s of now, the biggest issues facing Index are compliance with land management policies and management traffic. Each year more and more people come to Index, and that trend shows no sign of abating. While dex climbing today is less rogue, less libertarian, and less solitary than it once was–there are conspicuous vantages to the growing numbers of Index aficionados. Beyond the fact that more climbers also means more utes can remain clean and climbable year-round, more climbers means more bargaining leverage for the imbing community. The WCC is the voice for climbers in Washington, and everyone reading this should be supporter of that organization. The Access Fund and the American Alpine Club are also hugely important protecting our nation's crags, and it would behoove all of us to participate in and donate money to those oups.

r what it's worth, you can still have your adventure at Index. Go climb something at The Quarry, the Orc wer, or an obscure line at Lookout Point. Go find *Tie Me to A Length of That*, see if you can bushwhack your ay up anything at the Sentry Box, climb *Abraxas*, make your way to the Zappa Wall (without going on private nd). No matter how many people come to climb, there will always be a four star route without anyone on it. t a wire brush, an extra nut tool, and some tat on your rack, and go exploring. Adopt a crag. Go check out *rty Laundry*. Does it need a scrub? A new anchor? Does that thing actually go?

imbing at Index today means you can get the first ascent experience on something that was climbed decades o, and feel both the pride of re-opening that line for future climbers, and the humility of comparing your ettle to that of your predecessors. Get involved, have fun, and remember: always use stainless steel.

A NOTE ON SANDBAGGING

We often hear a critique of sandbagging which goes something like this: "People who sandbag their routes are just egotistical pricks." The line of logic is, essentially, that an insecure climber can feel better about his or herself by watching someone flail on a route he or she mastered, and can then declare "psh, that's only 5.whatever." This logic is incongruent with our own experiences, both as climbers, as friends of first ascentionists, and as first ascentionists ourselves.

Index is an area widely known for its sandbagging. Richard Ellison's famous Index t-shirt, with a list of routes on the back almost all rated 5.11b (though most are not), is an obvious nod to this fact. From beginners, to experts, visitors to locals, everyone has been on at least one Index route that raised a skeptical eyebrow. Is *Godzilla* really a 5.9? Don Heller and Don Harder thought so in 1972. Is *Thin Fingers* really a 5.11a with that one impossible slab move? Paul Boving felt that was the case in 1977. Is *Iron Horse* really only 5.11d to the ringing flake–even though Sonnie Trotter purportedly thought it felt more like 5.12c? When Peter Croft climbed it in 1981, that was the number he deemed appropriate.

The problem with the theory of the arrogant sandbagger is that Index's strongest climbers, and most prolific first ascentionists, are anything but egotistical. All that we have met are humble, talented climbers, who do it for the fun of it. Mikey Schaefer may be the only fully professional climber–in the modern sense of the word–to ever come from Index, and he's the definition of humility. What is a far more plausible explanation for Index's apparently stiff grades is a combination of two factors: geology and weather.

First of all, Index's geology is unique for American granite. It does not form in vertical fractures like Yosemite, or other areas where "splitters" predominate, but rather fractures horizontally in long bands. It's incredibly fine-grained, almost like New River Gorge sandstone, which makes it different from Squamish, Yosemite, the High Sierra, or anything in Colorado, Utah, or Wyoming. We can't think of any other granite as grippy as Index under proper conditions. The knobs are less extruded than many chickenheaded areas; the rock is steep but usually just slightly under vertical; few climbs remain pure to a single style. *Terminal Preppie* is a slab climb with a fingercrack roof finish. *Japanese Gardens* is a face climb to a hand crack to an offwidth to a finger crack, to a stem box, to a layback. Even *Slow Children*–one of Index's most splitter cracks–involves walking a plank, stemming, laybacking, and friction smearing. Very few routes at Index feel remotely reminiscent of any another, or to routes anywhere else. So the climbing is unique, and there's little that any climber can do to prepare for it other than to climb at Index. Hence visitors will find the area peculiar, uncomfortable, and stiff.

Furthermore, most visiting climbers will come to Index during the heat of the summer. Almost nothing at Index is a straightforward plain and simple crack, which means you have to face climb. Face climbing is incredibly conditions-dependent, especially somewhere like Index where friction is so important. That crux on *Thin Fingers*? It feels significantly easier when the temperature is below 70 degrees. But most climbers come to Index in July and August, and climb during the hottest part of the day, in the sun. This can make routes feel harder than they actually are.

Yet even Index veterans who know better than to climb in the sun can think of a ton of sandbagged routes–what gives? Consider, for example, *Model Worker*. If you're taller than 6'5", the second crux will feel uncomfortably scrunched up. If you're shorter, the first crux requires either a crazy all-points-off sideways dyno, or you have to be as flexible and as strong as Lynn Hill. This is typical Index fare. Most of the routes have distinct cruxes, and most of those cruxes feel harder to someone who is short, or someone who is tall. In the end, there's just no way around it. In other words, everyone will find a sandbag somewhere at Index–no matter how long she or he has climbed here.

Index has a learning curve like anywhere else. If you climb here long enough, you'll likely succumb to the reverse-sandbag affect. After climbing predominantly at Index for four summers, our onsight and redpoint grades both increased significantly at the crag.

SAFETY RATINGS

One place where sandbagging is absolutely unacceptable is in safety ratings. Of course, like anything in climbing, safety ratings are subject to debate and disagreement. Hence, the safety ratings in this book are suggestions, not facts, and should be considered as such.

One of the incredible things about Index is that the vast majority of free routes here are relatively safe climbs. They may not be splitter cracks, but the walls are steep, the protection is good, and typically where clean protection is not abundant for safe climbing, first ascentionists have placed bolts. This makes for a very pleasant climbing experience that can still FEEL pretty spicy, while staying basically safe. Still, there are outliers. Below is what we mean by PG, PG13, R, and X.

PG: Ample opportunities for solid protection exist.

PG13: Somewhere between casual and dangerous. May involve tricky, specific, or marginal gear.

R: Protection is sparse, and there are places where a fall can result in serious injury.

X: Protection is almost nonexistent, and falls can result in serious injury or death.

Abe Traven catching air on Bat Skins. | Photo by Alasdair Turner

STARS

Climbing at Index is really freaking good. *Sky Valley Rock* was stingy with stars. This is due in part to Cramer's desire to offer beta on a route's quality as it would have been climbed at the time of publication. Of course, there are one star routes in his book that get four in this one, and vice versa. Time changes all. In this book, we have tried as much as possible not to rate the current experience of climbing a route, but to rate a route based on the timeless features of stone it ascends. If you come across a dirty four or three star route in this book, you should strongly consider cleaning it, climbing, it, and encouraging your friends to do the same. It's definitely worth it.

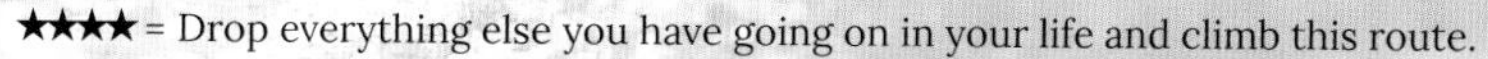

★★★★ = Drop everything else you have going on in your life and climb this route.

★★★ = Any other crag's four star route. Climb it.

★★ = If you're there, and it's convenient, climb it. It's still at least worth a try.

★ = May not be climbable in its current condition. Bring a brush, and climb it.

Blake Herrington has your rack for you.

GEAR

Index rock provides ample and excellent protection opportunities, and accepts a wide variety of gear options. Take the first crux of *Japanese Gardens*, for example. Some use a brassy RP, some protect with a bomber HB offset, some use a blue TCU, some use a green Alien, some use a blue X4. And truthfully, all of those catch falls over and over again at that same spot.

Choosing your gear is highly subjective, and hence it is difficult to provide exact recommendations. You will often see our suggestion: "Standard Index Rack" which is our humble advice for a reasonable onsight rack for any trad route at Index (though it can certainly be paired down).

The Standard Index Rack:

- 1 double set of cams, from tips (purple TCU/yellow X4/purple C3/blue Alien) to 3 inches (#3 Camalot)
- 1 set of nuts
- 1 set of RPs—preferably offsets.
- 5-6 quickdraws
- 5-6 slings

We have done our best to elucidate specific gear where necessary, and helpful. That said, just because we recommend one particular piece on a route does not mean a different piece will not also work. It's worth mentioning that a steel wire brush and other route cleaning materials are a good addition to the Standard Index Rack, especially if visiting more obscure crags. A quick once-over on a route that has not been climbed in a year goes a long way to maintaining the climb and will yield a much better experience overall.

Part of a Standard Index Rack.

ROPES AND RAPS

The bottom line on rope size at Index is this: **USE AT LEAST A 70 METER ROPE**. A 70 will get you through 99% of rappels and toprope situations at Index. If you don't have one, go buy one.

While many routes can be climbed, toproped, and rapped with a single 60, Index developers and climbers have been using 70s as the de facto length for a long time. We have done our best to provide details where a 70 will not suffice (e.g., two 60m ropes are required, a single 80m is necessary to set up a toprope, etc). We've also tried (for those of you too stingy or nostalgic to retire your 60) to note where a 60 will not suffice. But we have not been exhaustive with those efforts, nor did we intend to be since so many routes at Index have so many different rappelling options.

One way or another, if you don't see explicit information for a rope length, assume nothing. Always tie knots in your ends, and always watch your rope on rappels and while lowering climbers.

If you are not sure if your rope will safely get you down, swing around and open your eyes. Index has safe rap anchors all over the place, as routes tend to be packed close together. Just because you didn't climb it doesn't mean you can't rap it. Get creative, you'll figure something out.

A NOTE ON ETHICS

Index has a wild history with a lot of home-cooked, sometimes half-baked, shenaniganery and chicanery. From the very start, Index was a powderkeg of different ideas, ideals, and climbers of immense talents. It's actually kind of amazing the ticking ethics timebomb hasn't really blown up in a cataclysmic way. Aside from occasional internet feuds and genital-measuring competitions, things tend to remain pretty copacetic.

The best ethic you can employ at Index is one of tolerance. There are bolts next to perfect gear placements; there are cracks that get freed without bolts, then get bolted, and then get chopped; there are "tasteful pieces of aid" glued to the wall in some not-so-obscure corners. People stash cleaning tools, fix ropes in plain sight, hang draws, manufacture ... things... You know, whatever. Index has, historically, been a piratic zone of the "anything goes" persuasion. As one noteworthy Index climber said, "I will always side with the person who moves their hands instead of their lips." In other words, climbing at Index takes a lot of work, whether new routing or face-lifting. A premium is placed on simply getting after it, and doing your best to fix things up. That said, there are ten simple commandments that any pious Index climber should abide. They are as follows:

1. If putting in bolts at Index, the only proper materials are stainless steel (or titanium and glue) for both bolt and hanger. It's more expensive, but nothing else lasts, and old corroded bolts can be hard to identify and lead to major injuries or death. If retro-bolting old routes, remove the bolts and patch the holes. If possible, drill the old studs out of the original holes and reuse them. If you can afford it, place removable bolts.

2. If using fixed lines, be scrupulous about where and for how long. For example, fixing a line in a mossy gully near the back of the Inner Walls won't likely bother anyone. On the other hand, hanging a bright orange rope the entire length of the Upper Wall where non-climbers can pick it out from the middle of town is not acceptable. It's commendable to use that line to clean an amazing route—but if you plan to leave it all summer, choose a less visible color. Remember, the WCC owns the LTW, but not the other crags. Many Index crags lie on Forest Service and State Park land, and for now, climbing at those areas is a privilege that can be revoked.

3. Be tolerant of different climbers. If someone wants to aid *City Park*, let them. If someone wants to free it before you aid it, let them. If someone wants to climb only the first half of *Japanese Gardens*, put up with it. If someone offers to put up the full *Jap Gardens* on your rope and leave it for you to toprope, say thank you. If someone wants to rope-solo the same five routes day-in and day-out all summer, and they do everything in their power to keep the rope out of the way of other climbers when not in use, abide that soloist. Every climber should be friendly and amenable to every other climber. If you don't want to be, try climbing almost anywhere other than the LTW, and you won't see nearly as many people.

4. If you see vegetation, dirt, moss, or munge on a route, clean it up. Don't criticize the first ascentionist, rate it two stars on mountainproject, tell your friends that Index sucks, and walk away. Take a minute to pitch in: when clean, almost every route in this book is a top-notch climb. All of these routes deserve to be climbed, and many of them require routine maintenance.

5. Avoid spraying beta without asking permission. Onsighting at Index is an incredible experience that many climbers seek out. You may have your own personal beta dialed, and you may have the most high-tech ninja secret cam placement out left, but the person climbing might not want it. Ask first, spray second.

6. If aid climbing, be respectful of free climbers. Aid climbing takes a really long time, and can ruin or alter free climbs. Free climbing is lower impact. The best aid climbs at Index are not on the LTW. Aiding *City Park* is cool and all, and it won't typically interfere with free climbers, but it also won't really be that helpful in preparing you to climb El Cap. Try something more obscure, with less C1 nutting. And go light with the hammer. In fact, don't ever use a hammer on a route that has already been freed.

7. If you want to retro-fit an old route, contact the first ascentionist first. One of the authors of this book wanted to put a bolt at the start of *Agent Orange* until he talked to Jeff Smoot, and learned the story behind the line. That author is glad he didn't place that bolt. Placing a bolt is pretty permanent, so think before you act.

8. Do not chip holds, glue on holds that were not previously there, or otherwise modify routes to better suit your abilities. Drilling through an enormous flake and pounding a piece of rebar into it to secure it to the wall in a tasteful and inconspicuous manner is super awesome. Gluing a "piece of tasteful aid" into the middle of a route someone else free climbed 20+ years ago is not. Be respectful of those who came before, and will come after.

9. Respect any and all local authorities, local inhabitants, local businesses, and rules set down by any land managers. If there's a no parking sign, don't park. No trespassing, don't trespass. Remember, climbing here is a privilege, not a right. That privilege can be revoked. Don't screw it up for anyone. Follow the rules. There are so few of them that it should be easy to do.

10. Don't F!@# it up. When Darryl Cramer sat down and talked with us about writing this book, he gave us one distinct, and very valuable, piece of advice: "This is your Index now. What you do will affect everything that happens to Index in the future. A lot of us have spent a lot of time here, have worked our asses off here, really love it here. Don't fuck it up." That goes for all of us. If you are reading these words, consider yourself a caretaker of Index. The future of Index climbing is in your hands as much as anyone else's. Please respect and honor that awesome privilege.

Welcome to Index!

Chris Kalman replacing relic bolts at The Lower Town Wall.

Climbing is not the only adventure to be had at Index. Carl Mars walks a wild highline atop the Upper Town Wal

CHRIS' TOP 10 CLIMBS

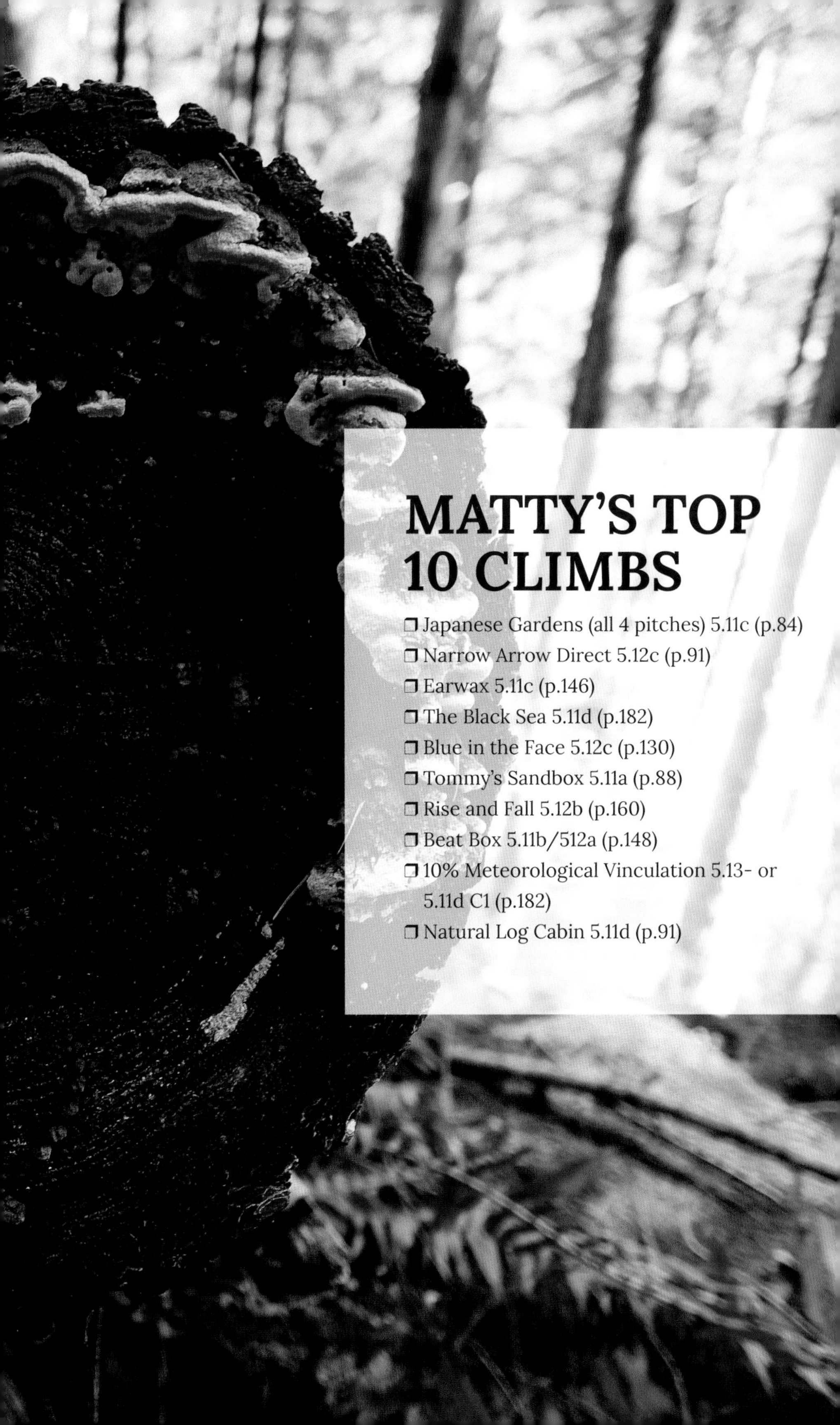

MATTY'S TOP 10 CLIMBS

- ❒ Japanese Gardens (all 4 pitches) 5.11c (p.84)
- ❒ Narrow Arrow Direct 5.12c (p.91)
- ❒ Earwax 5.11c (p.146)
- ❒ The Black Sea 5.11d (p.182)
- ❒ Blue in the Face 5.12c (p.130)
- ❒ Tommy's Sandbox 5.11a (p.88)
- ❒ Rise and Fall 5.12b (p.160)
- ❒ Beat Box 5.11b/512a (p.148)
- ❒ 10% Meteorological Vinculation 5.13- or 5.11d C1 (p.182)
- ❒ Natural Log Cabin 5.11d (p.91)

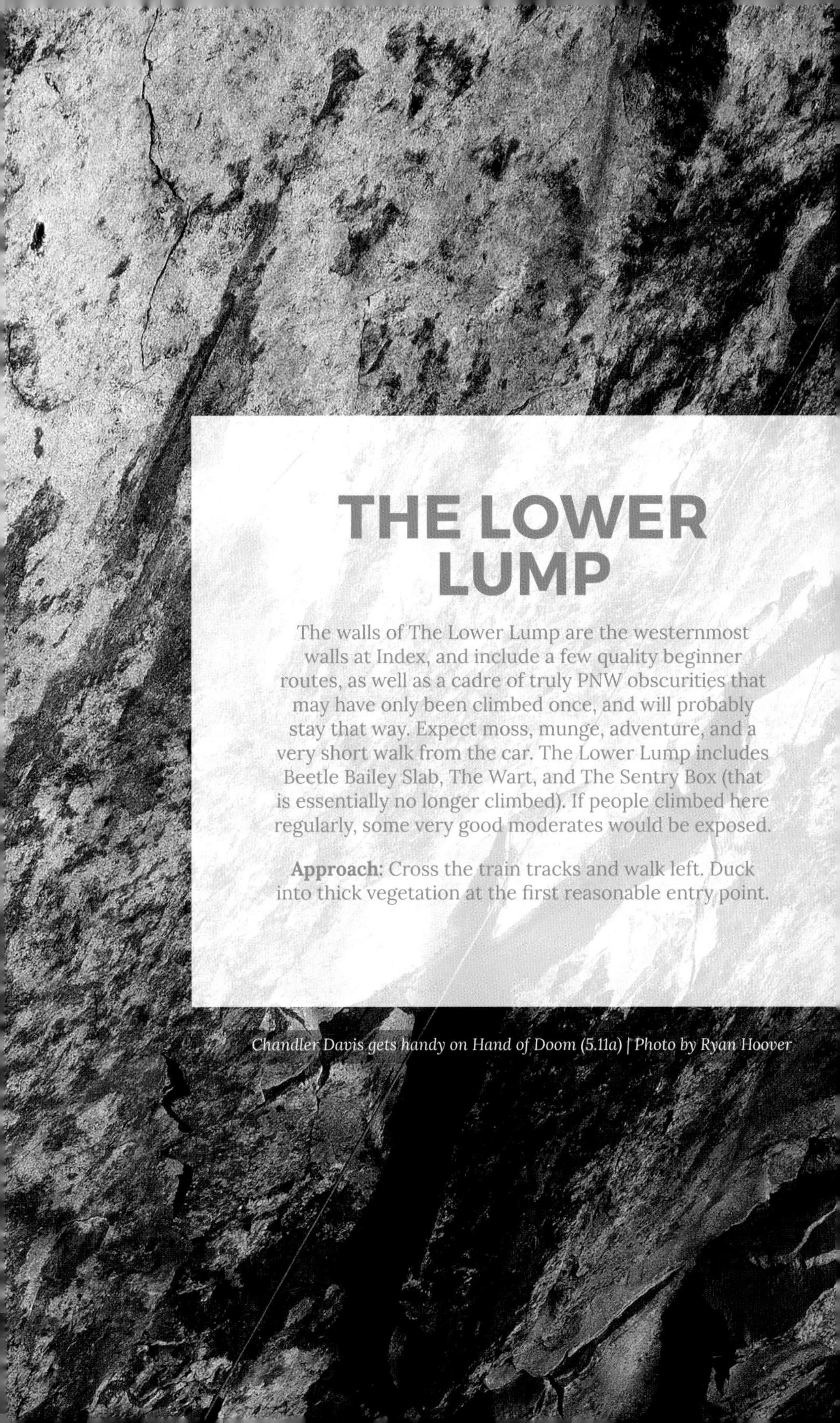

THE LOWER LUMP

The walls of The Lower Lump are the westernmost walls at Index, and include a few quality beginner routes, as well as a cadre of truly PNW obscurities that may have only been climbed once, and will probably stay that way. Expect moss, munge, adventure, and a very short walk from the car. The Lower Lump includes Beetle Bailey Slab, The Wart, and The Sentry Box (that is essentially no longer climbed). If people climbed here regularly, some very good moderates would be exposed.

Approach: Cross the train tracks and walk left. Duck into thick vegetation at the first reasonable entry point.

Chandler Davis gets handy on Hand of Doom (5.11a) | Photo by Ryan Hoover

BEETLE BAILEY SLAB

Beetle Bailey Slab is the farthest west crag at The Lower Lump. The rock is unbelievably good, with knobs and incredible friction. The wall tends to be dirty, and at the time of printing, most of the routes could use retro-bolting, but this wall should really not be overlooked!

Approach: Walk west along the train tracks from the parking lot for about a hundred yards, then dip into the woods on a faint trail after passing the clean south face of The Wart, on your right. Make your way to the base of the black slab and a smattering of bolts. There is currently only one clean entry pitch: the first pitch of *Beetle Bailey*.

Descent: Everything here can be rapped with a single 60.

1 RACER X 5.10B ★★★★

The most popular route on the Lower Lump. The third pitch is rarely done, and the first pitch is usually eschewed for the first pitch of *Beetle Bailey Arch*. The second pitch is the money–incredibly good Index knob-climbing on perfect stone. The bolts are well-spaced: safe, but exciting.

The route's second pitch is four stars; the other pitches are far less appealing.

Gear: Mostly quickdraws. A single .5 is necessary for Beetle Bailey's first pitch, and a #2 or #3 is needed for Racer X pitch 2.

FA: Darryl Cramer, Jon Nelson.

Pitch 1–5.7

Climb a jungly right-facing corner on the right side of a slight pedestal.

Or (much better) climb the clean first pitch of *Beetle Bailey* at stout 5.11a and belay at the chain anchor above.

Pitch 2–5.10b

From the anchor atop *Beetle Bailey* pitch one, traverse hard left past a bolt and an old pin (don't go straight up on bolts) and a crazy pocket which takes a good #2/3 (bring both and see which you prefer), extending draws on all these pieces. After the hole, continue straight up the bolt line past wild 5.10 knobs all the way to the anchor. The two farthest left bolt lines have been climbed (*Lying Lycra Piggies* 5.10b PG, Grafton, Russel; and *Congolindination* 5.10A3, Anderson, Carson), but are not recommended.

Pitch 3–5.9+

This pitch is rarely done. Climb up and over an arch.

2 METAL 5.11C PG-13 ★★★

Metal looks incredible, but could certainly use new metal (i.e. bolts). Climb the first pitch of *Beetle Bailey*. From the anchor, head left past a fixed pin, then straight up on bolts past cool slab climbing and friction. At the last bolt, traverse left (5.11c) to a left-facing feature, then cruise to the anchor above *Racer X*.

Gear: Quickdraws and a single 0.5 (for Beetle Bailey's first pitch).

FA: Terry Lien, Darryl Cramer.

3 BEETLE BAILEY ARCH 5.11A ★★★

Beetle Bailey Arch has a wonderful first and second pitch. The first pitch is certainly three stars. The second pitch, if retrobolted/clean, would be a three to four star affair.

Gear: Gear from purple TCU to #2 Camalot. RPs. A mess of quickdraws and slings. A single .5 is necessary for pitch one.

FA: Don Harder, Bruce Garrett; FFA P1: Darryl Cramer, Brian Scott; FFA P2: Terry Lien, Darryl Cramer, Brian Scott.

Pitch 1–5.11a

Climb the clean bolted slab (hard) and belay at the chain-anchor above.

Pitch 2–5.10b

From the anchor atop pitch one, climb straight up on flakes and features past pins to an awesome rightward diagonaling finger crack.

Heading right along a vegetated ramp/crack low on the pitch is a variation called *Larry's Gaily Colored Lycra* (5.10c, two stars, Grafton, Gerberding).

Leaving the crack and climbing knobs past two bolts at the end is a 5.11a variation (Bryan Burdo).

Pitch 3–A3 .

Cramer called this pitch "possibly nonexistent" 15 years ago. Don't expect anything to have changed. Be prepared to make and leave your own anchor.

4 CUPCAKE 5.10C ★

At the far right side of the Beetle Bailey Slab, walk uphill until almost on top of The Wart. Here starts *Cupcake*, a one star route that is almost impossible to see beneath vegetation.

Gear: Standard Index Rack, gardening shears.

Matt Sellick on the barely-there knobs of Racer X (5.10)

THE WART

The Wart is not the best crag at Index, but has enough good routes to warrant visit. It's a particularly good area for beginners.

Approach: Walk west along the tracks from the main parking area for about 50 yards until you see a small buttress in the trees on your right. Dip into the woods. The first routes you encounter are on the east side of the buttress.

For *Compound W* and *Meyah*, walk along the tracks a little further until a short trail breaks off leading into the woods, and the base of the south face.

Descent: All routes can be rapped with a single 70, most with a 60.

5 COMPOUND W 5.10A ★★

A quality left-facing corner featuring laybacking and jamming. This is the furthest left route on the south face. A 5.9 thin crack variation exists immediately right, ending at the same anchor.

Gear: Standard Index Rack

FA: Cameron Elias, Eric Lund.

6 MEYAH 5.10A ★★

Climb a short dihedral, then move right at a wide crack through the roof to a single-bolt lower-off.

Gear: Standard Index Rack

FA: Dave Repnik, Andy Cook.

7 SMILEY KYLEE 5.7 ★★

Climb the prominent crack system on the east face The Wart. If climbed regularly, this would become a good moderate.

Gear: Standard Index Rack

FA: Jesse Cirillo, Dave Repnik.

8 MEAN MUG 5.8 ★

This route climbs the right-facing chimney right of *Smiley Kylee* up to a ledge, then continues up cracks and face to the *Smiley Kylee* anchors.

There is a short variation which starts at the base of *Smiley Kylee* and heads up and right to *Mean Mug*, known as *Banana Hammock* (5.9).

Gear: Standard Index Rack

FA: Dawn and Jesse Cirillo.

9 WALKING BACK TO HAPPINESS 5.12A R/X ★

Begin immediately right of The Wart, and climb past expanding flakes, powerful underclings, and runout face to a difficult groove, past bolts, to a belay up and left.

Gear: Standard Index Rack, cojones.

FA: Greg Child, Greg Collum.

·IAND OF DOOM 5.11A ★★★

; is the leftmost bolted line on the wall to the right 'he Wart. It is rumored to be pretty good. A 70m e is suggested to lower. Climb past a funky slab to ›yable climbing higher up.

:r: About 15 quickdraws

Ryan Hoover, Michal Rynkiewicz.

VALKING LEGEND 5.10 ★★★

:cent addition to Index climbing, this enjoyable itch outing follows varying features up the heart he Lower Lump. Clean, fun, and totally worth ıbing.

ned, of course, for the incredible Pat Sullivan, who :ked from 35m at the top of *Thin Fingers*, and lived ell about it (and kept climbing, to boot)!

ır: 13 quickdraws. 70 meter rope mandatory.

Jesse Cirrillo, Dave Repnik.

ch 1—5.9

derate climbing through a shallow, right-facing ner leads to a belay atop a large block feature. It's gh to spot the chains from the ground. This shares start with another route (currently a closed proj-) and follows the righthand line of bolts.

wo star variation bolted first pitch exists: *Finger My* t, 5.11a, Cirillo-Repnik.

ch 2—5.10a

m the belay, step left then straight up balancy ves into a cool stem. Engage the slanting corner on holds and good rock up to the second belay.

ch 3—5.10c

is is the money pitch, and a full 35 meters in length. :nd up and left for a bit, then follow the bolt line aight up. Varied climbing, tricky movement, and an ›osed position with stellar views.

EXPONENTIAL EXCAVATION 5.8 ★

; questionable whether the excavation of this route l ever be complete. The route starts on blocky rain in a left-facing corner.

'ariation exists, leaving the route at a protruding ›w on the right, two-thirds of the way up: *Exponen- l Potential* (Michal Rynkiewicz, 5.10d, single rack to and draws, two stars).

ar: Standard Index Rack.

: Dave Repnik, Darby Summers, Jesse Cirillo.

HUBERT'S REVENGE 5.10A ★

ht of *Exponential*, climb past three bolts to the ht trending crack. Follow the crack with good foot- lds to the chains.

ar: Standard Index Rack.

: Dave Repnik, Jesse Cirillo.

⑭ DRUNKEN SAHARENITY 5.10B/C ★

A 40 foot sport route right of *Hubert's*. It shares the same anchor.

Gear: Quickdraws.

FA: Dave Repnik, Jesse Cirillo.

⑮ MUTUALLY ASSURED SATISFACTION 5.10A R ★

Start in the middle of the cave feature, on the tip of a little boulder. Commit to a bouldery sequence and trend right to an indentation in the rock, heading straight up from there to the chains shared with *Drunken Saharenity* and *Hubert's Revenge*.

Gear: Standard Index Rack.

FA: Danny Diamond, Stamati Anagnostou.

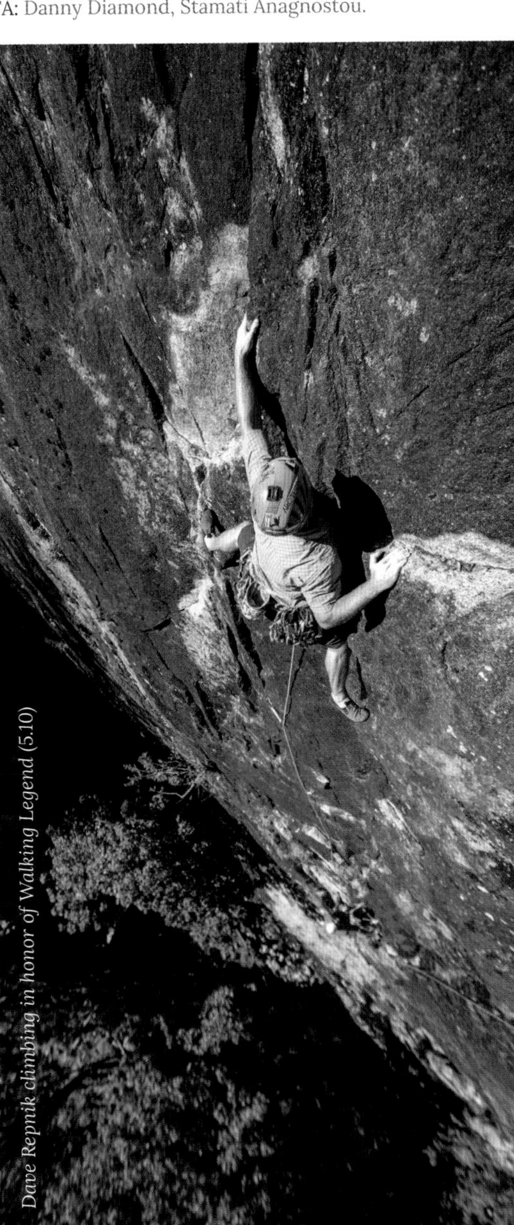

Dave Repnik climbing in honor of Walking Legend (5.10)

Jesse Cirrillo on the Walking Legend 5.10

'HE SENTRY BOX

is entirely possible that nothing on this wall has
:en climbed in the last ten years. Most of the
utes start out free and end on aid through the
verhangs. One of Index's most overgrown and,
urrently, least climbable walls.

pproach: Walk uphill and right from The Wart until
riving at the base of the overhang-capped walls.
ost of the routes begin near a lone evergreen at
e top of a short scramble. You should belay from
is spot.

escent: Rap with a single 70 and bring plenty of tat.

SNOWDONIA **5.10D ★**

onn Heller and Johnny Waterman's most infmaous
ute? Probably not.

imb the furthest left line, trending left up a ramp,
d passing small roofs.

ear: *Standard Index Rack.*

: Donn Heller, John Waterman; FFA: Jim Yoder, Matt
rns.

BILLY'S CORNER **5.10C ★**

imb a right-facing corner, right of *Snowdonia.*

ear: *Standard Index Rack.*

: Bill Crawford, Matt Kerns.

THE SENTRY BOX **5.10A ★**

ry little is known about this or any of the other
ntry Box routes. Though it gets a free grade, it is
ted in *Sky Valley Rock* that this is a good practice
l route. Start toward *Billy's Corner*, then head
aight up.

ar: *Standard Index Rack.*

: Don Brooks; FFA: Jim Yoder, Matt Kerns, Bill
awford.

FANG OVERHANG **5.10D ★**

ght of *Sentry Box.*

ar: *Standard Index Rack.*

: Jim Yoder, Steve Gerberding.

PAROLE **5.11A ★**

ght of *Fang*, climb corners to the right of a large
of.

ar: *Standard Index Rack.*

: Jim Yoder, Steve Gerberding.

TOP 10 MODERATES

- ❒ Pisces 5.6 (p.66)
- ❒ Asterisk 5.8 (p.206)
- ❒ Senior Citizens in Space 5.7+ (p.239)
- ❒ Toxic Shock 5.9 (p.50)
- ❒ Princely Ambitions 5.9 (p.75)
- ❒ Plum Pudding 5.9 (p.126)
- ❒ GM Route 5.9 (p.119)
- ❒ Godzilla 5.9+ (p.88)
- ❒ Rattletale 5.10b (p.216)
- ❒ Breakfast of Champions 5.10a (p.72)

Robin McArdel starting the day with Breakfast of Champions 5.10

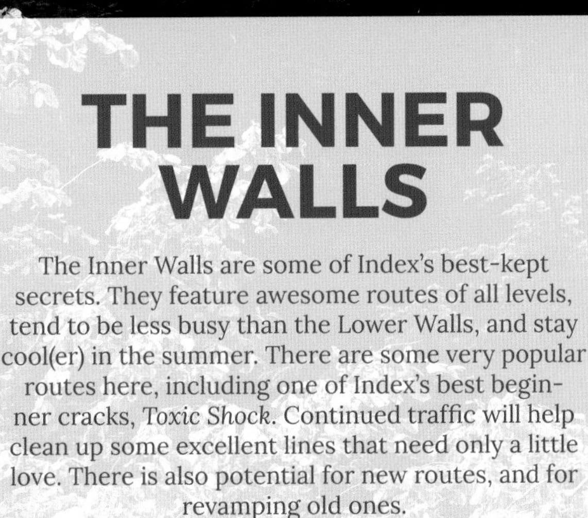

THE INNER WALLS

The Inner Walls are some of Index's best-kept secrets. They feature awesome routes of all levels, tend to be less busy than the Lower Walls, and stay cool(er) in the summer. There are some very popular routes here, including one of Index's best beginner cracks, *Toxic Shock*. Continued traffic will help clean up some excellent lines that need only a little love. There is also potential for new routes, and for revamping old ones.

Approach: Cross the train tracks and enter the woods. Just before The Great Northern Slab, a trail breaks off left. The Inner Walls all branch off this trail. After 10-15 minutes, the trail deposits you directly at the base of *Toxic Shock*, the most popular of the Inner Walls.

THE GARDEN WALL

This is the first bit of climbing you come to on your way to the Inner Walls. The trail takes you directly to the east face, whose *Knob Job* is more of a boulder problem than a route. The other lines are completely overgrown and unimpressive looking.

Approach: Walk the Inner Wall trail to the obvious boulder, with some cool knobs on a clean face, and a rusty old quarter-incher.

Descent: A single 60 is fine.

❶ KNOB JOB 5.10D ★★

Climb up to the bolt, clip it, and then traverse the crack left and up. Bring a finger sized piece to protect the finish.

Three other not-recommended routes reside around the corner on the downhill side. They can be reached by bushwhacking downhill from the base of *Knob Job* or by hiking up on top of *Knob Job*, and rappeling in. The lines, from left to right, are *Short But Dirty* (5.10d, TR, Cramer), *A Touch Too Much* (5.11b R, Cramer/ Strong), and *Weed-B-Gone* (5.10d, Boatsman).

Gear: 1 finger-size piece will do. You may want to bring a 60 FOOT rope, as a 60 meter one would just be over the top...

FA: Mark Boatsman.

THE SHAFT

The Shaft is an obscure little wall near the start of the Inner Walls with only two rarely-climbed routes that are in need of excavation if someone wanted to perform some community service. This is the farthest southwest of the inner walls.

Approach: Hike the Inner Wall trail until the trail junction to K Cliff. At this point, look across the ravine to a mossy and vegetated slab on the left. You may be able to see a bolt or two. Bushwhack your way over to the base.

Descent: Descend these routes with a single 60. You may want to bring tat for trees.

❷ PALPABLE THRILL 5.9 ★

A slab climb, and the leftmost of the two routes. The bottom is slightly runout and often wet. After the second bolt, move left to a 2-bolt belay.

Gear: Standard Index Rack.

FA: Dan Carter, Alan Belshaw.

❸ PRIAPISM 5.10C ★★

This is a drier, alternate start to *Palpable Thrill*. After the second bolt, climb up and slightly right to a tree belay.

Gear: Standard Index Rack.

FA: Dan Carter, Alan Belshaw, Oliver Ochs.

TOXIC SHOCK

The Toxic Shock area has the best routes at the Inner Walls, and is a great alternative to the Lower Town Wall when it is hot or crowded. Be prepared t see a crowd on *Toxic Shock*, and *Even Steven*. If you are here to climb *Toxic Shock* also consider *Corner Flash*, the nice 5.7 across the way. If everything up here is hopelessly crowded, your best bet for mode ates is K Cliff.

Approach: Follow the Inner Wall trail to the obvious splitters on the left where the trail meets the left wall.

Descent: All the routes here can be descended/TR'c with a single 60.

❹ A VIEW FROM THE BRIDGE 5.10D ★★

It's hard to tell that this thing is even a route, but in heyday it was regarded as one of the finest stemmir testpieces around. Climb the jungle stem corner lef of *Toxic Shock*. Just goes to show what happens wh routes don't get climbed!

Gear: A variety of scrub brushes and pressure washe

FA: Steve Strong, Jon Nelson.

❺ SLAPSHOT 5.11D ★★★★

For the ambidextrous arête enthusiast, this route is not to be missed! Powerful and tenuous arête slappi in the cruxy bottom leads to an interesting and delicate finish on the opposite upper arête.

Purportedly, the licheny cracks with death blocks o left of the upper arête have been freed. There could be an awesome route there but proceed with cautio

Gear: Quickdraws, a couple shoulder-length slings, a perhaps a .5, .75, or 1" cam at halfway.

FA: Jim Yoder, Matt Kerns.

❻ TOXIC SHOCK 5.9 ★★★★

One of Index's best moderates, and a great beginner crack climb. Either start left in a short layback crack or climb the twin cracks on the right side of the buttress (slightly easier). Follow the splitter into the corner, and onto the face on the left.

Gear: If starting on the left, bring cams up to .75 to reach the first pedestal. If starting on the right, bring doubles of hand-size pieces. For the upper crack, .5 to #3 is good with doubles in 1, 2, and 3.

FA: Steve Strong, Greg White.

rek Craig sampling the finer things on Toxic Shock (5.9)

7 EVEN STEVEN 5.11B ★★★★

Even Steven is one of Index's easiest 5.11b's, as such, is predictably popular. The crux itself is short and safe, but tenuous moves leading up to it could result in a ledge fall if you don't sew it up. Climb the twin cracks or the layback to start, and finish up the thin splitter crack right of the corner.

Gear: *See gear beta for Toxic for the start. Beyond that, bring a good collection of small cams and nuts to protect the cruxy thin crack above. Everything down to a gray TCU can be useful.*

FA: Dan Lapeska, Dick Cilley.

8 ROADSIDE FLORAL CURTAIN 5.12A ★★★

A difficult start guards the rest of this enjoyable arête. As it is currently missing lower bolts, a stickclip is a prerequisite.

At the time of printing, a tree has fallen across the top of the route, making it dangerous to climb.

A long forgotten 5.12b called *Stinkbug* (Cramer, Olsen) exists somewhere left of *Roadside* and is purportedly quite good.

Gear: *Quickdraws.*

FA: Darryl Cramer, Greg Olsen.

9 TANG 5.11B ★

The first pitch is rarely climbed; the second pitch hardly even exists any more. Climb the obvious thir crack next to the cave entrance.

Rumored to be quality. May be led in one long pitch Bust out the brush! (5.10b)

Gear: *A large rack of small nuts and RPs, and small camming units.*

FA: Jon Nelson, Terry Lien, Darryl Cramer.

10 WORKINGMAN 5.11B ★

About 6 feet right of the cave, climb up a right-facir corner and clip a bolt. Cruxy stemming leads to a 5. roof. There is a one star variation to the right called *Milanese Sandwich* (5.10b R).

Gear: *Standard Index Rack with emphasis on thin ge*

m Ramier harnessing the power of the forest to withstand Suckerpunch (5.11d)

THE FOODBAR/BEHIND THE 8 BALL

The Food Bar is the wall after the cave following the Toxic Shock area. Little is known about some of these routes, and some imagination must be used to discern which is which. That said, there are some good lines here that stay relatively clean in spite of little traffic. *Suckerpunch* is not to be missed.

Approach: Continue past *Toxic Shock* until encountering some cool overhanging features on the left past a large cave. This area is *Foodbar*. Just a bit past there lies *Behind the 8 Ball*.

Descent: Most of the routes end at a low anchor, but if you go questing, you may need a 70. The wall is taller than most of the routes.

⑪ WALL TO WALL FANNY 5.10A ★★

Climb a short chimney on the left side of the wall.

Gear: Standard Index Rack.

FA: Tom Ramier, James Wyland.

⑫ INNER THIGH 5.10A ★★

The next route over.

Gear: Standard Index Rack.

FA: Tom Ramier, James Wyland.

⑬ FUZZY UNDERCLING 5.11B ★★

Climb past a low bolt and a tricky roof with another bolt, then up lower-angle terain to an anchor.

Gear: Standard Index Rack.

FA: Tom Ramier, James Wyland.

⑭ HUMPBACK HUMPBACK HUMPBACK WHALE 5.10B ★★★

Climb past a low bolt to a ramp (crux), then continue up to the anchor straight above (as per *Foodbar*), or jaunt right to the *Suckerpunch* anchor.

Gear: Standard Index Rack.

FA: Tom Ramier.

⑮ FOODBAR 5.10C ★★

Climb up an imposing looking corner into a thin left-facing corner. Continue either straight up to a high anchor or blast right to the *Suckerpunch* anchor.

Gear: Standard Index Rack with an emphasis on thin gear.

FA: Darryl Cramer, Jon Nelson, Nicola Masciandaro. Retro'd by Tom Ramier.

⑯ SUCKERPUNCH 5.11D ★★★

This is an excellent route, and the best line at The Foodbar. Fantastic arête climbing and some wild moves define this difficult onsight. The end is hard, but the true suckerpunch might be finding out that it's only 5.11d!

Gear: Cams up to .5 to protect the easier entrance, then quickdraws.

FA: James Wyland.

⑰ BEHIND THE 8 BALL 5.10A ★★★

A splitter wide crack to the right of *Foodbar*. Would be four stars if clean.

Gear: Doubles from #3 to #4 and a #5, and a few medium sizes for the top.

FA: Kjell Swedin, Dick Cilley.

·IRE WALL

ɦis excellent wall is often overlooked, but it's well ·orth the trip. Two 5.11b routes, *China Syndrome* ıd *Yellow Cake.* are not to be missed, but the whole ea is amazing. Potential exists for new routes, or ıearthing old ones.

pproach: After The Foodbar, continue further back ·ong a trail that hugs the wall until you reach the ·illiant yellow lichen-streaked wall.

escent: You can probably rap these routes with a ·ngle 60, but watch your rope ends.

) CHINA SYNDROME 5.11B ★★★

ı excellent route that starts on the left side of the all, and moves right past a bolt on the face and a ·ugh move out right. Continue up and around the ête to a splitter crack terminating at the finish. ·atch the rope drag.

ear: Cams from tips up to hands, doubles in small zes, nuts, a few runners and about 5 quickdraws.

\: Dave Elder and James Wyland.

) YELLOW CAKE 5.11B ★★★

ıother brilliant route. Start on a thin, slabby hedral that ramps up and left. Make some cool oves through an overlap, and continually trend ɔ and left (crossing *China Syndrome*). Cool crack ıd face climbing with tricky gear brings you to a ·ought-provoking finish.

ear: Same as China Syndrome. Save some small wid-·ts for up high.

\: Dave Elder and James Wyland.

) LEATHER LUNG 5.10C ★★

ɔross the gully right of Fire Wall climb up a corner to a quality crack and take it to the chains.

ear: Unknown.

\: Unknown.

) TIE ME TO A LENGTH OF THAT 5.12A ★★★

ıis excellent climb lies deep, deep within the forest, rther back than Fire Wall, and on the other side of ·e gulch. There is no trail but the route is worth the ıshwhack. Expect some dirty terrain up high.

ear: Quickdraws and a #1 Camalot.

\: Dave Haavik, Darryl Cramer, Greg Olsen, Erik ıixton.

DELUSIONS OF GRANDEUR / AGENT ORANGE

These walls are directly across from Toxic Shock. The cleaner, smaller buttress features one good 5.7 offwidth crack, and an awesome PG13 face climb. The larger, more impressive, entirely overgrown wall on the left is Delusions of Grandeur Buttress. This wall was climbed via two routes: *Bobcat Bypass* (Cramer, Schimmel) and *Delusions of Grandeur* (White, Strong, Nelson)–both 5.10s. These old routes are so overgrown they are hardly worth describing. However, if anybody spearheaded a major cleaning, this buttress could sport 4 or 5 quality lines–or maybe those are just delusions of grandeur.

Approach: Follow the Inner Wall trail to the obvious splitters on the left near the end of the trail. Across the gulch on your right are *Delusions of Grandeur* and *Agent Orange.*

Descent: A single 60 will do.

22 AGENT ORANGE 5.11A PG-13 ★★★

This is a proud, bolt-free, route that deserves much more traffic from capable climbers.

Climb up to a decent hold on the blunt arête left of the offwidth crack. Place an OK tiny cam and make moves left around the corner. Continue up on cool horizontal cracks and face climbing moves to a 2-bolt anchor. The route now ends in a natural alcove at the end of the hard climbing with a 2-bolt anchor.

This route was X-rated in the Cramer guide, but modern gear has made the safety rating much more reasonable.

Gear: Doubles of thin gear up to .5. The start protects best with a purple-grey offset TCU, or a purple C-3. Some tiny nuts can be useful too.

FA: Jeff Smoot.

23 CORNER FLASH 5.7 ★★★

This excellent 5.7 is a fantastic intro to handcracks and offwidths. It is well worth the trip, and is one of Index's "easiest" pitches.

Gear: Hand-size pieces are best. Bring cams from .75 to 4, with extra 2s and 3s. If you have wide gear and want to play with it, you can certainly use a #5 as well.

FA: Steve Strong, Greg White.

MISSING BOTTLE BUTTRESS AKA TRAPPED BALLS

MBB is the large, interesting-looking buttress on the east side of the Inner Walls, across from the Toxic Shock area. It was orginally called The Milkman's Missing Bottle and is now more commonly known as Trapped Balls. Routes reside on the left and right sides, which are accessed by vastly different approaches. With more traffic, this wall could yield some very good lines.

Approach: *For Not in My House, and Trapped Balls* hike up to Agent Orange Buttress, then continue east uphill and to the right. A short trail deposits you at the base of *Trapped Balls; Not in My House* requires one last 4th/5th class scramble up and left, then step back right to the base.

For all other routes: hike up the trail towards *Toxic Shock.* Cross the creek, and keep an eye out for a small slabby boulder split by a handcrack (which you walk over). Here, head up and right, along a subtle trail, to the base of the buttress up the hill. A short 4th/5th class section gets you to the base of the routes.

Descent: All routes can be rapped with a single 60.

24 NOT IN MY HOUSE YOU DON'T 5.12A ★★

A short bolted arête with several difficult cruxes. To the left is a short but sometimes clean 5.8 handcrack called XL (wide hands).

FA: Darryl Cramer, Greg Olsen, Erik Thixton.

TRAPPED BALLS 5.10D ★★

s route's name derives from an accident with a rly-fit harness, so check your junk before you nb. Start in the chimney alcove uphill of *Agent Or-e*. From the alcove, climb out a roof and up a steep handcrack to a good spot to belay. The second h can either go straight up, or traverse left to a rappel at the top of the wall.

ır: Standard Index Rack.

Steve Strong, Jon Nelson.

THE BREADBOARD 5.10B ★★

furthest left of the right side routes (see ap-ach beta). Climb the thin crack to a 2-bolt anchor.

ır: Thin nuts and small cams.

Dan Waters, Ron Miller.

TROUBLED WATERS 5.11A ★★★

nb face and thin crack on cool features. After last bolt, escape right to a 2-bolt anchor. May be ;htly soft for 5.11a if you use the arête.

ır: Small cams up to purple BD, nuts, RPs, and 4 ckdraws and some slings.

Dan Waters, Ron Miller, Dave Hutchinson.

WHO PUT THE PURR IN MY PUSSY? 5.8 ★★

mb the obvious left-facing dihedral on the right e of the buttress using wide crack and stemming hniques. 2-bolt anchor.

ar: Doubles to #3, single #4, optional #5, nuts.

Unknown.

THE HAPPY PUPPY 5.9 ★★★

esponse to *Who Put the Purr in my Pussy*, *The ppy Puppy* is a fun crack climb to the right of the t-facing dihedral. It involves a crux fist crack, and hin handcrack. Ends at the same anchor as the evious two lines.

ar: A double set of cams from 0.75 up to #4.

: Darryl Cramer, Greg Olsen, Erik Thixton, Ron dinas.

SAM HILL / GILLIGAN'S TOE

This is an inspiring-looking buttress on the right side of the Inner Wall gulch, downhill and right from *Trapped Balls*. There are a few once-popular routes here, but now the entire wall is overgrown. This crag sees mostly shade during summer days and is definitely worth renovating (read: heavy scrubbing and new hardware) for those wanting cooler climbing on hot days.

Approach: Travel up the Inner Wall trail to where the regular trail crosses the creek. Just before this point, follow a faint/nonexistant trail up and right towards some buttresses hiding in the trees. Continue straight up, bushwhacking to the base of the wall's far right side. Here, you will find yourself beneath *Houseful of Hens* (the furthest right route on Gilligan's Toe). To reach Sam Hill, simply continue walking up and left hugging the base of the wall, past a slight break, to a bolted and moss-covered buttress. The routes are described left to right, starting with the furthest left route on Sam Hill.

Descent: A single 60 will get you down all these routes.

30 A DATE WITH DALE 5.12B ★★

An excellent slab testpiece with multiple cruxes. The rope drag can be bad if you don't backclean bolts (or use two ropes). There is often a wet section at the roof.

Gear: *Quickdraws, and long runners.*

FA: Erik Thixton, Greg Olsen, Darryl Cramer.

31 SIDERINDER 5.10A ★

Climb up and right past two bolts to some tough pro at an overlap, then continue past two more bolts to the anchor.

Gear: *Small cams, quickdraws, nuts, RPs.*

FA: Fred Grafton, Sabrina Kettle, Jim Gansky.

32 BOBCAT'S LAMENT 5.11B ★

A steep slab climb with cruxes at the top and bottom.

Gear: *Quickdraws.*

FA: Darryl Cramer, Erik Thixton

33 TEXAS, MY MILK FARM 5.12A ★

This is the first route encountered on the right side of the gully between Sam Hill, and Gilligan's Toe. Low-angle, delicate slab. There may be a loose block at the start.

Gear: *Quickdraws.*

FA: Greg Olsen, Darryl Cramer, Erik Thixton.

34 LEAVES AND GRASS 5.10B ★★

Probably the cleanest and best route on the wall. Start atop the large detached block, and climb up and right.

Gear: *Quickdraws.*

FA: Greg Olsen, Darryl Cramer, Erik Thixton.

35 HOUSEFUL OF HENS 5.11C ★

Varied climbing to the base of an open book. The start of the corner is insecure with difficult stemming. Jugs lead left to the belay at the top of the corner.

Gear: Quickdraws.

FA: Greg Olsen, Darryl Cramer, Erik Thixton, Ron Dedinas.

K CLIFF

K Cliff may have Index's best concentration of routes from 5.8 to 5.10. Most involve a mixture of bolts and gear. These are excellent climbs when regular traffic keeps them clean.

Approach: Hike up the Inner Wall trail until a faint junction branches up and right (if you reach the small creek, you've missed the right turn). If you keep an eye out, you'll be able to see K Cliff before the junction. After turning right, the trail brings you quickly to the base. Up and left of K Cliff is a scruffy wall that doesn't look like it's much worth climbing. It's not. But one route resides there: *Al's Armed Response* (5.8+), which climbs the crack system that splits the buttress.

Descent: All routes can be rapped/TR'd with a single 60. Also, all routes are easily TR'd by bumping the anchor over from pitch to pitch.

36 SPECIAL K 5.8+ ★★★

This may be the best route at the cliff, and is a great warm-up for the other lines. At the far left side of the wall, climb up a slightly dirty slab to the splitter cracks that arch up and right. Follow these to the anchor. The anchor is equipped for toproping, but not for rapelling. When you are ready to rap, simply move the rope a few feet right around a tree, and rap fro the anchor of *Rise Pumpkin Rise*.

Gear: Doubles through #1, perhaps a single #2.

FA: Unknown.

37 RISE PUMPKIN RISE 5.9 ★★

Follow the leftmost of two lines sporting glue-in bo through some blocky rock, up to a nice handcrack below the anchor.

Gear: Single rack to #2.

FA: Unknown.

38 TILT 5.11B ★★★

A fine line, with a tough move near the top. Follow righthand of the two lines with glue-in bolts.

Gear: Single rack through .75, quickdraws.

FA: Darryl Cramer, Ron Cotman, Jon Nelson.

39 KDAVR 5.10D ★★

This is a nice face-climbing route with some cool moves and interesting rock. Combining the upper part of *KdavR* with the lower part of *CF Route* would provide the cleanest rock and most enjoyable climbing, making this a three star route.

Gear: Small wires and cams.

FA: John Tetzlaff.

40 CF ROUTE 5.8 ★★★

This route starts in a fairly easy layback corner abou one-third of the way down the cliff (from left to righ It is popular, fun, and moderate. Follow the layback to a flake, then balancy moves gain a positive rail. Fu face climbing from here leads up to the anchor.

Gear: Single rack to #2.

FA: Cal Folsom, Debbie Brownstien.

Tom Ramier teching out high on Slapshot (5.11d)

41 BEND AND STRETCH **5.10B ★★★**

Another good line. Start immediately right of CF *Route*, and make cool face climbing moves past one bolt. From here, either continue up and left to finish on CF or up and right to join up with *Comes in Quartz*.

Gear: Single set of cams to #3, extras in small (tips) sizes.

FA: Cal Folsom.

42 COMES IN QUARTZ **5.10A ★★★**

This is one of the best lines at the cliff–not to be missed! Face climbing through a couple bolts brings you to some nice moves above gear at the latter part of the route. Clean, sticky rock, and interesting moves.

Gear: A double set of cams to 0.5 and singles from 0.75 to 3. Nuts, and a variety of slings and runners.

FA: Cal Folsom.

43 SPRING FALL **5.9 ★★★**

This route starts on an impressive finger crack, that would be one of the best climbs at Index...if it went for another 50 feet or so. Fortunately, cool climbing on good gear and neat features lie above.

Start on the finger crack in the right-facing corner, mantel past a little vegetation, and continue up on flakes and cracks.

Gear: Triples in blue TCU will all get used... but you can get by with a couple other similar size pieces if that's what you have. Single set of cams beyond that.

FA: Cal Folsom.

44 TURKISH HEELS **5.11A ★**

This route is 5.11a, with 0 stars, according to Crame guide; and 5.11 with three stars according to the Cli Cummins guide... We'd have to say it feels more like 5.12R/X, and 1.5 stars... The 5.11a grade is laughable, but hey, this is Index. If you plan on leading this, consider cleaning the tippytips layback on toprope beforehand, and sussing out the gear.

Gear: Tiny nuts, RPs, microcams, and ball nuts.

FA: Darryl Cramer, Terry Lien.

5 GO! 5.9 ★

'his furthest right route would be better if it were leaner, and better protected. For now though, it is he least quality route at K Cliff. Climb past a couple ow bolts. Trend up and left along a ramp to a 2-bolt nchor.

iear: Double set of cams .3 to 3, 4-5 quickdraws, 4-5 lings, nuts.

A: Unknown.

THE LIP

'he furthest east wall in the Inner Walls, and closer) The Great Northern Slab than most of the Inner Valls, The Lip is the first buttress uphill of the large lack wall adjacent to The Great Northern Slab. This rea has a few good routes, and is well-worth the isit.

pproach: The most direct way to get there is to ıake a short but steep bushwhack straight uphill om the first switchback after the Garden Wall, earing left of craggy rocks, to the base. It is also ossible to make a convoluted bushwhack downhill voiding cliffs) from K Cliff to get there. Neither pproach is well-established or obvious.

escent: All routes can be rapped/TR'd with a single 0.

A STICK AND A GUN 5.12B ★★★

his route (the first bolted line you encounter) is retty good, but involves a rather painful jam at the rst crux. At the time of printing, large tree branch-; have swallowed up part of the route. Climbing it ould require swimming through those branches.

he short dirty handcrack to the left is called *Cried rying* (Gerberding, Grafton, 5.10a).

ear: Quickdraws.

\: Darryl Cramer, Greg Olsen, Erik Thixton.

FIRST OFFENSE 5.10C ★★★

fun route deserving more traffic. Fantastic moves wildly featured, steep stone. The line starts on the r right side of The Lip, and angles up and left, then raight up, mostly following bolts and left-facing rners. An 5.11c direct start, *Head* (Cramer, Rosback) contrived, hard, and not as good.

oth *First Offense* and *Head* share a frustrating chor: three bolts (none of which have rappeling rdware), and a bit of tat hanging from a tree with nallion on it. Be prepared to walk off, or trust the ee tat.

ar: Mostly quickdraws, but bring small nuts and ms up to #2 for the start.

.: Bruce Garret, Fred Grafton.

Terry Lien climbing hard before climbing was a "thing."

TERRY LIEN

A HISTORY OF CLIMBING AT INDEX

started climbing at Index in 1975 a couple of years after the Pat Timson, Donn Heller, Don Harder years, rmed with about seven nuts and not really knowing for sure how they even worked. Our first climb was two-pitch 5.6 on the wall now known as *The Great Northern Slab*. It took all day. Needless to say at that me there were no people, no trails, no facilities. Just slugs. Index was a ghost town.

s the years rolled by, new faces appeared and a new local climbing community emerged. It was now not ncommon to see other climbers on the weekend. We even started recognizing each other's cars. It was bout 1979 that I met Jon Nelson and Greg Olsen who soon became regulars; a short time later came Daryl Cramer, Steve Strong, and Tom Michael. Of course, there were others but for the most part during the ext several years it was our little group that pretty much became the core of Index climbers.

lthough Peter Croft quietly came in and established Iron Horse in 1981, the beginning of new route activity really began in the spring of 1982 with the establishment of *Slow Children*. I remember the first time laid eyes on what was to become *Slow Children*. Jon Nelson and I were walking along the railroad tracks hen Jon stopped and pointed it out. "You see that crack up there." "You mean that line of weeds covered n dirt and moss?...Ya", "I think it would make a great new climb if we cleaned it". "Cleaned it?" I questioned. lthough common today, that was not a concept I had ever considered, but, somehow Jon convinced me it vould be a great way to spend time on cold rainy/snowy winter days.

Jncovering *Slow Children* opened all of our eyes as to what was really there. From that point forward we ecame aware of the new route potential at Index. More importantly, at least for me, was the realization hat it was ok for us to be the ones to spearhead the movement. In the beginning, I was a little intimidated vith the thought of putting up new routes. After all, that's what real climbers did, not us. Who were we idding? Climbing and cleaning soon became routine and although partners and routes changed from veekend to weekend, we all knew what everyone else was doing. Once a party established a new route he others would repeat it. It was a fun time. We were all totally committed. Though we all contributed, it vas Jon Nelson who really kicked things off. Jon was truly the visionary. He saw lines everywhere and was villing to get as dirty as it took to make them happen.

There were no rules, but we did have an informal code of ethics. As far as we were concerned there was o toproping, no hanging, and no chipping holds. A route wasn't free until it was led from the ground to he top. Yoyoing was ok only if there was a true no hands rest. Gear was placed on lead. Bolts were not o be added to established routes but could be chopped and replaced if they were perceived to be bad or langerous. Routes were rated based on their relative difficulty to other routes in the area. Pretty simple eally, basically the stuff we read about in *Climbing* magazine. Cutting trees down was ok, even encouraged if they interfered with the climbing (not endorsed by *Climbing* magazine). We were insignificant, on our own. No one cared, no one bothered us. It was a great time with great friends.

Although it may have been our little group that got the free climbing ball rolling. It was the next generation that truly put Index on the map, beginning with Todd Skinner's free ascent of *City Park* (5.13+) n 1986. Then by the mid 90s Index was flooded with new climbers. There were new faces everywhere and standards were being pushed higher and higher. A whole new set of rules and tactics came into play resulting in spectacular new routes. Lines that were never even considered were becoming reality. Index vas transforming. Thanks to the current set of extremely talented climbers, that transformation continues. I've seen the overall changes and they have been nothing but positive. Considering how passionate he current local climbers are, I see nothing but good things for the future of Index.

THE LOWER TOWN WALLS

The Lower Town Walls are the most popular collection of routes at Index, and the densest concentration of high quality climbs in the state, and possibly the country. These walls are tall, solid, safe, and awesome. No climber can resist their draw. For simplicity's sake, this chapter has been subdivided into five distinct areas from left to right: The Great Northern Slab, Winkie Dinkie Cliff, Roger's Corner, and the Lower Town Wall proper.

Approach: Just walk across the train tracks and you're there! You can also walk east along the tracks for a short ways and dip into the woods along a faint trail to arrive right beneath *Godzilla.*

SJ Lee pasted to the slab of Newest Industry (5.11a, p.74)

THE GREAT NORTHERN SLAB

The Great Northern Slab is a fantastic place for beginners to learn the arts of multi-pitch, gear placements, and crack climbing. That said, because of this reputation, and its proximity to the parking lot, this wall can often be crowded. Try to climb here early, or late in the day. If the area is too crowded for your liking, try The Mid Wall, K Cliff, or Private Idaho.

Most of the routes on The Great Northern Slab are technically multi-pitch affairs because of their wandering rope-dragging nature. Seasoned climbers, however, can often link pitches. Because of this, we have not listed all the original individual pitches on our route descriptions. Instead, we've tried to describe the pitch breakdown as we believe the routes are best climbed. Many belay options exist, and everything can be done in 1-4 pitches depending on your comfort level.

Approach: From the main parking lot, walk across the train tracks and into the woods and you're right there.

Descent: Everything at The Great Northern Slab can be descended with a single 60. Rap from the mess of chains above GNS to the railroad bolts, and rap again to the ground.

❶ THE GREAT NORTHERN SLAB 5.7 ★★★★

This may be Index's finest beginner climb. Climb it in one, two, or three pitches, as you like.

Gear: *Standard Index Rack.*

FA: Paul Guimarin, Philip Leatherman.

Pitch 1–5.7

Climb 15-20 feet to a large flat ledge. The easiest (but dirtiest) way is far left in a vegetated corner. Straight up a short clean corner is much more difficult, but the cleanest way. There are also options far right, but they require an extra very short pitch due to rope drag.

After the short plateau, climb up to the enormous eye bolts, and belay.

Pitch 2–5.7

Climb an initially difficult and challenging corner up to the slab proper, then cruise up fun twin cracks trending right to the top, and rap chains.

Lower here or climb one more short easy pitch to the top of GNS.

❷ PISCES 5.10A ★★★

This is a good intro to Index 5.10. The hard climbing is short, but sweet. Like GNS, it can be done in a single long pitch, or broken up into two.

Gear: *Double set of cams 0.3 to 3, 4-5 quickdraws, 4-5 slings, nuts.*

Gear: *Standard Index Rack.*

FA: Mike Berman, Mark Weigelt.

Pitch 1–5.10a

Climb up *The Great Northern Slab* route until a splitter off-hands crack right of the giant eye bolts. Follow that crack to the sloping ledge, and a perfect hand-crack in a slab. Rap off the mess of bolts and chains there, or make one more short pitch to the top.

Pitch 2–5.7

Climb up to the top via GNS, or a 5.7 ramp out right and then back left on bolts.

❸ LET'S GO BOWLING 5.11A★★

Short, but fun. Climb the bolted slab/arête right of *Pisces* past two bolts, then finish up *Aries*.

FA: Jim Yoder.

Tülin gives a finger-up for the splitter on The Great Northern Slab (5.7)

4 TAURUS 5.7+ ★★

Not as good as *The Great Northern Slab* or *Aries*, but smack dab between the two in difficulty. Starts up GNS, then cuts hard right, and eventually up the far right side of the slab.

Gear: *Standard Index Rack.*

FA P1: Ron Burgner, Tom Nephew; FA P2: Dave Anderson, Rich Carlstad, Carla Firey, Donn Heller.

Pitch 1—5.7+.
Climb up GNS, and bust right below the eye bolts and *Pisces'* splitter off-handcrack. Follow a short trough to an exposed and exciting traverse. Belay either before or after the traverse, depending on rope drag.

Pitch 2—5.7+
Instead of following the *Aries* roof out left, continue up and right on twin cracks, and then face climb to the top.

5 BLOCKBUSTER 5.9 ★

Climb the sickle-shaped crack right of the GNS route Surmount the block, or traverse around it, to join up with *Aries* or *Taurus*. A 5.10 variation is found to the left around the block.

Gear: *Standard Index Rack.*

FA: Ron Burgner, Tom Nephew.

6 AIR OVER ARIES 5.11A ★★

At the end of the *Taurus* traverse, move up and left over a roof, and climb the bolted slab up and left.

Gear: *Whatever you bring for Taurus. Mostly quickdraws.*

FA: Matt Kerns, Jim Yoder.

7 THE LIZARD ROUTE (AKA ARIES) 5.8+ ★★★★

This is the best line up The Great Northern Slab, as it winds its way through and around some very cool features. It was originally climbed/described in four incredibly short pitches. We recommend doing it in two (but watch the rope drag).

Gear: *Standard Index Rack.*

FA: Ron Burgner, Tom Nephew.

Pitch 1–5.8
Climb a short (only 20 feet or so), burly, wide hand-crack to a ledge. Belay here, or (recommended), continue up a left-facing corner to a ledge on the right.

Pitch 2–5.8
The infamous "Buttlips Chimney." It's every bit as good as it sounds. Grunt your way up and belay at the top, or (recommended) keep going out the roof to the left, and finish the splitter cracks up to a bolted anchor.

Lower here (recommended) or climb one more short easy pitch to the top of GNS.

8 VOYAGE TO THE BOTTOM OF THE VERGE 5.10D ★
Rarely done, this is a short pitch used to access *On the Verge*. A pin protects the finish but is often missing. If it is missing, the route is R/X. Climb up the face and arête to the right of *Aries*, under the Buttlips Chimney.

Gear: *A single rack of cams up to 3".*

FA: Greg Olsen, Jon Nelson, Mark Boatsman.

9 ON THE VERGE 5.11B ★★
This short arête right of The Buttlips Chimney is best combined with *Voyage to the Bottom of the Verge* for a single three star pitch. The arête was originally climbed without the advantage of modern sticky rubber—keep that in mind when you grease off!

Gear: *Single rack of cams, nuts, slings.*

FA: Dan Lapeska, John Tarver.

WINKIE DINKIE CLIFF

The Winkie Dinkie Cliff is aptly named, and features only two good routes. That said, they are both under 11, which makes them fairly popular, and worth visiting if you are looking for mileage, or a warm-up. Climbing these routes is also an excellent way to access The Mid Wall which lies directly above (plus some bushwhacking).

Approach: While it is possible to hike there by branching right off the Inner Wall trail below K Cliff, the best access is probably via climbing any route on the Great Northern Slab or *Roger's Corner*, and hiking a short trail to the base. BE CAREFUL in this area not to knock down loose rocks, as the very popular *Great Northern Slab* is directly below.

Descent: All the Winkie Dinkie routes can be rapped with a single 60.

10 HOUSE OF HAPPINESS 5.10B ★
This route is rarely done, though sometimes the top half is linked with the bottom half of *Timberjack*. Climb the layback/chimney crack on the left side of the cliff.

Gear: *A set of cams, slings, and 3 quickdraws.*

FA: Darryl Cramer, Erik Thixton, Ken Abeyta.

11 TIMBERJACK 5.8 ★★★
A fun moderate on laybacks and wide cracks. If you are comfortable at the grade, you can get by with a Standard Index Rack. If Index 5.8 gives you the willies, do yourself a favor and bring at least a #5. This is actually a pretty good route, and a rare Index 5.8. Don't let the wide gear fool you, it's a layback.

Gear: *Gear up to 6 inches.*

FA: Darryl Cramer, Erik Thixton, Ken Abeyta.

12 GORILLA MY DREAMS 5.10A ★★★
This is kind of a monotonous line, but if you enjoy laybacking, and clipping bolts, this one has your name all over it. If you enjoy laybacking, and clipping bolts, this one has your name all over it.

Gear: *Quickdraws, and optional small nuts or cams to protect the beginning.*

FA: Darryl Cramer, Erik Thixton, Charles Buell.

13 RETURN THE GIFT (TOPROPE) 5.12 ★
It's difficult not to fantasize about this route on the white face to the right of *Gorilla My Dreams*. It was originally envisioned as a free climb, but the unique white-colored rock is due to some sort of mineral deposit that drips specifically down this line, and is incredibly corrosive to bolts. The climb itself is very difficult, and somewhat contrived as one constantly has to avoid stepping left onto *Gorilla My Dreams*.

FA: Darryl Cramer, Erik Thixton, Charles Bluell.

Shaun Johnson dancing up Terminal Preppie 5.11c

ROGER'S CORNER AREA

Roger's Corner Area—the huge left-facing dihedral immediately right of The Great Northern Slab. It includes Roger's Corner and the pitches above and around it, as well as the routes on the Sonic Reducer Slab (the wall that forms the left side of the corner).

Overview topo for routes 14-23 on page 67.

Approach: Walk across the train tracks, through the woods and turn right at The Great Northern Slab. Shortly after passing the slab, follow a short steep trail uphill to a comfortable bench at the base of the corner. If you hit *Princely Ambitions*, you've missed the trail.

Descent: Roger's Corner routes are all rappable with a single 60.

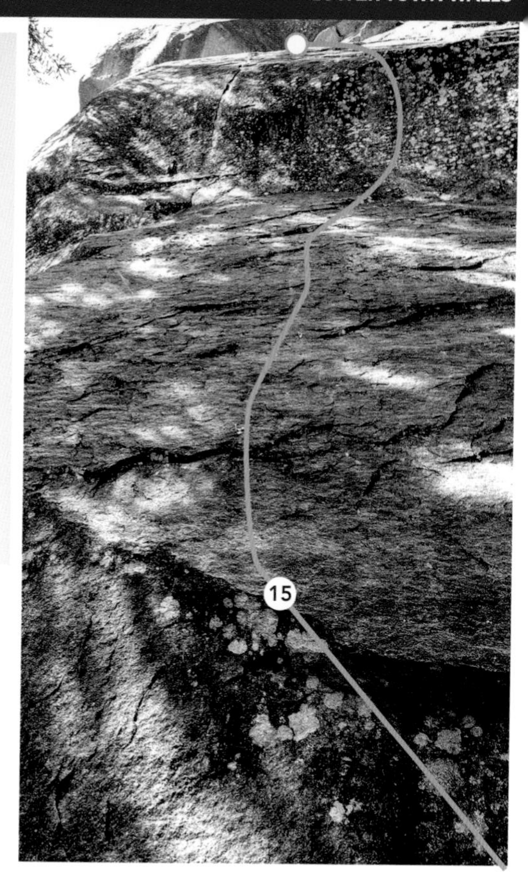

4 WALKIN' THE DOG 5.10C/C0 R/X★

This is the least quality route on the Sonic Reducer slab, and is rarely (if ever) climbed. The rock is friable, and the climb is neither a pure aid climb, nor a pure free climb.

Gear: *Unknown.*

FA: Don Brooks.

5 SONIC REDUCER 5.12A ★★★

This was actually Index's first official 5.12a, and it is still a proud testpiece. A befuddling slab boulder problem through the first three or four clips leads to significantly easier climbing above. This is the leftmost route that looks climbable, and the namesake or the area.

Gear: *Quickdraws.*

FA: Jon Nelson, Greg Olsen, Russell Erickson.

6 PRETTY VACANT 5.11D ★★★

A difficult start (stick clip) leads to a roof, and the slab above. Continually challenging edging and fantastic slab climbing make this a great route. Finish by moving left to *Sonic Reducer*'s anchors, or right to *Terminal Preppie*'s. If you head right you may need some gear.

Gear: *Quickdraws.*

FA: Darryl Cramer, Carmel Schimmel, Greg Olsen.

17 TERMINAL PREPPIE 5.11C ★★★★

This is the best of the routes in the Roger's Corner Area, and it is a doozy! Tricky moves at the first roof, sustained edging through the slab, and an airy traverse before the second roof make this an action-packed fun-fest. Don't celebrate too soon, the route isn't over til you clip the chains.

There is a rarely done second pitch called *Nick O' Time* which traverses right from the anchor to the top of *Roger's Corner.*

Gear: *Mostly quickdraws, small cams, nuts, and RPs for the bottom and top. A few long runners are nice.*

FA: Greg Olsen, Jon Nelson.

18 STRENGTH THROUGH BOWLING 5.10D/11A ★★★

This line used to get 0 stars and an X-rating. It is now a safe and excellent line, and a good warm-up for *Terminal Preppie*. Climb up right-trending cracks to the overlap, then up the right-most bolted line on the Sonic Reducer slab.

Gear: *Quickdraws and a single set of cams.*

FA: Greg Olsen, Jon Nelson, Bryon Trott; New Finish: Doug Taylor.

19 ROGER'S CORNER 5.9 ★★★

Though marred by a bit of lower quality rock in the middle, this is a great beginner's route, and the access point for *Breakfast of Champions* and *Marginal Karma*–two awesome splitters not to be missed. The obvious corner climbs through wide hands into some kind of junky (but safe) rock to an old anchor. Pass this, and continue through the steep dihedral to the anchor by the tree (base of BOC). You can lower from here with a single 70m rope, or rap to the first anchor, and then lower from there.

A short pitch that starts on *Roger's Corner* and climbs through awkward bulges out right to the same low anchor is known as *Sugar Bear* (5.10a, two stars).

Gear: *Standard Index Rack.*

FA: Greg Donaldson, Roger Johnson, Richard Mathies.

20 BREAKFAST OF CHAMPIONS 5.10A ★★★★

Breakfast of Champions is one of the best beginner handcracks at Index! A step up from *Pisces*, this one is steep but accessible if you are trying to break into the grade. Also, climbing *Roger's Corner* to BOC, is a great way to access the Winkie Dinkie Cliff (p. 69), which has more good routes from 5.8-5.10. Climb the splitter handcrack (the left crack) at the top of Roger's Corner.

Gear: *A variety of hand-size cams.*

FA: Dave Anderson, Don Harder.

21 MARGINAL KARMA 5.11B ★★★

The steeper, harder crack immediately right of BOC. This one is a finger crack but climbs like a sport climb. Not Index's hardest 5.11b.

Gear: *Small cams up to 0.75 and nuts.*

FA: Dan Lapeska.

22 VIRGIN ON THE RIDICULOUS 5.12A ★★

Immediately right of *Roger's Corner* are a few variations that lead up to a steep arête. Take any path you like (the furthest right is most challenging). The steep arête is not as good as it looks (unfortunately), and features some dangerously loose flakes.

Gear: *Small cams, nuts, quickdraws.*

FA: Greg Child, Larry Kemp.

23 5.12 INDEX AVE 5.12C ★★★

This recent Chris Henson line is a great addition to the LTW.

Begin at the bottom of the long line of bolts between *Roger's Corner* and *Dwarf Tossing*. The giant quarry ring that serves as the first bolt is considered aid and was not used on the first ascent.

Atypical holds through a series of boulder problems make up the lower cruxes. Fun 5.10 climbing in the middle to a sit down rest leads to more classic "Index Buggery." Rap it with a single 70.

Gear: *A lot of quickdraws (17), including two long runners for drag.*

FA: Chris Henson.

THE DIHEDRAL WALL

The Dihedral Wall is a small wall located up and right of *Roger's Corner*, between Winkie Dinkie Cliff and The Shield. It has a few decent routes, and is worth the visit, but shouldn't score high on your Index checklist. As of 2017, the wall was very closely crowded by a variety of trees, and the routes were generally dirty and in disrepair.

Approach: The easiest / best approach is to climb *Roger's Corner* -> *Breakfast of Champions*, *Princely Ambitions* pitch 2, or *Beak Beak Beak*. From the top of any of those, walk uphill and right along "The Terrace" which takes you past this wall on the way up to St. Francis' Ledge.

Descent: Dihedral Wall routes can be rapped with a single 60.

24 THE TERMINATOR 5.10B ★

A short knob climb. This and the following two route are certainly not the main attraction at this wall.

Gear: *2 quickdraws and medium size cams.*

FA: Doug Weaver, Jeff Wright.

THE DEFOLIATOR 5.7 ★

rely, if ever, climbed, this route goes up the ght-facing corner right of *Terminator*. The next cor-r over is a variation called *The Instigator* (5.8).

ear: *Standard Index Rack.*

: Doug Weaver, Scott Preuter, Jeff Wright.

WEEVIL'S WALK 5.10A ★

tle is known about this route. It is likely dirty, and climbed for some time. The long right-facing cor-r left of the *Defoliator.*

ear: *Unknown.*

: Unknown.

27 CUP AND SAUCER 5.11D ★★

This is a fun stemming corner which is now likely unsafe to climb. It would be a cool project to make this safe for lead, either by replacing the pins (which were gone in 2017), sussing out proper gear, or placing bolts (with permission from the first ascentionists, of course).

Gear: *May be impossible to protect without the pins, but try RPs and tiny offset cams.*

FA: Jon Nelson, Darryl Cramer.

28 JULIE'S ROOF 5.11A ★★

A painful thin crack in the third left-facing corner. At the roof you can continue straight up, or traverse left to join *Cup and Saucer*.

Gear: *Small cams, nuts, and RPs.*

FA: Larry Kemp; FFA: Julie Brugger, Tom Hargis.

29 GOGUM 5.11B ★★

A bold and awkward climb that is difficult to protect. Rarely done, but may be a pretty decent route if it got cleaned up and climbed more often.

Gear: *A good variety of small cams, nuts, and RPs.*

FA: Greg McKenna, Greg Olsen.

"Awesome and awkward" defines yet another classic Index addition. Chris Henson on his testpiece, 5.12 Index Ave. (5.12c)

LOWER TOWN WALL

The Lower Town Wall may be the best chunk of rock its size in the world. It has a little of everything, from 5.9 to 5.13+ but the majority of the lines are in the 5.11 and 5.12 range. The climbing is unique and funky, and it is pretty rare to tick all the routes on this wall, even for granite wizards. The rock quality, and climbing quality, almost always extend to the very top of the wall—so don't weenie out after the first pitch! Much more great climbing awaits you..

Approach: After crossing the train tracks, go right past The Great Northern Slab and Roger's Corner. The Lower Town Wall proper starts at the Princely Ambitions area.

Descent: You can climb a variety of LTW routes with a 60, but a 70 is mandatory to rap many of the most classic climbs..

30 ALL PURPOSE DUCK 5.11C ★

Twenty feet up and left of *Dwarf Tossing*, climb a dirty decomposing left-facing corner. Follow the corner, and traverse back right to join *Dwarf Tossing*.

Gear: *Standard Index Rack.*

FA: Terry Lien, Darryl Cramer, Tom Michael.

31 DWARF TOSSING 5.12B ★★★

This incredible climbs near the line known as *Snow White*, which is a two-pitch aid climb that goes at 5.11c A3. *Dwarf Tossing* starts around the corner on the arête uphill of *Princely Ambitions* with a gnarly V4 boulder problem. Continue up through a few separate 5.11 cruxes to a stopper seven-foot sideways dyno. If you can't make the dyno, it is easy to aid past by pulling on a draw. This route is easily toproped from *Princely Ambitions*. Rap to the base with a single 70, and make a short downclimb to the ground.

Gear: *Mostly quickdraws, but bring a variety of cams up to #1 and small nuts.*

FA: Rich Carlstad, Dave Hardinsty, Clint Cummins; FFA: Tom Ramier, James Wyland.

32 PRINCELY AMBITIONS 5.9 ★★★★

See p.75.

33 DR. SNIFF AND THE TUNA BOATERS 5.10D ★★★

From the belay atop *Princely Ambitions*' first pitch, maneuver right into a finger crack. Enjoy quality locks until the crack peters out into a short boulder problem. Work your way into a brilliant flare, and finish at the chains.

Gear: *Finger sizes down to RP's.*

FA: Terry Lien, Greg Olsen.

34 LAMAR'S TRUST 5.9+ ★★

A short slab outing up and left of *Beak! Beak! Beak!*. Rarely done, but not bad. If the anchor at the top is not in good shape, traverse right to the **Newest Industry** anchors.

Gear: *Mostly bolts, but an assortment of cams might be nice to protect the start.*

FA: Greg McKenna, Greg Olsen.

35 BEAK! BEAK! BEAK! 5.9 ★★

Climb an arching right-facing dihedral at the top of *Princely*'s second pitch to the 2-bolt anchor for *Newest Industry*.

Gear: *The same rack you brought for Princely Ambitions will do fine.*

FA: Greg Olsen, Jon Nelson.

36 NEWEST INDUSTRY 5.11A ★★★

Climb P2 of *Princely Ambitions* or *Dr. Sniff and the Tuna Boaters*. Once the terrace is reached move the belay 30 feet to the right to bolted anchors below a slab.

Climb up the bolted slab for five clips. After the fifth bolt, head to the dike and place gear up through a small roof and to the chains. Really good.

There is a second pitch that joins 10% *Meteorological Vinculation* (TPMV), and goes at 5.7, but most will choose to rap after the slab.

Gear: *5 quickdraws and 2-3 thin pieces 0.5"- 0.75".*

FA: Darryl Cramer, Greg Olsen, Max Dufford.

n the 1980s, *climbing Princely Ambitions (5.9) in the best possible style.* | *Photo by Larry Kemp*

37 NOBODY TOSSES A DWARF 5.12 ★★★

In 2014, Ben Gilkison freed this new pitch after some years of work and reconaissance. 5.12 is, for now, a suggestion. It's likely a sandbag, even for Index.

Climb the first half of *Princely*, and then continue right (where *Princely* traverses back left) to a 2-bolt anchor. Belay here. The second pitch goes straight up on bolts through a variety of challenging cruxes.

Roughly half of this route follows the original second pitch of *Snow White*.

Gear: *A variety of 0.3 and 0.4 size pieces, and 13 quickdraws (including 3-5 long draws), in addition to the rack for Princely to get up to the second pitch.*

FA: Ben Gilkison, Ryan Daudistel.

38 TADPOLE 5.11C ★★★

Tadpole is a fine pitch accessed via full *Model Worker, Frog Prince* or by climbing *Princely*'s first pitch, and making a 5.5 traverse right for 10-15 meters to the base. Climb up tight fingers to a bouldery move (crux). Finish up a 5.11a offwidth/chimey/flaring corner.

Gear: *Cams to 1", doubles of small stuff. Triples if you like to sew it up.*

FA: Dave Anderson, John Teasdale; FFA: Terry Lien, Greg Olsen.

39 MODEL WORKER 5.11C ★★★★

Welcome to Index 5.11c! If you are shorter than 5'6" (and not Lynn Hill), you may find yourself hurtling through the air sideways. If you are taller, the high step off the ledge might be stopper. Either way, this route is superb, and hard for anyone.

There's a low anchor, but do yourself a favor, and take it to the top. The principle difficulties are down low, and the upper climbing is fantastic. Climb it with a 60 or 70, but make two raps to the ground. An 80 will allow you to toprope, but tie a stopper knot.

Gear: *A variety of quickdraws, an inverted carabiner in the hole, and a #1 or 0.75 gets you to the first chains. A single rack from purple C3 to #2, and a few extra in the 0.2-0.4 range will get you to the top. Bring plenty of long runners.*

FA: Greg Olsen and Jon Nelson to 1st chains; Terry Lien, Max Dufford, and Greg Olsen to 2nd chains.

40 FROG POND 5.12C ★★

This is the improbable looking line right of *Model Worker*. Climb past two bolts into the thin crack leading up to the roof, and traverse left up to the anchors of *Model Worker*. Alex Honnold got the probable second ascent in 2016, and decided to stick clip the first bolt. So, you may want to do the same. But Greg Olsen says not to...

Originally a two-pitch route, the second pitch is never done. As Cramer said, "The second pitch should be avoided by those seeking even a modicum of quality in their climbing experience."

Gear: *Cams to 3", 2 quickdraws.*

FA: Dave Anderson, John Teasdale; FFA P1: Greg Olsen, Darryl Cramer.

41 NUMBAH TEN 5.12B ★★★★

Confounding Index trickery at its best is required t climb this narrow slot just left of *Iron Horse*. The lo crux is the most devious, but the route stays mostl 5.11+ throughout. One of the best sport lines at Inde

You may want to stick-clip the second bolt. Stay pa- tient with the low crux. It may feel impossible at fir but when you figure it out, it feels spot on for Index 5.12b. The rest of the pitch is a gift from the climbin gods.

There exists a rarely done 5.8 second pitch and a 5.1 third pitch.

Gear: *12 quickdraws.*

FA: Dave Anderson, Donn Heller; FFA: Max Dufford, Lary Kemp, Greg Olsen, Jim Purdy.

42 AMANDLA 5.13B/C ★★★★

Andy de Klerk, 1991, wow.

Climb *Numbah Ten* to the splitter through the roof out right, then pull through difficult finger locks around the corner to a steep and delicate arête. Tra- versing far right to cop a rest brings the grade dow to 5.13a... Index 5.13a, that is.

Ben Gilkison got the first ascent of the extension to this line (5.13d) in 2007, taking it through one more roof, to a more natural anchor point. You can also finish on the *Iron Horse* roof (also 5.13d). Bring extra RPs for this roof, or extra small cams for the *Iron Horse* roof.

Gear: *Quickdraws.*

FFA: Andy de Klerk; FFA extension: Ben Gilkison.

43 POWERHORSE 5.12D ★★★★

Climb the first half of *Iron Horse* into the second ha of *Amandla*. Killer.

It's 5.12c/d to the first *Amandla* chains, 5.13a to the second set above the roof. Blake Herrington coined the name *Full Horse Power* for the extension. It is, apparently, a less-contrived place to stop.

Gear: *Iron Horse rack, plus 5-6 quickdraws dependin on where you finish.*

FA: Justen Sjong.

Eric Child on Model Worker (5.11) in the early years. | *Photo by Larry Kemp*

48
54
66
52
35
68
36
48
54
65
44
58
57
51
53
33
44
38
48
37
41
63
61
62
64
54
55
60
67
69
41
49
31
32
48
63
39
41
44
54
60
69
42
45
62
64
56

㊹ IRON HORSE 5.11D ★★★★

This is the perfect-looking splitter on the clean face between *Amandla* and *Sagittarius* and one of the best pure trad routes at Index.

A couple low cruxes up to and through the first roof lead to a good rest. Climb some easier moves to the second roof, and a difficult exit (third crux) to a rest in the slot. There is an anchor here since the cruxes are beneath you; for full value, continue up through the slot, which is pure Index magic. Otherwise, clip the chains, and traverse right to finish on *Sag.*

If you want bonus points, go through the slot, and then pull the finishing roof of *Iron Horse* (5.11-) or *Sagittarius* (5.11).

Darryl Cramer rated *Iron Horse Full* 5.12a. Sonnie Trotter called it 5.12c to the first chains. Somehow, the grade 5.11d has become the accepted one, so that's what we're gonna call it.

Lower with a single 70. If you go through the final roof stand close to the wall and watch your rope ends.

Gear: *Cams from tips to .75, nuts, RPs, a couple offsets may be nice (red-black Metolius for upper crux, though other cams work as well). Bring a yellow C3, brassies, offset RPs, and small pro for the slot.*

FA to the flake: Roger Johnson, Doug Leen; FA full: Kit Hanes, Bob Lagenbach; FFA to flake: Peter Croft; FFA full: Dick Cilley, Dante Leonardi.

Pitch 1–5.11d
Climb the full route through the *Iron Horse* roof ou left to access upper pitches.

Pitch 2–5.10+
Climb straight up past three bolts (5.10+), or step o right to 5.8 terrain, until you reach a large ledge. Fr here, a number of options exist. Step left for *Numb Ten's* third pitch (5.10- finger crack), continue straig up *Iron Horse* P2 (5.10b stem, face), or step right to the third pitch of *TPMV* (steep fingers 5.10b to an e runout face).

㊺ SAGITTARIUS 5.11B ★★★

A fun route that packs a punch in the first 30 feet! There are two starts–either directly up the flare (harder to protect), or out right in a strenuous finge crack (harder to climb). Follow the huge arching fla out left underneath a roof, then pull over and chimney to some steep wideness and the anchor at the "ringing flake." Don't stop there–continue up the fir layback section to a second anchor. Stopping here i 5.10a/b, while finishing with the roof (recommende is 5.11b.

Gear: A *double set of cams up to #3 works. A single # protects the traverse fine. Bring plenty of slings. Rap with a 70.*

FA to the flake Pat Timson; FFA to upper roof: Mark Moore; FFA through upper roof: Terry Lien, Jon Nelson.

Jens Holsten takes it through the flare on Iron Horse (5.11d) | Photo by Ben Gilkison

TOP 10 SANDBAGS

- ❒ Rise and Fall (P1) 5.12b (p.160)
- ❒ I Am in Top a Shader 5.11c (p.233)
- ❒ Message of Love 5.11a (p.221)
- ❒ Swim (P1) 5.12c (p.166)
- ❒ Stern Farmer 5.12b (p.83)
- ❒ Normandy 5.12b (p.183)
- ❒ The Fifth Force 5.12b (p.116)
- ❒ Spooner 5.12b (p.116)
- ❒ Dirty Laundry 5.11d (p.134)
- ❒ Eraserhead 5.11b (p.236)

Greg Horvath negotiating with the Stern Farmer.

46 ARACHNID ARCH 5.12A ★★

This pitch rarely gets climbed, but deserves more traffic. It is the thin (often wet) roof beneath the big *Sagittarius* roof. Linking it into *Iron Horse* has not been done, but could be a pretty cool route.

According to Jeff Smoot, "Supposedly Ron Burgner toproped it in 1969... Dick Cilley TR'd it in 1984... In 1986, Russ Clune decided to give a lead attempt, but gave up because of a drip in a key jam. The next weekend, Clune was gone and so was the wet spot, so I gave it a go... I led out to the end of the arch (protecting with three rollers, a slider and a TCU–dicey!)... Protecting the rest of the flake was a challenge, so there was some hanging and fiddling with gear there. I went back up and figured out the sequence, pulled the rope, and led it. Definitely no style points there, but not out of line with the ethics of the day (I'd been hanging around Skinner too much)."

FA: Ron Burgner? Dick Cilley? FFA: Jeff Smoot.

47 TANTRIC BAZOOKA 5.11D ★★★

Tantric links the bottom of *Sagittarius* with the top of TPMV through some really cool climbing. Though originally freed on gear (wow and yikes), two bolts were recently placed next to the thin flake in the middle of the route with permission from the first ascent party. This route is now PG, and should become very popular. If you're short, the move getting back into TPMV may feel more like mid-12.

Gear: *Single set micros to #4 Camalot with emphasis on RPs and small cams.*

FA: Greg Child, Greg Collum.

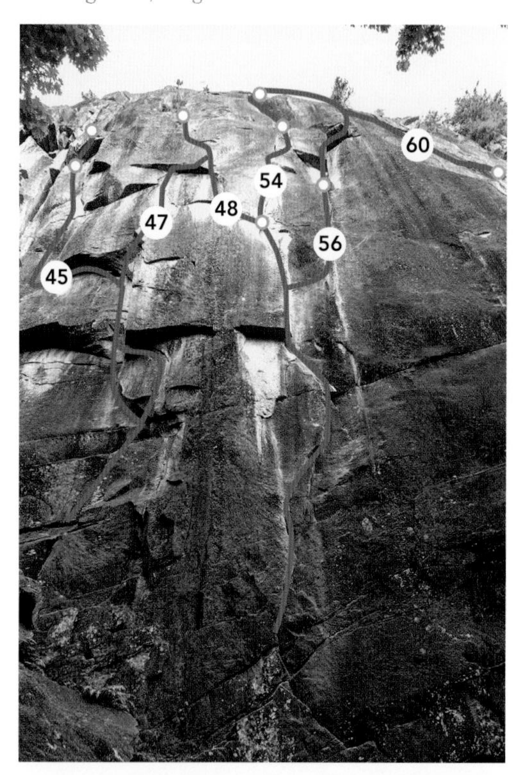

48 10% METEOROLOGICAL VINCULATION 5.13- OR 5.11D C1 ★★★★

This is a fantastic 5-pitch journey which goes the entire length of the LTW. The first pitch is usually done by traversing in from *Japanese Gardens* at the first chains, though the lower part of the route is good C1 nutting (and may go free eventually). Most people only do the first pitch, but the entire route is superb.

Gear: *A single set of cams, a few nuts, and some slings to the first chains of Japanese Gardens; after that, bolts and thin gear take you to the top. About 5-6 alpine draws and 5-6 quickdraws should work fine for the whole pitch.*

FA: Dave Anderson, Bruce Carson; FFA P1 (via JG): Larry Kemp, Max Dufford, Greg Olsen, Darryl Cramer. FFA P1 Full: Ben Gilkison. FFA: P3-5 Darryl Cramer, Greg Olsen.

Pitch 1–5.11d

Climb to the first chains of *Japanese Gardens*, and bust left. The chains are guarded by a couple challenging cruxes and a heartbreaker finish. This pitch is absolutely stellar.

Pitch 2–5.13-

If freeing this pitch, it is better linked with P1 from the ground, so your big whip happens with some rope out instead of right off the belay. Climb up above the first anchor to a difficult, height-dependent, boulder problem (5.12 to 5.13-) followed by a runout mantel and stemming in a corner up to an anchor on a ledge. Bring extra RPs, micros, and slings for this extension.

Pitch 3–5.10b

Climb cracks and face, angling left to an anchor below the obvious corner that starts the slab pitch (5.10-, slightly runout).

Pitch 4–5.11b/c

Another four-star pitch. Make a committing move to clip the first bolt. Climb the corner via bolts and gear, then proceed up a dike (runout 5.9) until you can step right to a ledge with an anchor.

Pitch 5–5.10d

Climb the slab past a bolt and some gear to a difficult mantel at another bolt. Follow cracks to an optional belay anchor and two options: either 5.8 R past a large hangerless stud, or 5.9 past two bolts. Both lead to the anchor atop the wall.

49 IT'S A DOG'S LIFE BUT YOU CAN PICNIC WITH US 5.11C ★★★

This is the farthest left of the four options above P1 of *Japanese Gardens*. Technical shallow corner climbing and stemming leads to a large ledge. There used to be two fixed pins on the route. They have since fallen out making this a bold lead. A 0.5 Camalot fits into a horizontal about halfway through the pitch.

Gear: *Singles from tips to 1".*

FA: Terry Lien, Jon Nelson.

50 IF GOD WROTE YOU A LETTER, WOULD YOU READ IT? A1 ★

This is the second crack from the left of *Japanese Gardens* P2. It is rarely climbed, and surrounded by excellent alternatives on all sides.

Gear: *RPs, beaks.*

FA: Unknown.

51 CHEESEBURGERS ON TRIAL 5.11B ★

Access from P2 of *TPMV*, or *Jap Gardens*. Start up a difficult-to-protect thin crack left of *Stiff Kittens.* After a bolt, cross *Stiff Kittens* and climb a thin crack to an anchor. The R part of this climb is much easier than the bottom half.

May be in disrepair. Use caution on lead.

Gear: *Whatever you brought up TPMV.*

FA: Greg Olsen, Darryl Cramer, Terry Lien.

52 JOURNEY TO PITAR 5.11D ★★

From the anchor of *Stiff Kittens*, difficult and runout knobby slab leads up and left to the end of *Japanese Gardens'* fourth pitch.

Gear: *Whatever you brought for JG or TPMV.*

FA: Greg Olsen, Darryl Cramer.

53 STIFF KITTENS 5.11C ★★★

Access from P2 of JG. This is one of the best pitches on the upper part of the Lower Town Wall. Not to be missed! It ascends the curving flake left of the third pitch of JG.

Gear: *Whatever you brought for JG.*

FA: Darryl Cramer, Greg Olsen, Larry Kemp.

54 JAPANESE GARDENS 5.11C ★★★★

See p.84.

55 TROUT FARM MASSACRE 5.11C ★★★

This may be the best P2 variation to *Japanese Gardens.* Climb up the true *JG* P2 until the first moment you can step right into a parallel crack. Continue up past some wild moves on twin cracks and flakes and hold on tight through the finish. If you don't see chalk, bring a brush.

Gear: *A good variety of small cams, and singles up to .75 and nuts and RPs.*

FA: Jon Nelson, Terry Lien.

56 STERN FARMER 5.12B ★★★★

The best 5.12b at Index, and maybe the world, and a 100% beautiful, fantastic world-class sandbag.

Climb to the middle of the first handcrack on *Japanese Gardens*, clip a bolt on the face, and traverse right into the shallow slot. Fight your way up through strange slot funk and thin fingers stemming past two challenging cruxes to a rest below the anchor. A little bit more 5.11 gets you to the first chains.

From here, either a) stop and lower, b) continue up and left finishing on the upper crux of *JG* (*Sushi Farmer*: still 5.12b, bring an extra blue TCU and a piece for the roof), or c) continue up and through the roof for the extension, a full value 5.12c/d (PG13). The left exit of the extension is cleaner, and more natural.

Gear: *A few finger and hand sized cams and nuts gets you to the bolt where you traverse right into the slot. Beyond that, it's all thin-finger size cams and stoppers (three 0.3-size pieces will not go unused), bring a few extendable draws.*

FFA P1: Terry Lien, Tom Michael; FFA P1 Full Right: Mikey Schaefer; FFA P1 Full Left: Mike Patz.

57 KLAUS VON BULOW & THE ALGORITHM OF LOVE 5.10C ★★

This is an alternative to *JG* P3. It is not as good, or as clean, or as consistent with the difficulty of other *JG* pitches, but still an enjoyable finger crack. It climbs the thin crack to the right of JG P3, and can also be done through a number of different variations (*Trapped by a Hampster*, and *Stern Jr.*, both one-star routes).

Gear: *Thin gear.*

FA: Darryl Cramer, Greg Olsen.

58 GIANT SIZED BABY THING 5.11C ★

This pitch goes up a few yards right of *Klaus Von Bulow*, starting with two bolts leading up to a small roof. The upper part of the route is runout, but significantly easier than the crux. It eventually traverses hard left to the JG P3 anchor.

Gear: *Standard Index Rack.*

FA: Greg Olsen, Darryl Cramer.

Marc André Leclerc soaks up the no-hands on the *Sushi Farmer Variation of Stern Farmer* (5.12b)

(54) JAPANESE GARDENS 5.11C ★★★★

Japanese Gardens is simply as good as it gets! All four pitches of this route are high quality, fairly clean, and safe. If you have never done the full route, consider it a must-do, paralleling the *Slow Children* linkup in consistent quality.

There is a low anchor which was put in at some point to provide a convenient 5.9 warm-up. The 5.9 is a two-star route; the 5.11c is a two-million-star route. Please be considerate of parties wanting to climb the full line.

Gear: *A single set of cams, a few nuts, and some slings will get you to the first chains. For the full pitch, add to that rack a couple blue TCU size pieces, a #4, and an extra #1 or #2.*

FA: Lowell Anderson, Dave Page (the famous Seattle cobbler), Jim Stoddard; FFA: Terry Lien, Jon Nelson.

Pitch 1—5.11c

Climb up moderate ground to a somewhat strenuous wide-hands crack. At the first chains, continue up the ow layback to the small roof. A crux here leads to a step-across move to gain the shallow dihedral out right. Climb through one more crux, and hang on through the pump to the chains!

Pitch 2—5.11b

Climb the thin crack out left, past a short, thin crux. A few options exist for the second pitch, but this is the best. A fierce move above good (but thin) gear brings you to the chains. A variety of finger and tips-sized pieces on each side of your harness should do.

Pitch 3—5.11a

This pitch is almost as good as *Slow Children*. That is not a typo. It really is that good! Climb the thin slot, pull the cool roof, and cruise to the anchors. Doubles of thin gear, and cams up to #1. Two purple TCUs could be nice.

Pitch 4—5.11c

Excellent climbing! Tricky dihedral smearing, stemming, and arête-pimping leads to a tough move left. Ancient pitons have now been replaced by intelligently spaced bolts. This thing is clean and hyper-classic. Small cams and quickdraws are all you need for gear.

Jenny Abegg hoping for good friction on the first pitch of Japanese Gardens.

82
81
83
84
66
68
90
52
81
73
54
54
68
53
58
65
89
57
75
72
81
70
76
80
55
61
63
64
74
85
60
54
69
79
87
56
63
72
86
76
81
78
64
60
71

59 BWANA DIK 5.11D ★★★

Named for the Bwana Dik himself, Dick Cilley, this route is appropriately overshadowed by the world-class lines immediately left and right of it. Though powerful and exciting, the *Dik* is a bit short, and anticlimactic. That said, you should still get on it–it's worth a ride. Just take caution as parts of the Dik can sometimes be wet.

Gear: *Purple TCU, doubles in finger sizes with some variety. Couple quickdraws.*

FA: Dick Cilley, Dave Rosenfeld.

60 BAT SKINS 5.12B ★★★★

Bat Skins is subtle, sweet, and pscyhologically engaging. Difficult moves above gear make the 5.11a climbing to the first chains eyebrow-raising, while befuddling stemming above the first chains will have most 5.12 climbers scratching their noggins. Super cool knobs make the impossible possible on this awesome pitch.

Shorter climbers may want to hang the top draw on rappel from *Godzilla*–it's not unsafe to fall from that position, but it's nice to be able to clip before the crux. The second pitch is every bit as good as the first, and goes free at 5.11d.

Gear: *A single set of cams to #2, with an extra blue TCU for the crux gets you to the first chains (5.11a). Five more quickdraws get you to the second chains.*

FA: Bob Crawford, Pat Timson; FFA: Darryl Cramer, Max Dufford. P2 FFA: Darryl Cramer, Nicola Mascian-daro.

Pitch 1–5.12b

Climb up beneath the left side of the long arching roof, and follow the roof all the way right. A short side-pulling section leads you to an engaging move out left onto the face, and then some trickery to reach the first chains (5.11a). Above there, difficult stemming and subtle movements leads up through a couple cruxes, all capped off by a final techy move left to finish off the pitch.

Pitch 2–5.11d

From the P1 belay, trend up and left past two (new) poorly-placed bolts (helps to have a 3-foot runner pre-rigged on second bolt). Climb through classic stemming and knob palming into a crack. Pull a mantel move where the line meets up with the *Stern Farmer* extension, and continue up a thin crack through the crux. Clip a final bolt and follow easier, runout climbing to the chains.

61 GOLD BAR GIRLS 5.9+ ★

Just as enticing as it sounds. Almost nobody gets on *Gold Bar Girls*. The climbing is friable, and it is the worst pitch in an area of high quality classics. The most logical approach is via *Godzilla*, then traversing to the far left side of the park benches, and stepping down and left.

Gear: *Standard Index Rack.*

FA: Max Dufford, Dante Leonardi.

62 ARTIFICE 5.10 A4 ★★

Artifice is the hardest aid route on the Lower Wall, and apparently not a good candidate for a free climb. Indeed, a few sections of each pitch look impossible. That said, there are some interesting free climbing possibilities throughout this route, which might make cool variations in the future.

FA: Dave Anderson Bruce Carson.

Pitch 1

Start on *Bat Skins*, then go up the thin seam at the first overlap. Belay at the second anchor (*Bat Skins Full* anchor). Sustained copperheading, technical trickery, and a tension traverse.

Pitch 2

Continue up the elevator shaft, through the roof, and up to the park benches (A3). Then aid the furthest left and thinnest right-facing dihedral (A2). This is a long pitch, and might feature loose rock.

63 CITY PARK 5.13+ ★★★★

The first pitch tips splitter is one of the most eye-catching natural cracks at Index. It is piss-hard, and better suited to pre-pubescent children than burly adults due to the wincingly small constrictions.

The route has been freed five times. First by Todd Skinner, second by Hugh Herr (a double-amputee) who manufactured feet to fit in the cracks (don't get wise, even with perfect feet this thing is absurd), third by Chris Schlotfeld. The first three ascents were all done by pinkpoint. Finally, in 2006 Mikey Schaefer did the first proper redpoint ascent, placing gear on lead. Recently, Blake Herrington made the fifth ascent.

Gear: *A ton of nuts, RPs, and small cams will get you to the first anchor whether you are freeing or aiding it. The second pitch (most commonly done after climbing Godzilla) takes a single set of cams to #1, two #2, and a small RP for the start.*

FA: Roger Johnson, Richard Mathies in 1966! FFA: Todd Skinner 1986.

Pitch 1–5.13+

Aid C1 or free the first pitch. Belay at chains.

Pitch 2–5.10b

Up and left from the anchor, clip a bolt and place a high RP. Pull difficult stemming moves into a perfect fingers to handcrack. Follow easy terrain to the chains. (Then climb *Slow Children*!)

Pitch 3–5.10a

Used to be A2. Recently retro-bolted and renamed *Park Ranger* 5.10a (p.88).

64 GODZILLA 5.9+ ★★★★

This is probably the best pitch of 5.9 in all of Washington. (Some might call it 5.10a.)

Climb up past an awkward first move and easy terrain to the top of a pedestal beneath a right-facing corner. Go either right or left, and continue up the corner past a series small roofs. When chalk runs out, step left around the corner, and pull a couple stemming moves (crux) on finger locks to another step out left to the chains.

The second pitch of *Godzilla* actually traverses hard right from the anchor (going left and up is the second pitch of *City Park*). This second pitch is called *Leapin' Lizards*, and it's really good.

Gear: *Standard Index Rack.*

FA: Don Harder, Donn Heller.

Pitch 1–5.9+

The first pitch is the incredibly classic right-facing corner. Stay right until the last possible moment, then traverse left to the anchor. A variation (*Bambi*) traverses left 15 feet lower at 5.10a.

Pitch 2–5.10c

This excellent pitch is best done as an extension to *Godzilla* and can be led with a single 70 from the ground. Move right from the anchor, clip a bolt, right again, then head up a crack to a V-slot with a pin and another bolt. Step right (third bolt) and stem/mantel to the chains. (Bring some extra cams from 2-inches down and small nuts).

There is a third pitch to *Godzilla* which is rarely done, dirty, and not recommended.

65 SLOW CHILDREN 5.10D ★★★★

One of the best pitches at Index, this V-slot finger-crack is as good as climbing gets–don't miss it! The stinger in the tail is classic Index. May feel like a sandbag.

The best way to get here is to climb *Godzilla*, then the second pitch of *City Park*.

Walk the plank to get started–it's awkward, but safe. Then climb flares and finger cracks up to an exciting "climb smarter, not harder" finish. Rap with a 70.

Gear: *Lots of finger sizes, with a focus on 0.3 (4 of these will not go unused), nuts, and cams up to 0.75. A purple TCU for the finish.*

FFA: Terry Lien, Jon Nelson, Jon Carpenter, Pat McNerthney.

66 TOMMY'S SANDBOX 5.11A ★★★

Awesome! Why rap at *Slow Children* when you can climb another classic pitch?

Step left from the belay of *Slow Children*, and enter a stem box. Continue through a small roof followed by tricky slab moves. Up and right, maneuver through an awkward body flare and undercling left. Pull wild moves out the huge roof with a finger crack to the chains.

Slightly up and right of the base of this pitch is an anchor at the start of a 5.9 called *Last Flight* (Henson), which takes you to the top of the wall.

Gear: *Standard Index Rack.*

FA: Mikey Schaefer, Chris Henson.

67 DEAL WITH IT RANGER 5.11B PG13 ★★

This is the original finish for what became *Natural Log Cabin*. It is scruffier, and dirtier, and not as good as *NLC*. That said, if you put it anywhere else, and cleaned it up, it would turn into an area classic.

The PG13 rating comes from the start of the route. After the bolt, the protection is good. When *NLC* steps right at the top, continue straight up.

Gear: *Standard Index Rack.*

FA: Dick Cilley, Jon Nelson, Greg Olsen.

68 PARK RANGER 5.10- ★★★

This two-pitch route is reached by either climbing *Leapin' Lizards* then climbing up and left to a chain anchor, or by traversing right along the park bench from the base of *Slow Children*, to the anchor below a groove with a thin crack.

Recently excavated, and still a bit scruffy, more traffic will keep this fun pitch clean.

From the anchor, climb the groove with a thin crack (hard to protect but a couple micro cams will keep you safe) up to a bolt. A cool crux leads into a flare and fun flake climbing to an anchor above.

The second pitch is 5.9 and less commonly done, but good.

Gear: *Standard Index Rack to #3 Camalot, bring extra micro cams (gray Metolius, purple C3, etc.)*

FA: Tom Ramier, Craig Rankin. Excavated and retro bolted by Blake Herrington in 2015.

Zenon Seeliger lifts his body weight in rope to make the clip on Godzilla (5.9+)

Super Dave climbing better than you can on Natural Log Cabin (5.11d) | Photo by Ben Gilkis

9 NATURAL LOG CABIN 5.11D PG13 ★★★★

n amazing display of geologic perfection—this might e the best 5.11d at Index. The climbing up to the rst bolt is spicy, giving the route a PG13 rating, (but oes at 5.10). If you're getting on this route (which lex Honnold called "the hardest 5.11d in the world"), ou probably are solid at that grade, so don't let the afety-rating deter you.

'limb up right of *Godzilla* through easy terrain to the rst bolt. Make wild moves out left, then up a stren-ous slot. Cop a no-hands rest at the top of the slot, ıen traverse right into the coolest V-slot around. ave some gas for the burly finish!

ı 2014, Dave Moroles placed a couple of bolts exiting ft out the bottomless stem box. It's probably not as lassic a finish as the original line, but it is still really ool, and worth doing. It is graded tentatively at 5.11d, ıt feels a touch harder than the original finish.

ear: *A single set of cams up to #1, with doubles from -.5; 7 draws and a few extendables. An 80m rope is andatory for toproping.*

A: Darryl Cramer, Nicola Masciandaro, Terry Lien

) SALAD FINGERS 5.11C ★★★

ıis arching corner lies above *Natural Log Cabin/ eal With it Ranger*, and can be accessed via either, by traversing right from *Leaping Lizards*. Climb up shallow chimney and into a shallower right-facing ıre on improbable moves. Engage the flare and apply ur repertoire of Index trickery to reach an imposing of. Hero moves to the chains up and left!

ear: *4 draws and gear to 2", emphasis on thin cams ıd fingers.*

: Tom Ramier, Tom Coe

NARROW ARROW OVERHANG .13A ★★★★

ıe impeccable and inconceivably good *Narrow row Overhang* may be the best 5.13a in the world. lay feel like 5.13b).

mb up through a thoughtful overhang to the first chor (5.11a), then out a wild stem box (small, tricky ar) to the second anchor. This alone is a superb 1c.

r full-value, continue past the second anchor up arête made of God's own stone, a wild boulder oblem through a roof, and a head-smearing finish. ıazingly, this all goes. Every bit of this route is top-tch.

e rating has been hotly debated, and while Blake rrington even suggested 5.12a, we think most will d 5.13a to be fair.

ar: *Quickdraws, nuts, RPs, and a single set of cams to #1. Single 70 will get you off.*

. Greg Donaldson and Richard Mathies in 68; FFA the middle anchor: Darryl Cramer, Terry Lien? FFA : Ben Gilkison.

72 NARROW ARROW DIRECT 5.12C ★★★★

This route is pure gold. The climbing is stellar, varied, and interesting. All four pitches are worth climbing. If pitch one is a bit above your head, you can finagle your way in from the anchor of *Shirley* to do the final three pitches.

Gear: *A single set of cams to #3. Doubles of 1" down. Yellow Metolius or alien protects the roof. Bolts protect most of the cruxes on P1. Wide gear for the final pitch.*

FA: Ron Burgner, Mark Weigelt; FFA P1: Dave Moroles; FFA P2-3: John Stoddard.

Pitch 1—5.12c

Cruise up easy terrain to a slightly runout (PG-13) stem below the roof. Pull the roof, and keep your cool through the corner all the way up to the baffling finish. Onsighting this thing would be pretty darn proud.

Pitch 2—5.10d

Technically two pitches, the orginal P2 and P3 are better linked. Layback up a corner (5.10) and then follow a thin crack up over a small roof (awesome 5.10d) and into a chimney. Belay at the anchor.

Pitch 3—5.10b

Climb the ow to the large ledge on top of the *Narrow Arrow Pinnacle*. This pitch takes big gear (to 6 inches), but is fairly secure to runout if you are solid on OW.

73 NO MAN'S LAND/HIGHER LEARNING 5.9 ★

From the top of *Narrow Arrow* tower, step across to the main wall and climb up the dirty slab through nowheresville to the base of *Bicycle Day*. A unique position. This pitch is not so incredible on its own, but it does provide access to the cool pitches directly beneath St. Francis Ledge (upper pitches of *Free At Last*, et al.)

Gear: *Standard Index Rack up to 2".*

FA: Tom Ramier, James Wyland.

74 I'D RATHER BE GOLFING 5.11B ★★

This is a challenging, but not as good, alternative right of *Narrow Arrow Direct's* 2nd pitch. Difficult to protect at the start. The righthand branch is a variation called *Chokin' the Chicken* and goes at the same grade.

Gear: *Standard Index Rack.*

FA: Terry Lien, Ron Kusera; Chokin' the Chicken: Terry Lien, Jon Nelson.

75 DEATH TO ZEKE 5.11B ★★★

This awesome pitch can be accessed by the first two pitches of *Narrow Arrow Direct*, and then stepping right, or by climbing the second pitch of *Shirley*. Layback out the clean orange arch, followed by a face traverse to the right. The corner above can be dirty.

Gear: *Standard Index Rack.*

FA: Terry Lien, Jon Nelson.

76 SHIRLEY 5.11C ★★★★

A fantastic intro to Index stemming. This attention-getting route may feel a little desperate, but just spread your legs and trust the rubber!

Begin between NAD and *Thin Fingers*. Moderate climbing leads to cruxy stemming right where the pro gets tricky. Keep it together, and fiddle something in before you pull the crux. Extra points if the train comes while you are sending—that makes it feel almost alpine... somehow.

Gear: *Single set of cams up to #2, with a good assortment of small camming units (such as purple and gray TCUs) and RPs.*

FFA: Greg Olsen, Dick Cilley, Jon Nelson.

Pitch 1—5.11c

The four star first pitch of *Shirley* goes up the awesome stem box left of *Thin Fingers*.

Pitch 2—5.10b

Continue up the crack on the right and belay at a small tree-this and the third pitch are rarely done. Another second pitch variation to the left is called *Freedom Fighter*, and is also rarely done.

Pitch 3—5.10b

Rarely done. Joins the offwidth portion of *Hard as Hell*.

77 SHIRLEY, YOU CAN'T BE SERIOUS 5.12C/D ★★★

This route adds an easier start and a hard variation finish to *Shirley*.

First clip a bolt and climb into the corner system righ of *Shirley*, place a thin piece or two, and when the corner ends step left and rejoin *Shirley*.

Continue up *Shirley* to the hand-jam pod below the crux stemming. Reach left and clip a bolt on the arête then downclimb until both hands are on the jug flake on the left side of the *Shirley* pillar. From here, climb up and left past two bolts, encountering two distinct boulder problems on the way to the NAD ledge.

Gear: *Gear for Shirley, plus four quickdraws.*

FA: Chris Tirrell.

78 24HR BUCCANEER 5.11B PG13/R ★★★

This is a short, good route with tricky pro and difficu climbing, but is not such a bad lead with modern technology. It starts about 15 feet left of *Thin Fingers* and climbs up powerful laybacks and tough slab to a left-leaning seam.

Gear: *A good variety of small cams and RPs will get yo through. It would not be a bad idea to dial in the gear on toprope.*

FA: Terry Lien, Jon Nelson, Greg Olsen.

79 THIN FINGERS 5.11A ★★★★

Thin Fingers is one of the poster-childs of Index. Moderate climbing leads to a stopper slab crux at the first anchor. Above lies a splitter handcrack—one of the best at Index—and some fun laybacking to the finish.

Many have wondered why this hand crack is so named. Back when Paul Boving freed the route, the crux parallel crack used to be much thinner. A huge rockfall later significantly widened the crack, coincidentally making it much easier.

Tragically, Paul Boving died on this route shortly afte succeeding on its first free ascent—one year before the invention of the cam, which probably would have saved his life. It is now safe and easily protectable, but think of Paul in 1977 when you plug your cammir devices, and imagine the climb as he climbed it.

For a fun variation, after leaving the handcrack, continue farther right and climb a challenging thin crac to the finish (*Big Toes*, 5.11a/b).

Gear: *A double set of cams to #2, micronuts and RPs for the crux. A single #3 may be useful. 70m rope mandatory.*

FA: Paul Boving.

80 HARD AS HELL 5.10B ★★

Above *Thin Fingers* and *Tattoosh*, *Hard As Hell* under clings out an arching flake, and then follows a wide crack up and left to *Narrow Arrow*. Rarely done.

FA: Kit Hanes, Don Heller.

"The Walking Legend" Sullivan display-
proper stemming technique on Shirley
) | Photo by Stamati Anagnostou

Chris Heason enjoying the goods on Thin Fingers (5.11a) | Photo by Ben Gilkison

81 TATOOSH / FREE AT LAST 5.10D ★★★★

Tattoosh is a phenomenal route just right of *Thin Fingers*, and one of the best pitches of 5.10 at Index. It is also the first pitch of a 4-pitch route called *Free at Last*, which is an excellent (although often dirty) excursion to the top of the LTW with no climbing above 5.10.

Gear: *Standard Index Rack.*

FA Free At Last: Ron Burgner, Mark Weigelt; FFA P1: Mead Hargis, Jim Langdon; FFA of VOTMGET: Tom Ramier, Craig Rankin.

Pitch 1–5.10b

Just right of *Thin Fingers*, climb a funky slot (crux) to some easy climbing. Difficult stemming takes you to a split. Either way is fun right slightly easier. Save some small gear for the top, and stem and jam your way (second crux) to the anchor. If you plan to keep going, continue past the chains, and belay on trees on the ledge above. Be careful not to knock off loose blocks.

Pitch 2–5.9

Step left on the ledge and climb the dirty second pitch. This is the worst pitch of the route, but the rest is quite good.

Pitch 3–5.10

Continue up a steep, splitter handcrack that pulls through some cool flakes and wild terrain. Walk right out a slab, and belay at a 2-bolt anchor.

Pitch 4–5.10d

This pitch starts on *Path of Righteousness*, and finishes on *Voyage of the Majestic Glass-Eyed Tuna*. It is a very good pitch. From the anchor, step left and make some awkward moves to get started. Climb through a few bolts (cruxy), and some finger–sized gear, until you are at a small ledge, and the base of a V-slot with a splitter handcrack (*Voyage*). This slot is really good, and is not to be missed. Exit right to reach St. Francis Ledge, and the top of the LTW.

82 KUNSELMAN'S PHYSICS 5.12B ★★

The positioning on this pitch is out of this world. B gin on the 4th pitch of *Free At Last*. Climb the first of *Bicycle Day*, then negotiate past three nicely sp bolts up the technical face of the headwall.

Gear: *Cams to 1".*

FA: L. Thorne, James Wyland.

83 BICYCLE DAY 5.10 ★★

Shares the first 30'. of *Free At Last* P4, but traverse hard right beneath the roof, eventually pulling the roof on the right. Then traverses hard left back to anchor. Watch rope drag.

Gear: *Whatever rack you used to get you here shoul plenty. Gear to 3" should do fine.*

FA: T. Budden, James Wyland.

84 SHIVER ME TIMBERS 5.10A C1 ★

From the P3 anchor of *Free at Last* aid hard right o bolts to some steep, friable flakes and climb them very carefully. This would be a four-star route if it went free and if the flakes were safe.

Gear: *Cams to 2".*

FA: S. Bangs, James Wyland.

85 JUST SAY NO 2 5.12B ★★

The start of this route has a couple burly cruxes. T top is rarely done. Most will traverse right for *Like Honey*. The bolts on the upper part of the arête are poorly placed and difficult to clip. If retro-bolted, t would be a more popular route.

Gear: *Mixed bolts and thin gear.*

FA: Jim Yoder, Larry Kemp.

Unknonw climber on Tatoosh (5.10b)

ian Ebert taking it to the tippy top of the lower wall on Free at Last/VOTMGET (5.10)

86 LIKE HONEY 5.12A ★★★

This is a great line which links the better parts of *Just Say No* and *Apologies* with a pretty wild face-climbing sequence. Climb past a bolt to a stance, then make cruxy moves past more bolts to a confuddling traverse right into *Apologies*. Finish up the splitter of *Apologies*.

Gear: *4-5 quickdraws, and a single set of cams get you to the crux. A few more cams from .4-1 are nice for the finishing crack.*

FA: Chris Henson.

87 WITH APOLOGIES TO WALTER B 5.11A ★★★

The highlight of this route is a tricky leftward traverse halfway up, and the splitter crack finish.

Start in somewhat rotten rock and climb fun moves to a rest. Make a difficult traverse left, and finish up the crack.

Gear: *Standard Index Rack.*

FA: Kjell Swedin; FFA: Dan Lepeska.

88 QUARRY CRACK 5.9 ★★

This is a really dirty, crumbly, chossy climb. If it became popular, it might be more enjoyable.

Climb the vertical choss gully around the corner from *With Apologies to Walter B*. This is the rightmost route to leave the ground on the LTW.

Gear: *Standard Index Rack.*

FA: Don Harder, Don Heller.

89 BOB AND DORIS 5.11B ★★

This is a good thin crack, but rarely climbed. If you step into the left corner at the start it's significantl easier. Access this pitch by finishing *Like Honey*, *Ap ogies*, or *Quarry Crack*. It is most likely dirty, and m feature loose rock.

Climb up the thin crack to a small ledge and two right-facing dihedrals. The left of those is called *Let Barbecue* and, according to Terry Lien, is recommer able. Climb the farther right one to a slung block be at the top. This belay is kind of sketchy, and would better replaced by a 2-bolt anchor.

Both left and right variation aren't worth the effort.

Gear: *Small cams, nuts, and RPs.*

FA: Terry Lien, Jon Nelson.

90 OLD MAN HUBBARD 5.11 ★★

A recent James Wyland addition above *Bob And Dor* The grade and quality are an estimate.

Gear: *Quickdraws.*

FA: James Wyland.

St. Francis the patron saint of animals, including monkeys

ul Tomlinson finishes up the splitter of With Apologies to Walter B (5.11a) | *Photo by Ben Gilkison*

The unequivocally stunning Lower Town Wall.

ACQUIRING THE LTW

MEMORY OF DOUG WALKER, 1950-2015

Trespassing. These are the signs you never want to see at your local crag. For five decades, climbers oyed nearly unfettered access at Index–so what changed? History has a way of repeating itself: the private downers of the Lower Town Wall quarried granite until redirection of the railroad brought the operations a screeching halt in the 1960s. In 2009, they saw a renewed opportunity to quarry some of the granite. The ns were posted and local climbers raised the alarm. The best way to answer a threat to access, like "No spassing" signs, is to respond with an alternative opportunity.

t months earlier, I managed the acquisition of Heybrook Ridge in partnership with Index town residents and ohomish County, as a young project manager for our local land trust, Forterra. When 100 acres of mature est were slated for a clear cut, the local community fought to preserve the ridgeline and make Index a sce- gateway to the Wild Sky Wilderness that surrounds it.

w, with "No Trespassing" signs just across the river, we found ourselves with another critical conservation portunity. It was time for local climbers to step up. I had recently joined the Access Fund as Access Director, ving just moved out of my home state. I jumped at the opportunity to combine my two passions: conserva- n and climbing. I was in charge of building a new program, the Access Fund Climbing Conservation Loan ogram: a tool for local climbing organizations like Washington Climbers Coalition (WCC) to protect their eatened local crags. It just so happened to be my favorite climbing area, too. My thought from the beginning s to repeat the same strategy used for Heybrook: secure an option agreement to give us the sole right to rchase the 20-acre parcel that contains the Lower Town Wall, Inner Walls, and Quarry with enough time to se the necessary funds.

der the leadership of former Access Fund Board President Dan Nordstrom and Executive Director Brady binson, the Access Fund raised enough from philanthropists and leaders in the outdoor industry to provide first-ever loan for Washington Climbers Coalition to secure the Option. WCC General Counsel and Access nd Regional Coordinator, Jonah Harrison, negotiated the deal on behalf of WCC. The landowners accepted CC's offer of a $10,000 nonrefundable option payment to go towards the total purchase price of $110,000 if CC exercised the option within 18 months. For the landowners, a voluntary sale of the property proved to a better alternative than contracting with a quarrying operation. The plan was for WCC to purchase and nporarily hold the property with the long-term goal of transferring the Lower Town Wall to the surrounding rks of the Sky State Park. The Option was recorded on June 2, 2009 and a team of WCC and American Alpine ıb (AAC) volunteers led the fundraising charge. That team included Andy Fitz, Dave Haavik, Darryl Cramer, die Espinosa, Jason Keith, Jeremy Park, Mary Hsue, Porter Hammer, Steve Swenson, and other dedicated mbers.

amwork paid off. The conservation strategy worked. But there was one climber I did not list above that was the heart of the effort: Doug Walker. It is thanks to Doug that so many of the pieces came together. When old friend "Stim" Bullitt, a philanthropist that found his love for climbing and Index later in life, passed away, ug saw a special opportunity to save Index and give Stim's family and friends a way to honor him. Doug was o a leading donor of the Access Fund's loan program and he served on the AAC board, energizing the club's twork to donate. Nearly half of the $300,000 raised for the acquisition and long-term stewardship of the dex Town Walls came from Doug's outreach and his idea of honoring Stimson Bullitt.

e foundation of the recreation and conservation movement cracked on December 31, 2015 when Doug Walk- passed away on Granite Mountain. For those of you who climbed with Doug, you know first-hand he had a ack for "out schooling" his partners in American history trivia, post holing, and sprinting to the summits of local favorite peaks. He mentored young conservationists and climbers across the Northwest, encouraging em to pursue their passions and protect our outdoor playgrounds. He shared a contagious enthusiasm with yone he roped up with. And Doug wore many hats; his work cannot be credited to any single group, and his luence is still felt everywhere we go.

CC is working hard on the next chapter at Index: finalizing plans with the county for a vault toilet, drafting limbing management plan and a deed restriction that will preserve the original spirit of climbing at Index, arantee our right to climb here forever, and keep it a remarkable place for climbing and wildlife, alike. Index one of the most amazing places to climb in the country and, for many of us, it is the best. Let us pass on the story of generosity by sharing our love for Index with everyone that walks up to its walls and cranks their ck back in awe.

oe Sambataro, Northwest Regional Director, Access Fund

Dan Aylward taking his time on Zoom (5.10d).

THE COUNTRY

The Country is a fine place to climb, and one of Index's most popular zones. The approach is short, and many excellent sport climbs can be found here, as well as some sensational trad lines. Though not quite as busy as the LTW itself, this area can be crowded at times. Still, with only a couple of exceptions, you probably won't have to wait in line for a single route.

For the sake of convenience we have included The Quarry and The Orc Tower in this chapter. As you will read in the subchapter descriptions for those walls, they are very much their own unique and special crags, quite separate from The Country in all ways save for geographic proximity.

Approach: The Country is accessed by hiking a short way along the train tracks and dipping into the woods along an access road to the tunnel.

THE QUARRY

Smack dab in the middle of the two most frequented walls at Index–The LTW and The Country–lies a zone so obscure, so strange, so frighteningly unknown that few have, or ever will, climb there. Welcome to The Quarry: a piratic zone best left to true Index Locals. You can expect to find dangling monkey-fists, missing bolts, fixed boat lines, dirty approach pitches, and tree climbs, along with some hidden diamonds in the rough.

Instead of trying to describe each nuance of this area in minute detail, we will let the chief architect of the majority of the routes do the talking–and take him at his word. Consider the descriptions, grades, and number of stars gentle suggestions from a sample size of 1. If you're looking for an adventure, this is the place for you.

Approach: For left side routes, approach from the right end of the LTW. For the routes on the right side, head to The Country proper, and bushwhack up a brushy trail on the far left side. Many of the far right routes are accessed via routes on the far left side of The Country.

Descent: Better bring a 70 to be safe, who knows what shenanigans you'll get into here.

❶ MINI AIR DANGLER / OTHERS 5.8 ★★

Between *Quarry Crack* and the first route on The Quarry Wall are a number of low quality, dirty routes on questionable stone. One of these routes doesn't even exist any more, having disappeared in a massive rockfall some years ago. *Mini Air Dangler* is probably the best of these pitches. It is a handcrack that is rather steep and starts in munge. While the rock high on this pillar looks amazing, it is full of death blocks, and better left unclimbed.

Mini Air Dangler starts uphill of *Quarry Crack* and goes up a handcrack a short ways before it traverses left on a flake.

Gear: Standard Index Rack.

FA: Various.

❷ STAMPER HOLLAND 5.9+ ★

Start on the far left side of The Quarry Wall, at the bottom of the gray pillar, after a bit of a 4th class scramble. Look out for loose death blocks.

Gear: Standard Index Rack.

FA: James Wyland, Jeff Ellerbrook.

Pitch 1–5.9
Climb 4th class into the safest, cleanest terrain beneath the clean white overhangs on the pillar left of The Quarry Wall. Near 30m or so, when it starts to get steep, step down and right to a fixed anchor belay.

Pitch 2–5.7
Do a short traversing downclimb onto The Quarry Wall proper, crossing a vertical gully. Make a natural gear belay in a good stance.

Pitch 3–5.8
Climb up and slightly left on The Quarry headwall or rather good stone. Stop at a 2-bolt anchor close to the top.

Pitch 4–5.9+
DO NOT go straight up from the anchor. Traverse hard right along ramps and cool features. You can to it out and walk off at the first possible moment, or continue traversing right until you reach the anchor for *Tour of Duty*, and rappel that.

❸ FRONT LINE ASSIGNMENT 5.11B ★★

This is an alternate 5th pitch to *Tour of Duty*. Climb out the overhang, pass three bolts, and then continu up a finger crack.

Gear: Your Tour of Duty rack will cover it.

FA: John Tetzlaff, James Wyland.

❹ TOUR OF DUTY 5.11B ★★

The leftmost route encountered on The Quarry Wall proper. This and *Jonah Benkert's World Famous Humble Pie* share the first pitch. After pitch one, *Tour of Duty* heads left.

Start from a gold-colored bolt atop a pedestal on the left side of the wall.

Gear: Standard Index Rack.

FA: Aaron Clifford, James Wyland.

Pitch 1–5.11b
The first pitch is bouldery and hard, but on clean roc for the start. The second half of the pitch is 4th class to the base of the steep headwall. Belay at a bolted anchor.

Pitch 2–5.11b
Continue up and left (right is *Humble Pie*), starting with a finger crack and then climbing a friable face. This is the worst pitch of the route.

Pitch 3–5.9
Start with a finger crack, then continue up face mov passing another bolt (last on the route). Continue up a splitter handcrack to the base of the obvious black corner.

Pitch 4–5.10b
This is the second best pitch of the route. Climb the crack in the corner with a variety of gear options fro small to large. Belay at an anchor below the roof.

Pitch 5–5.10c
This is the best pitch of the route! Climb out the righ side of the roof on a handcrack which angles back le through an undercling to the top.

Exiting the roof on the left is *Front Line Assignment* - 5.11b.

17
10
11
15
16
9
3
6
8
2
4
5
19
25
28
14
13
12
26
18
27
20
44
37
45
29
30
32
38
35
36

Note: *Topo for routes 5-21 on P. 103.*

5 JONAH BENKERT'S WORLD FAMOUS HOMEMADE HUMBLE PIE 5.11C ★★

The 4th pitch of this route seems inviting until you consider the climbing to get to it. Awkward, difficult, dirty, and chossy could describe the first two pitches. The third pitch follows a nice feature with improved climbing but is often dirty.

Unfortunately the hardware installed is not completely stainless and while it is good as of 2017, climbers are advised to use caution.

Start from a gold-colored bolt atop a pedestal on the left side of the wall.

Gear: *12 quickdraws should be fine, and an optional blue TCU.*

FA: Nic Rosser, James Wyland.

Pitch 1–5.11b
The first pitch is bouldery and hard. The second half of the pitch is 4th class to reach the base of the steep headwall. Stick-clipping the second bolt is recommended as the first bolt hardly protects an obvious ledge fall. Belay at a bolted anchor.

Pitch 2–5.11b
This pitch begins a bit bouldery as well. Climb a sloping rail right under an overhang to easier ground, and a set of chains (for *Tour of Duty*). Don't stop here; continue out right to another bolt station.

Pitch 3–5.10b
Climb up the cool black pillar to the base of the headwall.

Pitch 4–5.11c
This is probably the best pitch of the route–face climbing on a blank-looking orange and black streaked face. Belay in an alcove.

Pitch 5–5.10b
Climb up moderate terrain to a ledge that traverses right along a rail. Finish at a belay on a large ledge with two trees. Either rappel from here, or climb the last pitch (5.11c) of *Tales From Zahajko.*

6 TALES FROM ZAHAJKO 5.11C ★★

Zahajko begins just right of *Humble Pie* on bolts through a bouldery section (previously known as *Whipnatize*). This is a fine route with some cool climbing. The last pitch is airy, steep, and fun!

Gear: *12 quickdraws ought to do. If you plan to climb the 5th pitch, make sure to bring a single rack of cams to 3".*

FA: Brad Lignoski, James Wyland.

Pitch 1–5.11b
Bouldery climbing leads to a 4th class section, followed by a bolted face, that ends at a large treed ledge and a 2-bolt anchor.

Pitch 2–5.10c
This fun pitch climbs through some steep terrain on jugs up to a hanging belay below a triangular roof.

Pitch 3–5.11c
Climb up and right from the belay. One super cruxy move (i.e., 5.11c sandbag) passes the slight roof and gains the headwall. Climb up to a small ledge belay to the right of the only tree on the headwall.

Pitch 4–5.11b
Climb a discontinuous crack to a two-tree ledge. There is an open project to the left of this pitch.

Pitch 5–5.11c
The 5th pitch uses gear in a crack to start then traverses left under a roof to a flare with bolts. Also known as *Constructive Mathematics.*

7 COBBS FREEZER 5.11D ★★★

A worthy variation to P4 of *Tales From Zahajko*. From the belay climb the overlap left, passing bolts.

Gear: *Quickdraws.*

FA: James Wyland.

8 COACH'S FABLES 5.11D ★★

This is an alternate ending to *Tales from Zahajko*, splitting off right in the middle of the third pitch.

Gear: *Quickdraws and gear to 1".*

FA: John Tetzlaff, James Wyland; FFA: Cole Allen, James Wyland.

Pitch 1–5.11c
After P1 and P2 of *Tales from Zahajko*, head right as per *Tales'* third pitch. Where *Tales* goes straight up, continue right towards twin roofs. Belay beneath the left roof.

Pitch 4–5.11d
Climb out a flare to thin face climbing past bolts and two pins in a discontinuous crack to a belay. This is one of the best pitches on the wall.

Pitch 5–5.10a
Climb up a knobby overhanging block past a bolt to easier gear-protected climbing through ledges and roofs to the top.

9 ALTERNATIVE FACTS 5.11C ★★★

Start 15' right from the start of *Coach's Fables*. An ear dyno leads to technical face climbing higher up.

Gear: *Quickdraws.*

FA: S. Eves, James Wyland.

10 CONSTRUCTIVE MATHEMATICS (AKA SOME BULLSHIT) 5.11C ★★

Essentially a final pitch to *Tales From Zahajko*. Climb up a short wall, then traverse left on knobs under a roof, then up an awkward, flaring slot to the chains.

Gear: *Quickdraws, gear to 1".*

FA: Brad Lignoski, James Wyland.

25 OVER ORCSPOSED 5.12A ★★★

So long as the Orc Tower itself does not fall down, this is an excellent, and completely safe route. Climb *Zoom -> Leave My Face Alone / Kite Flying Blind*, and then make a short 4th class walk through the trees to the base of the Orc Tower headwall. Be careful not to knock loose rocks onto your partner!

Gear: Quickdraws.

FA: Greg Collum, Mike Massey, Matt Kerns.

Pitch 1–5.11b

Beginning beneath the steep white wall, climb up and left past a hanging chain through cool, steep terrain, to a bolted belay around the corner on the west side of the Orc Tower.

Pitch 2–5.12a

The start is a doozy, but there's a late crux, too. Layback the improbable and bouldery arête right off the anchor, then traverse right. Another crux is encountered pulling a bulge, and then the route and finishes in an amazing position between two minarets on the top of the Orc Tower.

Chris Kalman battling demons on Over Orcsposed.

⑪ RUFUS TUFUS **5.10B ★★★**
From the anchor of *Alternative Facts* bolts lead up to an exciting roof and easier climbing above.

Gear: Quickdraws and cams to 3".

FA: Michael Dom, James Wyland.

⑫ DEVIL MAY CARE **5.11B ★★**
The third pitch of this route is great, but the first two are forgettable. Climb past bolts right of *Tales*.

Gear: Quickdraws.

FA: P1&2: Brad Lignoski, James Wyland; P3: Dave Morison, James Wyland.

Pitch 1–5.7
Ledge climbing reaches a belay at a copper-colored block.

Pitch 2–5.11b
Traverse 12' right from the anchor and climb an awkward corner system to a large ledge above. Continue up the detached blocks to the belay.

Pitch 3–5.11a
Fun face climbing leads to an exciting last move to the chains.

⑬ BABA YAGA **5.11C A0 ★★**
Climb *Jimmy Who* or use the secret access portal to reach the base of the route. It starts 100' above the base of the cliff.

Gear: Quickdraws.

FA P1: Brad Lignoski, Nic Rosser James Wyland; P2: S. Eves, James Wyland.

Pitch 1–5.11c
Find the start. Then progressively harder face climbing leads to a tricky corner below the chains.

Pitch 2–5.11c
Traverse out right, face climb into a corner, and continue up and right through a wild roof.

Pitch 3–5.11a A0
Easy aid climbing accesses a ramp traversing rightward to the ledge.

⑭ RAGNAROKKR **5.12A ★★★★**
Mandatory tree climbing and a bolted face lead to a scary second pitch. Up and right of *Baba Yaga*.

Gear: Quickdraws.

FA: S. Eves, James Wyland.

Pitch 1–5.12a
Climb the topped tree and step across onto a bolted face. Multiple cruxes lead to a final showdown just below the anchors.

Pitch 2–5.12a
Poor climbing on large blocks accesses a diagonal seam. Exit the end of the seam through a crux and up a striking golden face (better toproped).

⑮ CASTLE JIMMY **5.10D ★★**
Accessed via RAGNAROKKR. From the single bolt b lay, climb a crack on an arête, then traverse left un a roof. Pass two pitons, then climb up an obvious w flake to a ledge. From here work your way up the f through unique water runnels to the top of the clif Often wet.

Gear: Gear to 3".

FA: Sketchy Jim, James Wyland.

⑯ CHEETAH LALA **5.10B ★**
Accessed via RAGNAROKKR. Traditional crack clim ing with a thin face finish.

Gear: Gear to 2".

FA: Michael Dom, James Wyland.

⑰ HOOHOO OWL **5.8 ★**
Above *Cheetah Lala*. Continue up another short pit to an anchor.

Gear: Gear to 2".

FA: S. Bangs, James Wyland.

⑱ BIG BAD WOLF **5.10C ★★★**
Easier climbing for 60' ends at an arête where the r of the pitch climbs progressively harder terrain wit climactic last move. There is no easy/obvious way t access this route without climbing in the trees.

Gear: Quickdraws.

FA: S. Eves, James Wyland.

⑲ THE BAD LIEUTENANT **5.12A ★**
This route is not-so-easily accessed via *Big Bad Wo* It is rarely done.

Gear: Quickdraws.

FA: Greg Collum.

⑳ JW SPECIAL (AKA FECOPHILIA) **5.10C ★**
Forgettable climbing early on leads to a clean and f slab with large moves on thin face holds.

Gear: Quickdraws.

FA: Michael Dom, James Wyland.

㉑ ORC WALL **5.10 A3 ★★**
Approach via *Ted Nugent in a Basket*, in The Countr This route is rarely done. It ascends the west side o the Orc Tower.

Gear: A rack of cams, and a major emphasis on thin pieces.

FA: Mike Martin.

Pitch 1
From the top of *Ted Nugent*, climb up and left throu some aid and easy face to a belay in a white corner.

Pitch 2
Climb the corner to cracks leading up and right to a alcove.

Pitch 3
Climb the thin A1 crack to the top splitters.

THE BRIDGE OF KHAZAD DUM 5.10D ★★★

e Bridge of Khazad Dum is a really fun climb, but on mewhat lower quality rock. If it were right off the ound, it'd be rather popular.

st accessed by climbing *Zoom -> Leave My Face ne -> P1 of Over Orcsposed*. From the P1 anchor, averse left around the tower into the chasm be-een Orc Tower and The Quarry Wall. Begin on a ke on the backside of Orc Tower with your back to e Quarry Wall. When the bolts run out, traverse to e edge of the tower, and make a wild stem across to e Quarry Wall. Continue up the face past chopped lts and cracks, and rap from the slung tree above.

e second half of this pitch climbs the last pitch *Opportunity of a Lifetime*, which was climbed by nes Wyland without bolts.

ar: Single set of cams, and 8-10 quickdraws.

: Chris Kalman.

OPPORTUNITY OF A LIFETIME 5.10B ★★

is route climbs the splitter cracks deep within the asm between the Orc Tower and The Quarry Wall. can be reached either by climbing 116 *Orc Tower* and then tunneling through to the chasm, or by versing around the tower after climbing *Over Orcs-sed* P1 or *Orc Tower* to the end of the third pitch.

mb via wild stemming, protecting with a thin crack The Quarry Wall until under the roof. There is a bolt hanging belay here on The Quarry side which necessary only because of rope drag. From here, ntinue west out the roof, and onto The Quarry Wall, ishing on somewhat dirty handcracks. Rap down m a slung tree.

: James Wyland, Nic Rosser.

ORC TOWER 5.8 A3 ★

hard to recommend anything about this adven-ous aid climb, that starts above *Patrick's Flake*. It rts the enticing cracks high on the Orc Tower. The ticing cracks are a variation called *Rubble without ause* (Greg Child, Greg Collum, 5.11b). If *Rubble* is at catches your eye, and you're thinking of free mbing potential, climb *Zoom -> Leave My Face Alone Over Orcsposed* P3 -> *Rubble* for an awesome link-that goes at 5.11.

: Al Tarrington, Steve Trafton.

OVER ORCSPOSED 5.12A ★★★

e page 101.

㉖ 116 ORC TOWER RD. 5.10C ★

Accessed via *Zoom -> Leave My Face Alone* or *Kite Flying Blind*. This route climbs out the right side of the Orc Tower.

Gear: *Standard Index Rack.*

FA: James Wyland, John Tetzlaff.

Pitch 1–5.10b

Climb a super dirty flake/crack past a bolt.

Pitch 2–5.10c

Heralded as the best pitch on Orc Tower by the first ascentionist.

Gear: *Standard Index Rack.*

The following two routes are accessed via a convoluted, exposed, somewhat sketchy trail. If you want to climb them your best bet is to find a local.

㉗ CREAM OF THE COUNTRY 5.10B ★★★★

Bolts early lead to a thin corner crack system above. This is a quality splitter!

Gear: *Quickdraws, cams to 2".*

FA: W. Haugland, James Wyland.

㉘ MANDATORY PIANO LESSONS 5.11D ★★★

Essentially the much harder variation to *Cream of the Country*. A worthy find for finger crack enthusiasts.

Gear: *Many 0.75" and 1".*

FA: C. Rankin, James Wyland.

㉙ STEEL MONKEY 5.12A ★★★

This is a short, fierce tips crack with occasional pods on uncharacteristically smooth rock. An impressive little climb.

To reach this route, walk uphill and left from The Country about five minutes until you see the thin unbolted splitter tips crack.

Gear: *Thin gear to 0.75 Camalot. RPs.*

FA: Brooke Sandahl.

㉚ JIMMY WHO? / BABOON 5.11B ★★

Originally an unfinished Jim Yoder route, Greg Collum came and completed the line in style, adding the funny name *Jimmy Who?*.

The original line, *Baboon*, continues straight up a scruffy corner on undesirably mungy terrain where *Jimmy Who?* follows bolts left.

Located at the far left end of The Country, uphill and almost to The Quarry. It is the first bolted line right of *Steel Monkey*.

Gear: *Standard Index Rack for Baboon. Just quickdraws for Jimmy Who?.*

FA: Jim Yoder, Greg Collum.

㉛ CROWBAR 5.11B ★★

Clip three bolts then blast through two roofs. Gear is required after clipping the bolted section. Would be better if climbed more often. Just right of *Jimmy Who?*

Gear: *Single rack of cams from .3 to 3" and nuts.*

FA: Darryl Cramer, Jon Nelson.

㉜ TED NUGENT IN A BASKET 5.11C ★★

To reach this route you have to do a somewhat sketchy rightward, traverse along a narrow and brambled ledge, right of *Crowbar*. It would be a great project to clean up this ledge and install a fixed line; access this route and its righthand neighbors would no doubt clean up into nice lines, if they were safer and easier to access.

Ted Nugent is difficult the whole way through, but the crux is probably between the second and third bolt. This route may need a brushing. Farthest left bolted line on the ramp.

Gear: *Mostly quickdraws, with a few cams/nuts to supplement in the middle.*

FA: Jon Nelson, Greg Olsen, Darryl Cramer, Max Dufford.

PATRICK'S FLAKE 5.10D ★

is pitch looks better than it climbs. In actuality, s rather difficult to protect, and the climbing is kward and off-balance. It ascends the layback flake the right of *Ted Nugent.*

ar: Small camming units and nuts.

. Al Tarrington, Steve Trafton; FFA: Terry Lien, Jon lson.

TOTAL SEAWASH CALYPSO 5.11D ★★★

is is probably the best climb in the immediate inity. TSC features hard moves on excellent, pos-e edges. Stick-clipping the second bolt is highly commended.

e of the bolts in the middle of the pitch is currently ashed due to rockfall.

ar: Quickdraws.

: Darryl Cramer, Greg Olsen, Jon Nelson, Larry mp.

35 WILLING SLAVE 5.11D ★★

Willing Slave and *Savage Gardens reside* at the far right end of the thin vegetated ledge. Use caution accessing them, as a fall from this ledge could be fatal.

Willing Slave goes straight up from the anchor at the base, and joins *Savage Gardens* briefly before moving back left. The original finish has been lost to incurable scruffiness. Finish at the first anchors you find.

Currently, the cleanest way to access this pair is to start on *Savage Gardens*, and finish on *Willing Slave.*

Gear: Quickdraws.

FA: Greg Collum, Greg Olsen.

36 SAVAGE GARDENS 5.11C ★★

Savage Gardens goes up and right from the anchor at the base. It joins *Willing Slave* briefly before moving back right. This pitch features some bold climbing.

Gear: Quickdraws.

FA: Greg Collum, Greg Child.

THE COUNTRY

The Country includes everything from *Wipe* to the start of the Upper Town Wall trail. It is a dreamy crag with nearly as many stellar lines as the LTW, but usually less climbers. There's no clear reason why–except possibly for fear of the monster lurking deep in the wall, behind the sealed tunnel. What is that toxic ooze seeping out from there, anyway?

Approach: Cross the train tracks, then walk east alongside them, paralleling the Lower Town Walls. After a few minutes, an obvious access road leads to a nice grassy area complete with picnic bench and a strange tunnel in the wall.

Descent: Rap anything here with a single 70. On a few routes, that may require some creativity.

37 WIPE 5.11A ★★★

A very good pitch! Best reached by starting from the chains atop the first pitch of *Kite Flying Blind* or *Frank Presley* (can also be accessed from the start of *Savage Gardens* via looser rock). Embark left on broken, but good rock. After a few feet head straight up past a bolt. You will reach a ledge with a set of chains. Bypass these and continue upwards past a short crux. Stay engaged up interesting face climbing peppered with gear placements. This leads to an awesome, tight flare that takes micro gear to the top.

Gear: *3 quickdraws, a single rack, small camming units and nuts/RPs.*

FA: Jon Nelson, Terry Lien.

38 KITE FLYING BLIND 5.11C ★★★★

This is a fantastic route. The second pitch features brilliant power laybacking with great position, and even a finger crack finish to keep your attention. Awesome.

Many prefer the neighboring route, *Frank Presley*, as a slightly easier first pitch warm-up for the second-pitch goods. *Kite Flying Blind* is a great way to access the Orc Tower and *Over Orcsposed.*

A 70 is mandatory to rap/toprope the second pitch.

Gear: *12 quickdraws*

FA P1: Greg Child, Greg Collum; P2: Greg Collum, Kurt Schmierer.

Pitch 1–5.11a/b

The lefthand of the two bolted lines at the far left side of The Country. The crux is down low exiting a tricky shallow corner of white rock.

This first pitch is also known as *Elvis-Nixon.*

Pitch 2–5.11c

This stellar pitch climbs up relatively moderate terrain until the base of a small headwall. Get psyched, and tackle the strenuous layback through two bolts to a good jug, then find your way up and around the corner to the right. Cool edges, stemming, and a finger crack take you to the chains.

39 FRANK PRESLEY 5.11A ★★★

This fun pitch takes you through some great friction climbing on knobs and a juggy finish to the chains. The crux move is harder if you're shorter than 5'5".

Gear: *Quickdraws.*

FA: Greg Collum.

40 JUST SAY NO TO FRANK SINATRA 5.11D ★

Rarely done, and usually climbed as a TR. There is one stopper move (harder if short) at the first roof, protected by dubious nuts. It would make for a nasty groundfall if the nuts pulled.

Begin deep in the alcove between *Zoom* and *Kite Flying Blind.* Pass the low roof, and continue up the scruffy crack past the bolt, or bail right onto *Mourning Star.*

Gear: *Standard Index Rack.*

FA: Mack Johnson, Steve Risse.

41 MOURNING STAR 5.8 ★★★

This is a nice moderate, or warm-up pitch for other routes in The Country. At 5.8, it is a rare "easy" Index route, and certainly worth climbing! Climb up easy terrain to the blocky left-facing corner. Climb the corner to chains.

Gear: *A single set of cams to #3, extra finger sizes, and a variety of slings and quickdraws.*

FA: Fred Grafton; FFA: Fred Grafton and Sandor Nagy

42 LONGLIFE 5.12A R ★

Almost never climbed, poorly protected, dirty, and much more difficult than it looks. *Longlife* can be toproped from the anchor of *Mourning Star.* To lead it, begin just left of *Zoom*, and head up and left on scary moves to access a bolt. Then continue roughly straight up.

Gear: *Small cams and RPs, a handful of quickraws and runners.*

FA: Jim Purdy, Greg Olsen.

TOP 10 KNOB CLIMBS

- ❒ Echolocation 5.11d (p.183)
- ❒ Racer X (P2) 5.10b (p.40)
- ❒ Zoom 5.10d (p.112)
- ❒ Wham 5.11c (p.115)
- ❒ The Orangutan/Bonobo 5.11 (p.218)
- ❒ Sisu (P1) 5.11b/c (p.172)
- ❒ Bat Skins 5.12b (p.87)
- ❒ Phone Calls from the Dead 5.11a (p.119)
- ❒ Tempitchuous 5.11d (p.148)
- ❒ Little Jupiter 5.13a (p.114)

Jonathan Cooper moving with precision on Zoom

You know it's a jug in Index when...

43 ZOOM 5.10D ★★★★

This bold route is one of the best of its grade at Index and possibly the best line in The Country. Wild knobs and a thin seam that opens up just enough to keep the meat of this climb traditional, provides for some thought-provoking moves above small, but bomber, gear placements. Not to be missed! Shorter climbers should stick-clip the first bolt, or bring a tall friend.

This route has a dirty second pitch, and a quality third pitch which are rarely done.

Zoom can be linked with *Leave My Face Alone* for a full 70 meter thriller–but bring about 18 quickdraws, in addition to the gear for the first pitch. *Zoom -> KFB -> Over Orcsposed* is one of the best linkups on the Lower Town Wall.

Gear: A handful of slings and quickdraws. Single rack 0.3"-2" camming units. Micro nuts/RPs. May want an extra blue TCU.

FA: Jon Nelson, Steve Strong, Tom Michael.

Pitch 1–5.10d
Climb the stellar first pitch via knobs and cracks. Belay at chains.

Pitch 2–5.8
A funky dirty 5.8 traverse hard-right leads to a set of anchors below an offwidth roof and left-facing corner.

Pitch 3–5.10b
Climb out the roof and up the left-facing corner.

44 LEAVE MY FACE ALONE 5.11A ★★★

This is a fantastic climb on high quality patina–an Index anomaly. The route gets tougher and tougher until the heart-breaker finish, so milk those rests! If you do *Zoom*, there's no good reason not to do this one as well.

Climb the bolt line directly on top of *Zoom's* first pitch. The bolt line leading right is *Hairway to Stephan.*

Gear: 13 quickdraws, good edging shoes.

FA: Greg Collum, Matt Kerns.

45 HAIRWAY TO STEPHAN 5.11A ★★★

From the anchor atop *Zoom* trend up and right following a line of bolts. A succession of progressively difficult mantel moves and a series of hand traverses characterizes this climb. Not as good as LMFA, but pretty darn good.

Gear: 12 quickdraws.

FA: Greg Child, Sally Oberlin.

TOP 10 SPORT CLIMBS

- ❒ Cunning Stunt 5.10c (p.116)
- ❒ Climax Control 5.11c (p.116)
- ❒ The Fifth Force 5.12b (p.116)
- ❒ Amandla 5.13b/c (p.76)
- ❒ Calling Wolfgang 5.12a (p.158)
- ❒ 12 Gauge IQ 5.12b (p.129)
- ❒ Biology of Small Appliances 5.12a (p.146)
- ❒ Kite Flying Blind (P2) 5.11c (p.110)
- ❒ Infinite Jest 5.12+ (p.192)
- ❒ Numbah 10 5.12b (p.76)

47 LITTLE JUPITER 5.13A ★★★

This climb is usually only done to the first set of chains out right, and goes at 5.11d to there. Either way, the route offers fantastic knob climbing and is more difficult than it appears. Short climbers may like to place a nut between the second and third bolts.

This route is easily identifiable by the hanging chain draw left of the tunnel. The full first pitch continues straight up passing a 5.13 crux instead of traversing right to the anchor at half-height. There is now an anchor before the 5.13 finish that you can lower from. The climbing to there is 5.12.

Gear: Quickdraws.

FA: Jim Purdy, Greg Olsen, Max Dufford.

Sonya Kepler gets cosmic on Little Jupiter. | Photo by Ben Gilkison

WHAM 5.11C ★★★★

s enjoyable knob climb has a fierce start, in a shal- dihedral right of *Zoom*, and left of the tunnel. The d start leads to technical and enjoyable climbing, a final crux traversing left. While not quite as ssic at *Zoom*, this one still gets four stars.

ar: 10 quickdraws.

Greg Collum, Greg Child, Tim Wilson.

LITTLE JUPITER 5.13A ★★★

page 110.

BIG SCIENCE/SCIENTIFIC AMERICANS 12B ★★★

Science is actually the first pitch of a four-pitch te called *Scientific Americans.*

ariation start called *Little Science* fires straight up t a single bolt (5.11a) below the crux, rather than versing in from the right.

ar: Cams up to 1" and RPs.

Greg Child.

ch 1–5.12b

Big Science, traverse left from the sloping ledge of the tunnel through some cool overlap features the bolt line next to *Little Jupiter.* Continue up ough some cool features and knobs past more ts to a 2-bolt anchor.

ch 2–5.12b

mb up through overlaps past four bolts and gear cements to a 2-bolt anchor. Clip one of the anchor ts, and continue upwards past a hard (5.12b) crux, and a few more gear placements to the next 2-bolt anchor.

This pitch originally went on fixed copperheads and a railroad spike! Yikes! It was also chipped.

Pitch 3–5.9

An extremely dirty, short pitch traversing right under a roof, and then up the right side of it to a 2-bolt anchor on a treed ledge beneath a right-facing dihedral.

Pitch 4–5.9

Climb the dirty right-facing dihedral. There is an unsent project to the right of this pitch that was climbed on TR by Greg Olsen, but never sent on lead.

49 S.S. ULTRABRUTAL 5.7 ★★★

One of the easiest routes at Index and very popular. Though the climbing is not superb, it's not bad either.

Climb the rightward trending ramp on the left side of the tunnel. Make a traverse right at the end to chain anchors.

Gear: Standard Index Rack.

FA: Jon Nelson, Steve Strong.

50 TUNNEL VISION 5.10D ★★★

This is the bolted extension to *Ultrabrutal.* The quality hard climbing is short-lived, but certainly worth the effort. Climb *Ultrabrutal*, clip the chains, and follow bolts up to the next anchor. Descend with a 70.

Gear: Quickdraws.

FA: Chuck Boyd, Greg Collum.

51 CONDITIONED RESPONSE 5.11B ★★

From *Tunnel Vision's* anchor, climb up and left another six bolts to a 2-bolt anchor. Stop here, or fire up another six bolts (5.11b) to the top of *Angora Grotto.* May be dirty, but purportedly a very good climb.

Gear: Quickdraws.

FA: Greg Collum, Dan Cauthorn.

52 UPTIGHT 5.11+ ★★

This sport climb is directly above *Tunnel Vision.* Climb up past a funky mantel and some weird body tension moving left to the 2-bolt anchor. You can either clip these chains and lower, or continue to the top of *Conditioned Response.*

Gear: Quickdraws.

FA: Rod Fox & Jason?

53 ANGORRA GROTTO 5.11A ★★★

This fun line climbs easy terrain on top of *Tunnel Vision.* While it is not superb, it is worth doing. Follow easy terrain right up to a chain anchor. Clip this anchor, and climb the crack to a funky mantel, and pumpy finish.

Gear: Standard Index Rack.

FA: Dan Cauthorn, Greg Collum.

54 BIG BIG FUN 5.11D ★

Starts from the 2-bolt anchor at the beginning of *Angora Grotto's* layback flake, and heads right. If you take the name seriously, you might be in for a big big let down. The start is often wet, and the crux is a single move.

Gear: Quickdraws.

FA: Jim Purdy, Greg Olsen.

55 CLIMAX CONTROL 5.11C ★★★★

This is a fantastic sport climb which was originally done (and still could be) as a trad climb. One of Index's softest 5.11c.

Right of the tunnel, scramble up to a flat ledge beneath two nice looking sport climbs. This is the left line.

Gear: Quickdraws.

FA: Greg Collum, Cal Folsom, Larissa Collum.

56 CUNNING STUNT 5.10C ★★★★

This is another superb sport line, and a good warm-up for *Climax Control.* Climb up the right bolt line, enjoy some cruxes, and clip the anchor. It's not runout–that's just your inner sport climber talking.

While *Climax* feels soft for 5.11c, this one feels hard for 5.10c. At 5'5", I think they're about the same. But people insist I'm wrong.

A 3-bolt extension on friable rock does not change the grade, but allows you to hang a TR on *Fifth Force.*

Gear: Quickdraws.

FA: Greg Child, Greg Collum.

57 THE FIFTH FORCE 5.12B ★★★★

Pure Index trickery! This is the incredible bolted lin right of *Climax Control* and *Cunning Stunt.* Short pe ple may find one of the cruxes frustratingly difficul Welcome to Index 5.12b.

Climb up easy terrain just right of *Cunning Stunt,* making an awkward traverse right at the first bolt. Climb through three distinct cruxes, and keep an ey out for the stinger in the tail.

There is a variation called *Force Fed* which supposec goes at 5.11d, and traverses right at the fourth bolt t join *Spooner.*

A rarely climbed second pitch, *Last Man Standing* (5.12a, Wyland) continues from the anchor up a line bolts through progressively harder moves ending w a heel-hook dyno.

Gear: Quickdraws.

FA: Greg Collum, Greg Child, Greg Olsen.

58 SPOONER 5.11D ★★★

This route may be a contender for Index's biggest sandbag. If you are shorter than 5'6" it may feel impossible. That said, the climbing is immaculate. Kud go to the first ascentionists, 1983.

Prehanging the draws is a good idea. The second bo is also very hard to clip, and could result in a groun fall. Stick-clip advised.

This is the first left-traversing bolt line right of *Fifth Force.*

Gear: Quickdraws.

FA: Darryl Cramer, Jon Nelson.

ss Campbell harnessing the power of the Fifth Force. (5.12b)

59 G IS FOR GINERS 5.12A ★★★

If *Spooner* wasn't enough you can keep going for a second pitch through difficult cruxes and quality climbing. Bring some gear for this pitch, though.

Gear: Draws, cams to 2", emphasis on finger sizes.

FA: James Wyland.

60 HIERONYMUS BOSCH 5.11B ★★

HB starts just right of *Spooner*, and goes straight up. Short, and much harder than 5.11b. Clipping the third bolt is challenging, and if you blow it, you'll deck.

Gear: Quickdraws.

FA: Greg Child, Andy de Klerk.

61 D IS FOR DICTORY 5.11B ★★★

Begin on the huge detached flake at the base of the wall which has easy offwidth climbing on either side (most people climb the left side).

From here, climb into some beautiful golden rock, until you reach the top of a large flake. Traverse left and up to a belay in an alcove. Not the hardest 5.11b at Index...

Gear: Standard Index Rack. If you want to protect the starting flake, you'll need large (#5 and #6) cams.

FA: Darryl Cramer, Greg Olsen, Jeff Walker.

62 FOOLS GOLD 5.9+ ★★

Start on the big flake and climb it however you like.

Above the flake, climb through a featured golden section reminiscent of Tuolumne stone. At the top o the golden stone, traverse right to join the *GM Route* at its first belay ledge. Use many long slings and well spaced gear to minimize drag.

Gear: Same as D is for Dictory.

FA: Don Brooks, Chris Syrjala.

63 HEART OF THE COUNTRY 5.11B ★★★★

This is a really darn good route. Almost anywhere else, it'd be the area classic. This route climbs attrac tive orange rock through quality crack climbing, and a couple wild face moves. Can be done in two or thr pitches, and rapped with a single 60 or 70.

Gear: Double set of cams from tips to hands. Bring plenty of long slings, especially if you plan to combine P1 and P2.

FA: John Stoddard, Randy Stout.

Pitch 1–5.10d

Climb the large detached flake of *D is for Dictory*, and continue up and right to a wierd move around the corner to the bolted anchor on GM's first pitch. Alternately, if you don't care for the crux on this pitc follow a diagonaling crack up and right, and around the chains at the top of GM's first pitch. If you go thi way, don't link the first two pitches. This variation is called *The Right Ventricle* (Tetzlaff, Gamache. 5.10a/

itch 2–5.11b

ıis pitch is outstanding, especially if linked with the ·st pitch (if linking the two pitches, don't step right ound the corner at the end of pitch one). Climb the ɔod cracks in the orange, left-facing dihedral. Don't averse right again until you clip the pin, then hand averse the higher of two horizontal cracks. Tricky oves around the corner gain the next belay. Excel-nt rock on this pitch.

itch 3–5.11a

ɛrfect crack climbing. Climb the arcing splitter out ght. If you lower at the first chains, this pitch is only 10a. For full value, both difficulty and star-wise, imb the perfect splitter up and left to the next ıains.

GM ROUTE 5.9 ★★★

his is another stellar multi-pitch. All the anchors are ıared with *Heart of The Country*, so it's easy to com-ne both routes in a number of different variations.

ɔu can descend with a single 60, or make two full ppels with a single 70.

ear: Double set of cams up to #3; a single #4 could nice.

\: Ed Gibson, Greg Markov.

itch 1–5.8

etting established on this pitch can be a little funky vet and dirty) especially in early season. Ascend 4th ass terrain far right, then make a tenuous 4th class averse back left. Clip the bolt, and climb a left-fac-g corner to a ledge. Walk the ledge left, and belay at e chains.

boulder problem direct start goes at solid 5.11, and is nprotectable.

is possible to link P1 and 2; or P2 and 3. In reality, if ɔu run it out a bit to keep the rope drag down, you ın link all three pitches. Done properly, one long tch is the best way to do the whole route.

itch 2–5.9

his pitch is short, pumpy, and awesome. It may feel little tough for 5.9. Go straight up into roofs, and ıll a difficult move out the overhang. Continue up e cracks to chains up and left. If you're not solid at e grade, you may want a #4, or even a #5 to protect e start.

itch 3–5.9

imb the sort of weird, grovelly wide handcrack to e left. Or climb the perfect awesome handcrack to e right (*Heart of The Country*'s 3rd pitch) to keep the ar-value high.

65 PHONE CALLS FROM THE DEAD 5.11A ★★★

This is a fantastic knob climb with a tricky mantel finish. From GM's first pitch anchors, step right, and climb past knobs and bolts to a cool mantel, and the chains.

You can continue upwards above the *Phone Calls* anchor for a longer, even better pitch, that goes at 5.12a A0 (or better yet, free it!) The extension requires more small cams and nuts, and three more quickdraws. The full pitch is called *Long Distance Phone Calls From the Dead.*

Gear: Small cams and nuts, quickdraws.

FA: Greg Olsen, Jon Nelson; FA Long Distance Phone Calls from the Dead: Doug Taylor.

66 THE SCOOP 5.11D ★★

Difficult but fun knob climbing. This pitch is located about 15 yards right of *Phone Calls*' anchor. To access it via GM's first pitch is a bit scruffy and not recommended. Your best bet is to make a traversing rap in from *Phone Calls* anchor. It may also be possible to access the base by walking out on the ledge on the right-hand side.

Gear: 6 quickdraws, cams to 2".

FA: Greg Olsen, Darryl Cramer.

67 WHIPPED CREAM OVER THE CLOTHESLINE 5.12A ★★

If you continue walking right past GM and what appears to be the end of The Country, you'll reach the base of this bolted line in about 50 yards. It is in decent shape, with freshly replaced hardware, and probably worth climbing, even if a bit dirty.

Above this pitch are two other short scruffy pitches which are rarely climbed: *Freeze Dried Lizard Antlers* (Cramer, Olsen, 5.10d) and *Dead Bobcats Travel West* (Olsen, Nelson, 5.10a).

Gear: Quickdraws.

FA: Greg Olsen, Max Dufford, Jon Nelson, Jim Purdy.

Drew styling Amandla 5.13b/c (p. 76) back in the day. | Photo by Ben Gilkison

ANDREW PHILBIN

N DEFENSE OF STEWARDSHIP

cut my climbing teeth on the angular, compact granite at Index. The climbing is so subtle and refined hat it takes years to master. The devotion to this refinement along with the incredible quality of Index ranite are what have made this such a special place for me. It's an endlessly rewarding place to climb. It's lso incredibly important to me, and—along with gushing praise of the climbing—I feel obligated to offer ome advice upon that note.

Jnlike many of the best trad climbing areas in the United States, Index is mostly safe. By that I mean that you're up to the challenge, and if you take advantage of the available gear and place it well, you can fall lmost anywhere on most routes at Index. It's not generally a place where if you slip at the wrong time, ou're going 40 feet onto a ledge and breaking your legs. There's a time and a place for those types of outes, but for the most part, the precedent just isn't there at Index. Approaching a route for the first time t Index is, as a result, more fun and far less intimidating than at other areas.

'his convenience comes at a price, however. I am, of course, referring to fixed gear such as bolts. There lways will and should be a debate about how many bolts should protect a route, but all too often, the more is better" argument wins the day. Excessive convenience bolting can utterly destroy the aesthetics f a crag. There are already examples of new, extremely closely bolted routes on the Lower Town Wall and lsewhere at Index, that—aside from other potential criticism—just don't fit into the general aesthetic. If olting is too much of a grey area, then consider that both a rebar ladder (which accesses a ledge shared y many climbs) and at least one artificial handhold (on a route that went free without it) were installed at ndex in the past year or so. These are outdated tactics that are considered completely unacceptable at early every crag in the United States. Why should Index be any exception?

ndex is already massively popular and this guidebook will undoubtedly increase that popularity. I have nixed feelings about this, but the cat has been out of the bag, so to speak, for a long time. On a weekend, 's very common to see topropes on almost every route at the LTW. It's possible to arrive on such a day nd never have to lead a pitch. This is a boon for those of us who have already taken the lead on these itches or for someone showing up solo just looking to get in some laps. However, I think it's incredibly mportant for people to take to the sharp end. The routes at Index are, by almost any standard, as safe as limbing can be. In order to preserve a sense of adventure, casting off on the lead is an absolute necessity.

Ay defense for this assertion is this: without experiencing a little piece of that doubt, insecurity, and yes, ear, it's impossible to develop a relationship with the aesthetic sense of a climbing area. Without that ense, it's impossible to have an opinion about how a route fits into the overall vibe of an area. Lack of ngagement of this type results in a lack of critical input on new developments at the area. At Index, this neans that excessive logging, overbolting, and worse will increase at the expense of our beloved resource.

Community consensus can squelch these issues before they become issues. I urge everyone to become tewards of Index as well as consumers of the amazing rock: learn the sorcery required to climb there and have fun, yes, but also keep a critical eye on what route developers are doing; pick up your trash; control your dogs; get on the lead and cast off onto the magical Index granite!

THE MIDDLE WALLS

The Middle Walls are some of the least known, least crowded, and least sunny at Index. As such, they can be a little dirtier, more obscure, and more difficult to reach than some of the better known areas. At the same time, they offer solitude in the forest and can be cooler on hot summer days. These walls have a wealth of good routes. The Blues Cliff, in particular, is a real gem. If you are a moderate climber, you will especially enjoy the The Middle Walls proper.

Approach: The approach varies radically from wall to wall, and there are quite a few different ways to get to The Middle Wall crags. For each wall, we've attempted to describe the best approach–but that doesn't mean it's the only one. Whatever approach you take, always use caution when you walk, as you are often above popular LTW crags.

Stamati Anagnostou is a hound for splitters on Black Cat Bone (5.11c, p.130).

THE MIDDLE WALLS

This is an excellent beginner's wall, not to be missed. Classic routes here such as *Robin's Ramp, Plum Pudding*, PBR, and *Folsom Blues* will keep climbers happily busy well below the 5.11 range.

Approach: The shortest approach is to start on the Inner Wall trail, and then branch off right towards K Cliff. Pass K Cliff, and Winkie Dinkie Cliff, and go hand over hand (or ascend) a fixed rope through a narrow slot. Above here, two more short fixed ropes take you above St. Francis Ledge, and a short bushwhack brings you to the cliff. If you go this way, use extreme caution not to knock off loose rocks as popular climbing areas are directly beneath you.

If you don't want to mess around with fixed ropes, you can also hike in via the Upper Town Wall trail. Take your first left off that trail. Stay left at the first branch, and right at the next. This trail will take you to the cliff edge (best access for *Starfish* and #9 via rappeling), and then beyond. You'll pass an old bridge (may be sketchy) and some long-abandoned stairs. This approach has some places of questionable safety, and so is less recommendable.

Finally, you can simply top out a variety of routes at K Cliff or Winkie Dinkie Cliff which will put you close to the base of The Middle Walls.

Descent: Everything at The Middle Walls can be toproped and rapped with a single 70—a 60 is probably fine as well.

❶ SEAMSTRESS 5.7 ★

This route is only included because it provides one way of accessing The Middle Walls. It is dirty, ugly, and isn't fun to climb. But it gets you to the The Middle Walls quickly. Just before you reach Winkie Dinkie cliff on the approach trail, go uphill to the dirty slab, and climb it.

Gear: *Standard Index Rack.*

FA: Geoff Georges, Bill Ayre.

❷ ALL MY FRIENDS ARE ALIENS 5.10A ★★

This is currently the farthest left route at The Middle Walls. Start in a shallow left-facing corner/seam. Make a balancy move over to the arête (crux), and then follow the left-traversing undercling until it is possible to go up towards a tree. Continue up the crack system, trending left then right to an anchor.

An alternate start in the offwidth on the left may sport a bolt to link up with this pitch.

Gear: *Single set of cams from tips to 2 inches. Extras in finger sizes. Aliens are nice, as the name implies. RPs.*

FA: Geoff Georges, Jessica Todd.

❸ KEITH'S CRACK 5.11C ★★★

See page 125.

❹ WILD BOAR 5.11D ★★

Climb the bolted dike just right of *Keith's Crack*. This route can be dirty/wet, but when it is clean it is a three-star route.

Gear: *Quickdraws.*

FA: Cal Folsom, David Rosenfeld.

❺ STEMS AND LEAVES, ET AL. 5.10A ★

There is a huge flake just right of *Keith's Crack* and *Wild Boar* along the base of the wall. It sports three low quality munge-fests: *Stems and Leaves* (5.10a, left side of flake), *Dinky Twinkies* (5.9, bolted front of flake), and *Flee Fly Flue* (5.7, right side of flake). None of these routes should be priorities.

Gear: *Standard Index Rack.*

FA: Cal Folsom with David Rosenfeld, Fred Grafton, and Debbie Browstien.

❻ HIPS AND VALLEYS 5.8 ★★

Climb the handcrack to the sloping ledge, then traverse left and climb up the wide chimney/offwidth. Cool moves and a finger crack pull you through the roof. Traverse right at the top to the anchors of *Robin's Ramp.*

Gear: *A single set of cams from .3 to #4. If you are uncomfortable with fist cracks, you can use two #4 Camalots in the beginning.*

FA: Unknown.

❼ STEMS AND VALLEYS 5.11A ★★★

Start on the handcrack of *Hips and Valleys*. At the sloping ledge, make some interesting face moves pas[t] bolts, traversing left, and then continue upwards pas[t] four more bolts, stemming until you step back right. Pull through the overhang and continue on to *Robin's Ramp*'s anchors.

Gear: *Single rack to #1, 5 or 6 quickdraws.*

FA: John Tetzlaff, Doug Taylor, Uros Lukic.

EITH'S CRACK **5.11C ★★★**

w a thin crack to a small roof/overlap (5.11b), continue up the thin crack above, with 5.11c face es to the finish.

r: *Tips to 1" cams and RPs.*

Keith Blumhagen, Monty Westgard.

hal Rynkiewicz stepping up to Keith's Crack (5.11c). oto by Stamati Anagnostou

⑧ FLIPPO 5.10B ★★★

Same start as the past two routes. At the sloping ledge, climb up and right on bolts to a stance then back up and left to the anchor.

The middle bolt line is unnamed, but was climbed by Uros Lukic on gear and later bolted by someone else who didn't know it had been climbed. From the sloping ledge continue up the slot on laybacks and finger locks to a cool stem move out right on knobs. Climb the face, then pull through a juggy overhang and continue up and left to the anchor on *Robin's Ramp*.

Gear: *Single rack to #2 Camalot, handful of quickdraws, rack of nuts.*

FA: Jon Nelson, Darryl Cramer.

⑨ ROBIN'S RAMP 5.11 VAR. 5.11A/B ★★

This short but enticing variation leads up to the finish of *Robins Ramp*. Splitter fingers to the ramp. Try hard.

Gear: *Smattering of finger sizes.*

FA: Unknown.

⑩ ROBIN'S RAMP 5.7 ★★★

This is one of the best 5.7s at Index, and a great intro to trad climbing on granite. Start on the right, and follow a leftward trending ramp up and left around a corner to an anchor.

This is also a good way to access Blue Tile Lounge. Continue past the anchor and belay at a tree at the base of a slab.

Gear: *Standard Index Rack.*

FA: Cal Folsom, David Rosenfeld, Robin Brownstien, Debbie Brownstien.

⑪ PLUM PUDDING 5.9 ★★★★

This one is straight outta Yosemite. Splitter parallel sided crack climbing in a rightward-leaning corner. It's as good as *Plum Pudding* can be! For extra point continue on past the first anchors for the 5.10a finis to *PBR*—you may want an extra set of cams to #1 for that.

There's a new route which starts on *Plum Pudding* and breaks hard left at the first visible bolt past thre techincal boulder problems, and some insecure, but easier climbing to the anchor. This is *Seams Alright* (Lowy, Redon, 5.11+, three stars)

Gear: *Triples from blue TCU to purple Camalot. Rack of nuts.*

FA: Ron Miller, Dan Watters.

Always good to have a brush on hand.

Fred Knapp getting his fill on Plum Pudding (5.9)

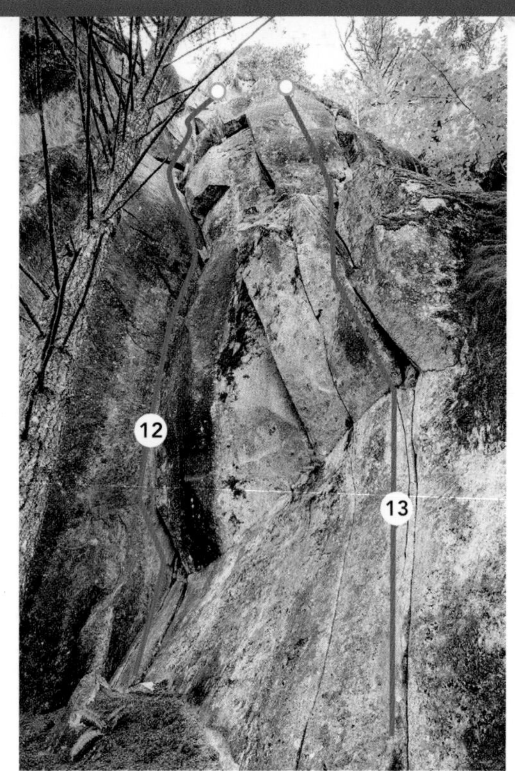

⑫ PBR 5.10A ★★★

This is an excellent recent addition to the wall which required chopping a pretty sizable shrub out of the crack halfway up the pitch. The route features nice crack climbing. Climb up the corner between *Plum Pudding* and *Folsom Blues.*

Gear: Three 0.3-sized cams. Doubles from 0.4 to 0.75, single #1 and #2, 8-10 quickdraws and slings, nuts.

FA: Geoff Georges.

⑬ FOLSOM BLUES 5.10C ★★★

A low layback crux in a splitter finger crack leads to nice crack climbing for another 40 feet. At about 50-60 feet, step left for a beautiful 5.10 finger crack through a blank face. This takes you to the anchors.

Gear: Triples tips to fingers. Single set of cams from 0.75 to #2, 6-8 slings and quickdraws, a rack of nuts.

FA: Ron Miller, Dan Waters.

Waiting for the Sun, and the following two routes, are all part of the Blue Tile Lounge directly above The Middle Walls, and can be reached via most of the right side The Middle Walls routes.

⑭ WAITING FOR THE SUN 5.9 ★★

This is a fun route, and a nice 5.9 knob climb for th beginner Index climber. Climb the knobby face pas small gear and three bolts to a bolted anchor.

Gear: 3 quickdraws plus a green Alien (or red C3 or TCU) to protect the start. Also nice to have a few oth finger size pieces to make an anchor to belay from at the base.

FA: Eric Lund, Brent Swee.

⑮ FRENCH CANADIAN 5.10 ★★

Climb the left-facing corner right of *Waiting for th Sun.* May be dirty. Traverse back left at the end to t anchor for *Waiting for the Sun.*

Gear: Standard Index Rack.

FA: Eric Lund, Derek Pearson.

⑯ JADED 5.11 ★★

On the right side of the Blue Tile Lounge, climb a slabby face past two bolts to a flared chimney whic tapers down to a thin crack.

Gear: Standard Index Rack.

FA: Eric Lund.

The following route is not on the The Middle Walls proper, but lies uphill from the first staircase east of The Middle Walls. It is rarely visited, and even more rarely climbed.

Jack Taylor enjoying the sinker fingers of Folsom Blues (5.10c)

BEHIND THE GREEN DOOR 5.11C ★★

ficult climbing past five bolts leads to a cruxy ntel and a flake to a contrived finish following bolts ht across a face. The thin crack to the left has also en climbed. The slab to the right is an open project.

ar: Standard Index Rack.

Dave Tower, Bruce Anderson.

BLUES CLIFF

The Blues Cliff has some stellar climbs, and really good rock. It stays shadier than many other walls which makes it a nice choice in the heat of summer. Definitely make sure not to miss this outstanding wall.

Approach: Hike up the Upper Town Wall trail until the first trail junction, and take a left. At the first trail branch you reach, go left (right goes up to Rhythm Cliff). At the second trail branch, go left again (right goes to the The Middle Walls). This will bring you shortly to the base of the climbs.

Descent: Most of the routes at Blues Cliff can be rapped with a single 60, but watch the ends on some of the longer routes.

The following two routes, #9 and Starfish, are at the top of Blues Cliff's left side, but they are best accessed by passing the trail to Blues Cliff, and continuing past Rhythm Cliff, to the first obvious clearing at the edge of a cliff. Approach the edge carefully. The first chains you see are for Starfish. A semi-hidden set lies to climber's left just out of sight. Both routes have their own anchors, above and below. Rap in to a 2-bolt anchor (70m required for the rap), and TR the climbs, or pull the rope, and lead out!

18 #9 5.10A ★★★

Rap in from above, and enjoy unique, Gunks-esque horizontal holds and gear placements. #9 is the left line.

Gear: Tips to #2, with extras in finger sizes if you like.

FA: Chris Henson.

19 STARFISH 5.9 ★★★

Similar in character to #9, *Starfish* is the right line.

Gear: e.

FA: Chris Henson.

20 ACCIDENTAL DISCHARGE 5.11B ★★★

The farthest left route along the base of Blues Cliff. Delicate slab and cryptic arête climbing make this a fantastic line.

Gear: 9 quickdraws, possibly some small cams for the beginning.

FA: Greg Collum, Matt Kerns.

21 12 GAUGE IQ 5.12B ★★★★

This is a fantastic line. Low difficulties lead to a cruxy section on slippery rock right before the roof. The roof climbing is difficult and pumpy, but everything is there. This route was 5.12c in the Cramer guide, but feels significantly easier than that. Some have suggested 5.12a (that is... Index 5.12a).

Gear: 11 quickdraws.

FA: Greg Collum, Matt Kerns.

22 BLACK CAT BONE 5.11C ★★★★

Originally freed on gear then mysteriously retro-bolted, the bolts have since been chopped which improves the aesthetic and climbing of this cool finger crack. The standard start is OK, but features an exasperating first move dyno if you are less than 6 feet tall. That start can be avoided by climbing the opening section of *12 Gauge IQ*. You can also climb the finish of *12 Gauge* for a nice extension.

There may be a remnant first bolt next to a splitter crack which can be removed at any time, and currently serves no purpose.

Gear: Double set of cams from tips to 1", emphasis on purple to yellow TCU sizes (blue to yellow Alien). RPs, and a few slings/draws.

FA: Cal Folsom, David Feinberg.

23 CRY BABY/UNICORN BLUES 5.12A ★★★

Unicorn Blues is a fantastic route–pure sport climbi at its best. Start with increasingly difficult moves through a featured dike to a short bouldery crux before a ledge. The route *Cry Baby* (5.11c) originally stopped here. Now, there are another four bolts of excellent arête climbing above, at roughly the same grade. For many, the low crux on *Cry Baby* will prov harder than the upper arête.

Gear: Quickdraws.

FA Cry Baby: Greg Collum, Larissa Collum, Matt Kerns; FA Unicorn Blues: Chris Kalman, Allesandra Patz, Mike Patz.

24 BLUE IN THE FACE 5.12C ★★★

Climb a ledgy chimney right of *Unicorn Blues* to the first bolt. Steep climbing leads to a powerful and technical crux sequence to turn the arête and enter the corner. The climbing stays proud as it continues up the corner and surmounts another bulge.

Gear: Quickdraws.

FA: Greg Collum, Matt Kerns.

Mike Patz on the FA of Unicorn Blues (5.12a) | Photo by Chris Kalman

㉕ WRITTEN IN STONE 5.11B ★★

A tenuous start leads to enjoyable edges and jugs. Near the top the features thin out and friction moves provide a tricky crux before clipping the chains. From the anchor it is possible to carefully traverse left to rig a toprope for *Blue in the Face*.

Gear: 10 quickdraws.

FA: Cal Folsom, David Feinberg.

㉖ BB CLING 5.11D ★★★

This pitch climbs the slabby arête that hangs high above the center of the Blues Cliff. The moves and position are both excellent. Approach via *Written in Stone*, *Etch a Sketch*, or *Blues Riff*.

Gear: Quickdraws. Between the second and third bolts is an old threaded sling which you clip for pro. Someone should get rid of that tat and just place a bolt.

FA: Greg Collum, Will Catlin.

㉗ ETCH A SKETCH 5.11B ★★

Though often wet (right at the crux, to boot!) this is actually a really fun climb. Climb out the arching left-facing dihedral past bolts and some funky moves traversing hard left, then back right. Keep it together through the easier but tenuous finish.

Gear: 8 quickdraws.

FA: Greg Collum, Matt Kerns, Oleg Ashirov.

㉘ BLUES RIFF 5.11A ★★

About as good and as hard as *Etch a Sketch*. This route climbs the bolt line immediately right through some corners and face to the same anchor. The start is cruxy, and requires noticing a semi-hidden hold that is often wet. The rest of the route is not as difficult.

Gear: Quickdraws.

FA: Larissa Collum, Greg Collum.

㉙ RHYTHM AND BOLTS 5.11A ★★★

A good warm-up—this route used to be the most popular one at the cliff according to Cramer's guidebook. A short boulder problem at the start gives way to fun slab climbing with technical foot work. Unique holds and cool features allow an improbable passage up to the large roof where you will clip dangling chains below a bizarre mineral deposit that looks like (but isn't) spray paint. Freeing the roofs above would certainly make for an interesting project.

Gear: 6 quickdraws.

FA: Greg Collum, Matt Kerns.

㉚ COLOR OF PAIN 5.12A ★

Rarely, if ever, done. This is the bolted corner right of *Rhythm and Bolts*.

New tat on the anchor as of 2015.

Gear: Quickdraws.

FA: Matt Kerns.

㉛ PREVIOUSLY EXPOSED 5.12A ★★

The thin crack right of *Color of Pain* is as hard as it looks. Originally led on pre-placed gear, an onsight attempt could be R-rated.

Gear: Tiny cams and RPs up to 1". Emphasis on the small stuff.

FA: Greg Collum, Matt Kerns.

th a brush, rack, and the shirt off his back, Greg Horvath charges up Stud Farm (5.11c, p.135).

32 WEDGIE 5.12A ★★

This is an interesting-looking route in a tight slot with a thin crack in the back. The crux is pulling out of the wedge onto the right face above the slot.

The bolts are likely in need of replacement.

Gear: Quickdraws.

FA: Ron Farrell.

RHYTHM CLIFF

This wall may not have many routes on it—but two REALLY good lines make it worth the trip for sure. *Stud Farm* and *Unnatural Act* are both classics in every sense of the word. These routes combine with nearby routes at either Blues Cliff or Little Elvis for a great day.

Approach: Hike up the Upper Town Wall trail until the first trail junction, and turn left. At the next trail branch you reach go right (left goes down to Blues Cliff). The wall will appear shortly on your right.

Descent: Both routes can be rapped and TR'd with a single 60.

33 STUD FARM 5.11C ★★★

Climb the left-leaning bolted arête. The entry move may be very difficult if you are under 5'9". The crux i actually higher up, though, establishing on the arête

Gear: Quickdraws.

FA: Greg Collum, Andy Selters.

34 UNNATURAL ACT 5.11C ★★★★

Climb the first four bolts of *Stud Farm*, then bust right. Wild moves take you continually right through overlaps and roofs on great rock, and fantastic climbing.

Gear: Quickdraws.

FA: Greg Collum, Andy Selters.

LITTLE ELVIS

This wall, like Rhythm Cliff, features at least two awesome routes (*Love Buttons* and *Dirty Laundry*). It is worth a stop off on your way to the UTW, or combined with Rhythm Cliff or Blues Cliff for a great day.

Approach: Hike up the Upper Town Wall trail until the second trail junction, and turn left. After a short hike on a well-established trail, you will see a mysterious looking buttress up and right with no reasonable trail to access it. Just bushwhack the path of least resistance to the cliff. Trust us, it's worth the effort.

Descent: A single 60 will do.

35 SHARK BAIT 5.11B ★

Dirty and obscure, climb the left-facing corner (gear on the left side of the cliff up to some bolts along an arête. Most people lower off a single bolt at the end of the good climbing. You can also climb runout 5.8 to a tree at the top.

Gear: Rack of cams, quickdraws.

FA: Greg Collum, Chuck Boyd.

CORNERED 5.12A ★★

contrived route just left of *Love Buttons*.

ar: *Standard Index Rack. Fixed nuts (may be miss-g).*

: Greg Collum, Cal Folsom.

LOVE BUTTONS 5.11C ★★★★

very cool knob route through a couple of roofs, ding at a 2-bolt anchor. Most will lower at the bolt ove the upper roof, but you can keep on going to 2-bolt anchor. At time of writing, in bad need of trobolting.

ear: *Quickdraws.*

: Greg Collum, Andy Selters.

DIRTY LAUNDRY 5.11D ★★★★

is is a fantastic route on awesome stone, with some ry memorable knob climbing. It starts on *Love Buttons*, then climbs the rightward-trending line of bolts rough a series of intimidating looking overlaps and ofs. The cruxes are both up high, above the steeper ctions. Stem past some amazingly cryptic moves eminiscent of *Bat Skins full*) to the proper crux—a ight dependent, full-blown stopper move between rizontal cracks. This move certainly feels harder an 5.12b if you are shorter than 6'0". But don't let at deter you—the crux is easily aided, and the climb-g is incredible!

is route is officially 5.11d, but I think Cal and Greg ay have dropped a few sandbags along their way to at conclusion...

ear: *6 quickdraws, single finger size TCU optional.*

: Greg Collum, Cal Folsom.

ck Taylor on the rarely climbed Dirty Laundry 5.11d. | Photo by Chris Kalman

Justen Sjong honing his skills on Amandla (5.13b/c).

JUSTEN SJONG

BRINGING IT ALL BACK HOME

I grew up in Sultan, right outside of Index, but my love affair with climbing there really didn't start until 1992. I was living in Bellingham, and a bunch of us were hanging out at the house, and I remember someone dropped a copy of *Climbing* magazine on the coffee table. There was this picture of Alex Huber on the cover, on the Salathe Headwall—an old Heinz Zak photo—and I was just like, "Wow."

I was just your average 5.9 trad climber—but seeing that picture, I thought "OK, I want to free that." The next natural step was to buy a port-a-ledge, and head up to Index. I talked a friend into coming up to do *Town Crier* with me. It ended up taking us over two and a half days! We had a great adventure. The sheriff's office even came out late in the night. They were down in town with a big searchlight and a bullhorn yelling "DO YOU NEED A RESCUE?! FLASH YOUR LIGHT ONCE IF YES, TWICE IF NO..." It was hilarious.

For the next four years, I honed my skills at Index, and all over the northwest. There wasn't really anybody climbing there. It was incredible. I got pretty strong, pretty fast, and I guess my big prize before I left and moved to Colorado was sending *Amandla* in 1997. That was the apex of my career to that point.

I moved to Boulder for a while, and then California from 2002-2007. I was utterly obsessed with El Cap, and ended up finally achieving my dream from way back in the day in Bellingham by freeing the *Salathe* (5.13b) in 2004, and then *Golden Gate* (5.13) shortly thereafter.

A few years after freeing those El Cap routes, in 2007, I found myself with my wife, back in Washington on a transition back to Boulder. I was stunned to discover that *Town Crier*, and many of the other incredible Upper Town Wall routes still had not been freed. We were living in a van down by the river.

I decided to try to free *Town Crier*. I would scrub in the morning, then jump in the river and get all the grossness and lichen off of me, then in the evening I would go and mini-trac it. It was heaven. *Town Crier* went really well, and after just a week or so, I eventually freed it. Then, of course, I couldn't help but clean up and try *Green Drag-on*, and I ended up freeing that line, too with Ben Gilkison. All of this was within about a two-week period.

Index was really the proving grounds for me to learn how to navigate the really hard climbing in Yosemite. *Magic Mushroom* (5.13d/5.14a), which I went back and freed with Tommy Caldwell in 2008, has a lot of shimmying, feature climbing, and "oozing up the wall." And Index just has endless amounts of that. Yosemite granite is not as good, not as sticky, or grabby. But learning to navigate that granite funk at Index—that's what really made it possible for me to excel on the hard climbing in Yosemite.

Index is one of those places where, as one generation fades away, another one develops. That can feel like a good thing, or a bad thing, depending on how you look at it. The way I see it, the next generation always has to cherish what was there, but also take ownership and keep adding to it in a way that reflects *your* time at Index—*your* generation. It is such an amazing and spiritual place for so many people, that of course, you have to respect what came before. That said, you also have to respect what makes it special for you.

I think Index is the best crag in America, hands down. Or, at least, the best relatively unknown crag. But I don't think we should ever worry it's going to become *hugely* popular. It's not Smith Rock, it's not Squamish. It's never going to be that. If we don't keep the traffic up, it's always going to be overgrown, and fading away. How cool would it be to show up to Index and see a community of people where it's just like "Welcome, this is Index! Let me give you a tour!" If you are an Index local and a strong climber and you want to keep those routes clean, you've got to take that responsibility, and expose people to what Index has to offer.

Pressure Drop—a fine 5.11a crack hiding in the forest.

MISCELLANEOUS CRAGS

You're walking in the woods, off-trail somewhere, looking for new routes. The sun barely filters down through the thick canopy of trees. Everything is covered in beautiful green moss. Lost in your revelry, you just about stumble over the edge of a cliff. Whoa! Surely you've found something new, you think, as you scramble around to the base to look at your quarry.

There in the middle of another scruffy face is a perfect splitter. And it's clean! What is that thing?

As it turns out, new routing at Index is not as easy as you might think. Those Index climbers from back in the day were prolific! While not every square inch of stone has been expended, most of it has at least been looked at. And as for single pitch cracks, chances are they have been done.

We've done our best to be comprehensive with our coverage of all the routes at Index in this book. But for various reasons, there are a few smaller, scruffier, less visited crags that just don't exactly fit here, or there, or in any particular chapter. These are the Miscellaneous Crags. We encourage you to seek them out, explore, and if you find that mossy splitter, clean it up and make sure it has good anchors! Here is a small sampling of what you can find in the woods, lurking in the shadows.

PAJAMAS

A short ways past Little Elvis is this decent-looking wall, which has two routes: *Pajama People* (5.9, right facing corner, two stars), and *Smile* (5.7, thin crack, two stars).

SHADY LANE

Just before you hit the base of the Upper Town Wall, an indistinct trail heads out left along the base of a cliff called Shady Lane. That cliff sports three routes: *Free Range Chook* (5.10b, splitter crack, two stars), *Eso No Se Hace* (5.11a, three stars, Dedinas, Dedinas, Tower), and *Chronic Relief* (5.9, bolted face, two stars, Dedinas, Dedinas, Tower).

PRESSURE DROP

Just before you reach the first routes on the Lower Cheeks, duck down into the woods keeping an eye open for any faint trails. Soon you will come to a tree with three distinct trunks, and possibly a cairn. Head downhill and right to the base of Pressure Drop Rock. There, you can find *Pressure Drop* (5.11a, Swedin McDougall, three stars), *Blame it on Cain* (5.11b, thin crack, two stars), and *Errol Flynn on Piano* (5.12b, finger crack, three stars).

ICELICKER

Just southwest of *Pressure Drop* is another small cliff called Icelicker, which sports one route, *Pad in Hand, the Milk Flows Oh So Freely Every Sphincter Holiday* (5.9+, one star).

COFFEE ACHIEVERS

If you continue past the three-trunked-tree, you will soon come to a small cliff on the left called Coffee Achievers, which has a few short cracks and corners that are easily toproped.

THE RABBIT

Shortly beyond Coffee Achievers, past it's right (north) end is The Rabbit. Here is one fine route called *Concrete Lawn Critters* (5.12a, bolted face, Dufford, Baird, Crowley, Olsen, Cramer). For another point of reference, it is just below Black Planet area, on the Lower Cheeks.

Wally Barker on Pressure Drop (5.11a) | *Photo by Jon Nelson*

THE UPPER TOWN WALLS

When you cross the bridge on your way into Index it's hard not to stop and stare at The Upper Town Walls. Steep, sheer, huge, and clean, The UTW's domineering presence thwarts and belittles the more popular LTW from almost any vantage point. There are classics of every grade up here, and the views are some of the best in the northwest. The walk uphill is steep–but relatively short (no more than 30 minutes). And while it's understandably difficult to leave the LTW of your own volition, just keep in mind that solitude and perfect stone await just a short walk away.

Approach: Cross the train tracks, then walk east alongside them, paralleling the LTW. An obvious access road after a few minutes leads to a nice grassy area complete with picnic bench and a strange tunnel in the wall (The Country). Enter the woods at the right side of the grassy area, and follow the trail up steep switchbacks. Bear right at two different trail junctions (these go to Blues Cliff and other Mid Walls), eventually passing close to a medium sized cliff (Shady Lane). After Shady Lane, another five minutes takes you to the base of Davis Holland Area. Specific approach beta for all of The Upper Town Walls are described from this spot.

Luke Stefuriak and Kerwin Loukasa head into the final frontier on Starfish Enterprise. (5.12)

EARWAX WALL

The Earwax Wall forms the far left (west) terminus of the Upper Town Wall formation. It features a variety of impressive single-pitch routes which stay shady and cool in the heat of summer. Some very good climbing is to be had here, making this wall well-worth the walk. The rock is unique for Index with bizarre colors and strangely-sculpted holds. It can look a bit scruffy, but actually climbs quite well.

The routes from *Sportfishing* to *Squeeze It* are located just beyond (further left than) Earwax proper.

Approach: Follow the UTW trail to the base of the Davis Holland Area, then continue left to the final wall.

Descent: Most of these routes can be climbed with a single 70. For *Sport Fishing* bring two ropes.

❶ SPORTFISHING 5.10C ★

The furthest left route on the Upper Town Wall, this was also the first free climb in the Earwax area. Now, it is a rarely climbed three pitch route. The third pitch is quite good, but the first and second pitches are less than incredible. The whole thing could be climbed as one very long pitch.

Gear: *Standard Index Rack. 2 ropes and tat.*

FA: Don Brooks, David Whitelaw.

❷ VANESSA DEL RIO 5.12C ★

The bolt line left of *Everest without Lycra*. This and the route farther left are rarely done. If VDR was climbed more, it would be a fine line. The bolts are spacey, and the climbing is continuously challenging. The last 30 feet or so go on gear.

Gear: *Quickdraws. Single rack of cams up to 2.5", and RPs.*

FA: Greg Child, Rich Johnston.

❸ EVEREST WITHOUT LYCRA 5.11B ★★★

Climb the obvious bolted arête by starting up ledg terrain and then stepping left. Quality position, int esting moves, and an exciting finish.

Gear: *Quickdraws.*

FA: Greg Child, Greg Collum.

❹ SQUEEZE IT 5.11D ★

Squeeze It is the short bolt line climbing giant bloc to the right of *Everest without Lycra*. A piece or tw could be nice for the bottom.

Gear: *Quickdraws, and a couple of optional cams.*

FA: Matt Kerns, Jim Yoder.

❺ FRIENDS IN HOLY PLACES 5.11A A2 ★

At the far left end of the Earwax Wall proper, this w the first UTW route to be put up solo. Now this thi is rarely/never climbed. The second pitch could pe haps make for an interesting free climbing project. Climb up the dirty wet right-facing corner to a bol and traverse right on a funky flake. Rap, or enjoy ar A2 second pitch.

Gear: *Standard Index Rack.*

FA: Don Brooks; FFA P1: Darryl Cramer, Max Duffor

❻ SWEATSHOP 5.12B ★★

The farthest left fully bolted line on the cliff. Rarely done. It is not as blank as it appears from the groun There are two possible bolted starts. Either works.

Gear: *Quickdraws.*

FA: Greg Collum, Andy de Klerk, Matt Kerns.

❼ DOMESTIC VIOLENCE 5.11D ★★★

This challenging and excellent route climbs a thin crack using face climbing techniques up to the roof then pulls strenuous moves all the way to the chain

Gear: *Cams to 2". There may be a few fixed pins or bc as well.*

FA: Terry Lien, Jon Nelson.

'HE BLACK FLAG OF THE SCHWARZER AMIN 5.10D ★★★

ıb straight up the large boulder/flake lean- ıgainst the wall. Head up the first two bolts of *show*, then split off left and climb a groove/crack ure to the anchor about 10 feet right of where *ıestic Violence* turns the roof.

r: Quickdraws.

Eric Hirst, Jon Nelson.

SIDESHOW 5.10D ★★★

ney up small edges and sidepulls, continually ;onaling up and right through a blank looking wall. on-point all the way to the chains.

r: 8 quickdraws.

Greg Collum, Matt Kerns, Larissa Collum.

KILLSLUG 5.12B ★★★

: to the right of *Black Flag*, begin up bolts and gh edging. Where *Sideshow* crosses the route, you get a nice rest. A tough roof encounter leads to tinuously difficult climbing above.

ve the first anchor, two more bolts lead to a ond anchor. This does not change the grade, and can lower from the upper anchor with a 70 meter e.

r: Quickdraws. Optional small cam or nut after the th bolt.

Greg Collum, Greg Child; FFA: Andy de Klerk.

Dan Kluskiewicz enjoying the perfectly sculpted edges of Sideshow (5.10d)

Todorovich using thin finger locks and thinner gear on Earwax (5.11c, p.146)

Jon Nelson on an early attempt of Domestic Violence (5.11d, p.142). Barefoot. | Photo by Greg Olsen

JON NELSON

JAPANESE GARDENS, DOMESTIC VIOLENCE, YO-YOS, AND ROCK SHOES

In the early 80s, when Terry and I first started climbing *Japanese Gardens*, the first pitch had already gone free. I don't know who freed it, or even if it had been led yet. But one day, Terry led the first pitch. We liked it, and so on later days we came back to clean and lead the remaining pitches and their variations. I recall only two such days.

On one trip, we were driving up to do variations to the second pitch. As Terry drove, we thought up names. Terry first suggested *Trout Farm Massacre*, perhaps influenced by *Trout Farm Road* in Sultan. Next came *Light Bulb Sandwich*, both names announced with big Terry grins. I had to admit, he had mastered the three-word pattern (soon to dominate Index naming), and then voted for the trout. For my name, I momentarily reflected on the climber's picnic (which I'd never been to, alas), and thinking he'd never agree to such nonsense, blurted out "It's a dog's life, but you can picnic with us". But he liked it, and so it stuck. Now I don't actually remember climbing any of those second pitches, but I do remember their naming.

Sometime later, we went up to free the fourth pitch. This time, I got to Index and realized that I had forgotten my rock shoes. But Terry loaned me a pair of his Fires, the new sticky-soled shoe that had only recently come out. (He actually kept several pairs of "magic shoes," a pair once helping Greg Olsen free the 5.12a lower variation to *Sagittarius*). As I recall, the hardest part of that fourth pitch involved a thin, smearing traverse, protected by a pin. With the Fires, it did not seem very difficult. Later, in the parking lot, I saw Dick Cilley, who asked me how hard the pitch was. I replied that I had no idea, as it was my first time using the fancy new sticky shoes. I still have no idea, as I haven't been back. Concerning those shoes, he ended up giving me the pair, and I continued to use them off and on until 2013 when I lost one on an approach in Washington Pass. Of course, I still have the other one.

And about the ascent style–back then, we didn't worry as much about style as climbers do now, at least as I recall. If I got up the route, whether by yo-yoing or not, I simply called it done. After all, if you can yo-yo a route, then clearly you can redpoint the route. It becomes just a matter of patience, not ability: Try it a few more times and you will get it no falls, placing all your own pro. But I was never that patient. Why not just move on to another route? Doing something new is much more fun. In the case of *Japanese Gardens*, I cannot remember if we yo-yoed any pitches. If, after some FA somewhere, a person asked about our style, we'd tell them honestly; otherwise, we just moved on.

But I do recall one yo-yo case. It was the FA of *Domestic Violence* at the Upper Town Wall. I had tried it on a previous trip (in my bare feet). In this case, Terry went up, cruising quickly as he usually did, then lingered for the longest time up high. Belaying him far below, I couldn't see exactly what he was grabbing, and thought that he must have found a great rest stance above the roof. But in this case, (well OK, in nearly every case), there was no stance at all: Terry had been jamming on the pumpy, enduro-crux the whole time, putting in the pieces, working out the moves, all without weighting the rope. Eventually, he called out that he was coming down, and I went up. We didn't pull the rope, so I didn't have to put in any pieces to his high point. In fact, I didn't have to place any pieces at all. Instead, (this time, climbing with shoes) I desperately (and quickly) scraped my way through the part Terry had lingered on, being completely amazed that any human could place pro there, and continued as fast as I could to the anchors.

The oft-repeated joke back then was that if Terry was hanging around some section of a route for a long time, then he was probably clinging on some one-handed fingertip layback, a Terry Lien "rest".

⑪ SLUGSHOW 5.11C/D ★★

Start on *Killslug* and end on *Sideshow*. Not as good as either of those routes, but between them in difficulty.

Gear: *Quickdraws.*

FA: Greg Collum, Greg Child; FFA: Andy de Klerk.

⑫ EARWAX 5.11C ★★★★

This is a stunning line. Follow the thin crack right of *Killslug* applying a combination of crack and face technique to reach a very cool roof.

You can continue past the first anchor for a super-good full-value pitch of crack climbing. To toprope the whole pitch may require an 80m rope. Bring extra gear for the full pitch

Gear: *Standard Index Rack to #1 Camalot. Emphasis on thin gear.*

FA: Don Harder, Dougal McCarty; FFA: Terry Lien, Jon Nelson.

⑬ YOUNG CYNICS 5.12D ★★★

The first route on the Upper Town Wall to be established with a power drill. This thin edging testpiece climbs up the face and through a roof to the anchor of *Earwax*.

Gear: *9 quickdraws.*

FA: Greg Collum.

⑭ SOUL ON ICE 5.12D ★★★

Two routes left of the obvious arête (*Biology*) lies So *on Ice* and its two variations. Overhanging climbing mostly positive holds leads to continuous micro-ed ing on the headwall. The crux is very thin. The first variation (*Raggedy Andy* 5.12a/b three stars) heads left to the *Young Cynics* anchor at the fifth bolt. The second variation (*Raggedy Ann* 5.11+, three stars) tra verses to the *Young Cynics* anchor at the seventh b

Gear: *Quickdraws.*

FA: Andy de Klerk; FA Raggedy Andy: Jeff Baird, Max Dufford; FA Raggedy Ann: Jeff Baird, Max Dufford.

⑮ THE ANTIDOTE 5.13A ★★

Listed as 5.12d in the Cramer guide, but upgraded to 5.13a, this route is truly a neglected gem (just like most of the Earwax Wall). Just left of the obvious ar (*Biology*), climb past continuous, strenuous crimps difficult-to-decipher sequences on sloping holds. T route is still awaiting a second ascent.

Gear: *Quickdraws.*

FA: Max Dufford, Jeff Baird.

⑯ BIOLOGY OF SMALL APPLIANCES 5.12A ★★★★

Stunning. This is the first route you encounter on Earwax Wall (the furthest right bolted arête) and it i one of the best arêtes at Index. Incredible climbing past seven bolts brings you to a memorable crux an the chains. It may feel hard for 5.12a.

Gear: *Quickdraws.*

FA: Max Dufford, Greg Olsen.

Unknown climber on Biology of Small Appliances (5.12a) | Photo by Larry Kemp.

TEMPITCHUOUS AREA

he Tempitchuous Area lies between the Earwax Vall and The Heaven's Gate (Lamplighter) Area. here are some excellent routes here, including the amesake–*Tempitchuous*–which is not to be missed.

pproach: Head west (climber's left) along the base f the UTW, passing The Sport Wall, Heaven's Gate, nd the obvious bolted arch (*Dana's Arch*). If you hit arwax Wall, you've gone too far.

escent: You can rap these routes with a single 60.

THE BACK ROAD 5.8 ★

nere is rumored to be a four-pitch 5.8 back this way. arryl Cramer wrote, "Most who look for it–don't find Most who find it–don't climb it. Most who attempt –escape by rappeling from the top of the bulge." 'herever this route is, it probably has not been imbed in some time.

ear: Standard Index Rack and gardening tools

: Jim Langdon, Pete Sandstedt.

18 DGS 5.9 ★★

This moderate climb is a tribute to the famous Washington climber, David Gunstone. While a bit dirty, this route is really pretty good. It exists somewhere nebulous in The Back Road/Jungle Fun area.

Just after pulling up the hand line, trend right to a tree. Start with a rightward traverse to the corner-crack.

Gear: Standard Index Rack. Brushes & gardening tools.

FA: Bruce Anderson, Dave Tower.

Pitch 1–5.8+

Start with a rightward traverse to a flake and then jam a hand/fist crack to a large ledge with a big fir tree.

The Death of Abraham Lincoln by Mounties (5.11c) is a variation that goes up the steep face and corner just right of the regular first pitch.

Pitch 2–5.9

Start up thin face cracks, then traverse left into the long corner system. This pitch is about 150 feet and ends at a bolted belay.

Pitch 3–5.7

Traverse out right on the exposed ramp about 30', and belay at the bolted anchor.

Pitch 4–5.9

Climb a fantastic, steep arête, protected by bolts to a scenic overlook with a bolted anchor. Rap the route.

⑲ BEAT BOX 5.11D/12A ★★★★

A very good two pitch route that follows *Jungle Fun's* first pitch.

Gear: Quickdraws, nuts, and finger sizes.

FA P2: Sonya Kepler/Orion Watson; FA P3: Orion Watson.

Pitch 1–5.10b

Climb the first pitch of *Jungle Fun* (see below).

Pitch 2–5.10

Follow the bolted flake as for the start of P2 of *Tempitchuous*. After the second bolt, trend left and follow flakes and a featured face to a belay stance. By using slings, this pitch can be linked with P1 for a 180 ft pitch (20 draws).

Pitch 3–5.11+

Climbs through two fun 5.10+ bulges/roofs to a tenuous traverse left. A boulder problem through the roof (much harder than the rest of the route) brings you to the chains.

⑳ TEMPITCHUOUS 5.11D ★★★★

This is an excellent route–the final pitch is one of the best knob climbs at Index. The route is best approached via *Jungle Fun*, another classic line.

Gear: 10 quickdraws if not linking, 16 if you plan to link P1 with Jungle Fun.

FA P1: Jim Yoder, Steve Gerberding; FA P2: Matt Kerns, Greg Collum.

Pitch 1–5.10b

Climb the first pitch of *Jungle Fun* (described below).

Pitch 2–5.11a

Climb the left line of bolts next to a hollow flake. The right line is the second pitch of *Jungle Fun*. Head up the flake past a challenging mantel move, and continue up fantastic face climbing to a ledge and a 2-bolt anchor. Can be combined with *Jungle Fun's* first pitch with a 70m rope.

Pitch 3–5.11d

A four star pitch with a stinger in the tail! Climb past wild knobs and overhangs to a steep and strenuous finish. Do this climb!

㉑ JUNGLE FUN 5.11C ★★★

This route is very good–don't let the veg at the start fool you.

Gear: Quickdraws.

FA: Bruce Anderson, Dave Tower.

Pitch 1–5.10b

5.10 face climbing on bolts leads up to a nice ledge and a 2-bolt anchor. There is often a wet section that can easily be avoided by climbing to the left.

Pitch 2–5.11c

An excellent pitch. Climb the right bolt line up black rock to a difficult crux, followed by challenging friction climbing to a 2-bolt anchor.

22 PASTIME CO ★★

The next bolt line right of *Jungle Fun*. Aid past the first bolt, and follow bolts right and then back left.

Apparently this route has not been freed. The first bolt is aided at C0. There is a variant down and right of the start that was freed on toprope at 5.12d. It would be worth inspecting both ways to see if a nice free leadable pitch could be established.

Gear: Quickdraws.

FA: Erik Thixton, Marty Gunderson, Doug Duncanson.

23 FIRST AID 5.10 C1 ★

Up and left of *Dana's Arch*, a thin crack and bolts lead to an arching left-trending flake. It is not clear if this route has an anchor or not. This would be another route worth inspecting for free climbing.

Gear: Standard Index Rack.

FA: Fred Grafton.

HEAVEN'S GATE AREA

The Heaven's Gate Area (also known as Lamplighter Area) is home to what have become some of the most popular multi-pitch routes on the UTW, as well as a few interesting single-pitch lines. The first pitches often climb through some scruffiness–but the upper pitches feature immaculate edging on incredible patina and granite crimps. This section of wall includes everything from Tempitchuous Area to The Sport Wall.

Approach: Follow the Upper Wall trail to the base of the Upper Wall, then continue left to the obvious bolted arch (*Dana's Arch*). The routes on this wall begin just left of that arch.

Descent: Bring a 70 to be safe, but many of these routes can be rapped with a single 60.

24 PENCIL THIN MUSTACHE 5.12A ★★

Immediately left of *Dana's Arch* are two right-facing corners. This route climbs the one further left. The initial protection is thin, and difficult to place. Eventually the route arches up and right to a 2-bolt anchor. Above the 2-bolt anchor lies a project in a dike that has not yet been freed or bolted.

Gear: Small cams and RPs.

FA: Erik Thixton, Greg Olsen, Darryl Cramer.

25 IMPERIAL FUN 5.12A ★★

Would be more popular if easier to access. Climb the third pitch of *Dana's Arch* (bring your aid kit) up to a ledge (5.11b). Belay here, and continue up past tough climbing on bolts to a crux move and the top.

FA P1: Matt Kerns, Mike Massey; FA P2: Matt Kerns, Greg Collum.

26 DANA'S ARCH 5.11A A3 ★★★

The aesthetic first pitch to this route is often climbed by itself, since the remaining pitches involve much aid climbing (A3). The right-facing corner immediately left has been toproped at A3/4–whatever that means.

Gear: 8 quickdraws for P1, or a Standard Index Aid Rack for the full route.

FA: Bob Crawford, Leigh Nason, Pat Timson; FFA P1: Darryl Cramer, Terry Lien.

Pitch 1–5.11a
The first pitch has been freed to the first anchor at 5.11a, climbing the obvious left-leaning arch. If aiding continue past the first anchor another 20 feet or so of C1 to the second anchor.

Pitch 2–5.8 A1
Climb up a bolt ladder past pockets and bulges to a leftwards traverse (5.8) and a ledge (the Cheeto ledge).

Pitch 3–A3
Continue up more pockets, thin flakes, and bolts (A3) to a belay.

Pitch 4–5.11b
Free climb to a dirty ledge system and belay at the right side of it. Alternatively, if you want to climb *Imperial Fun*, belay at the first bolted anchor you come to.

Pitch 5–5.8 A2
Climb a dirty groove to a series of ledges and the top.

27 MYSTERY ROUTE A4 ★

Between *Dana's Arch* and *Another Man's Car* lies this obscure aid climb. Nobody knows who established it, or much about it. It climbs the thin seam in a steep corner.

Gear: *Unknown.*

FA: Unknown.

28 ANOTHER MAN'S CAR 5.11C ★★★

A true Washington rarity. Climb up into the maw of an overhanging wide crack. Offwidth trickery will get you through the crux and onto easier ground to the anchor. There is a bolted second pitch (also 5.11c) on good rock (11 bolts).

Gear: *Standard Index Rack with emphasis on wide cams.*

FFA P1: Don Brooks; FA P2: Darryl Cramer, Carmel Schimmel.

29 THE BRETT THOMPSON AND SCOTT FULLER MEMORIAL ROUTE 5.10+ ★★★

A nice, new (as of 2016) route that follows the obvious splitter corner above *Lamplighter* to the top of the wall. One of the easier full-length routes on the UTW, with airy and sustained climbing, often on small but solid gear. Go get it!

Gear: *12 draws, rack of nuts, RPs, doubles from gray Metolius to 0.4 Camalot, singles up to #3, optional #4 and #5. Rappel with a 70m rope.*

FA: Michal Rynkiewicz, Chandler Davis, Ryan Hoover.

Pitch 1—5.10c
Climb P1 of *Lamplighter* to the top of the chimney. Traverse left and follow the slab to the anchor.

Pitch 2—5.9
Enjoy steep but juggy crack climbing on good pro for a fine pitch of 5.9. The rest of the climb takes only smaller gear, so feel free to leave all gear from #3 up at the end of this pitch.

Pitch 3—5.10+
Pull a roof past a few bolts, followed by steep climbin on small gear. Finish up a leftward seam to the chain. Delicate and tenuous.

Pitch 4—5.10-
Climb straight up protecting with small cams. Clip a bolt and follow crimps up and right until reaching twin cracks. Traverse left at the bolt and continue up steep terrain to the anchor. The last pitch is all bolts, so leave the cams at the end of this one.

Pitch 5—5.10-
Climb the crimpy face to the top, clipping bolts the whole way.

LAMPLIGHTER 5.10C A3 ★★

ıe first pitch of this route is done regularly to access e more popular neighboring routes, including *aven's Gate*, but the remaining pitches are rarely mbed.

ıte: it is possible that this whole route could be eaned and retro'd into a very nice, and very popular l length UTW free climb.

ar: Standard Index aid rack.

: To the roof: Fred Beckey; FA Full: Dave Dailey, Al vler; FFA P1: Darryl Cramer, Carmel Schimmel.

tch 1–5.10c
imb the ow/chimney/face to a cruxy move in the of. Step out right and climb an awesome layback to anchor.

ar: Single set of cams; extra tips to ringlock sizes can nice.

tch 2–A3
d climb a thin crack between two bolted pitches en up and left past old bolts.

tch 3–5.8
ee climb the moderate wide crack to a large ledge th a huge detached flake. Dirty. Hard to protect.

tch 4–5.8 A2
mixture of free and aid climbing leads to a ledge ar the top. Beware of loose rock.

tch 5–5.6
short pitch of easy 5th class brings you to the top.

31 THE CRIMSON EYE 5.11- ★★★

A long-eyed somewhat meandering route with moderate climbing interrupted by short stout crux sections with an airy feeling. Named after the last verse in the Black Sabbath song *Planet Caravan*: "And so we pass on by the crimson eye, of great god Mars, as we travel the universe."

Gear: 14 draws and a single rack to 1" (single rack to 3" for Lamplighter approach pitch). Can be rapped with a single 70, but it is recommended to rap Heaven's Gate.

FA: Chandler Davis, Ryan Hoover, Michal Rynkiewicz.

Pitch 1–5.10c
Climb P1 of *Lamplighter*, but continue past it's anchor up and right another twenty feet to a second anchor.

Pitch 2–5.11-
From the belay break left to an obvious, short, right-facing corner. The corner leads to a left-leaning flake with bolts, eventually gaining a juggy, shallow, left-facing corner/groove. At the top of the groove, a tricky boulder problem to sustained crimping leads to a great belay ledge.

Pitch 3–5.10
Side-pulls, crimps and gastons lead up and left. Continue up slopers to a hard break left on jugs. At this point the climbing eases and follows face cracks to a huge flake leading to an anchor.

Pitch 4–5.11-
Step off the belay onto gorgeous patina and follow the incredible features to a no-hands rest underneath the crux. Boulder through the crux on thin holds to jugs leading slightly left. Continue right above a roof to a desperate move to slopers. Straightforward climbing leads straight up to the top of the wall.

32 HEAVEN'S GATE 5.11A ★★★★

Heaven's Gate is an exceptional route, and has become one of the most popular, multi-pitch climbs at Index. Considering that the climbing is fairly moderate, and with the exception of the first pitch, entirely bolted, this should come as no surprise. There may be parties in front of you at the base, if so, consider *Golden Road* as an excellent alternative.

Gear: Single rack to #3 for P1, 15 quickdraws, 70m rope.

FA: David Gunstone, Darryl Cramer.

Pitch 1–5.10+
Climb the first pitch of *The Crimson Eye*.

Pitch 2–5.11a
Excellent climbing up endless horizontals. This is a full on sport climbing extravaganza. Bolts lead a little right and then straight up from the anchor.

Pitch 3–5.10b
Another excellent pitch on good stone. Straight up the bolts, boys and girls.

Pitch 4–5.11a
Airy moves through jugs and a funky crux leads to fantastic jug-bashing to the top. An big ledge provides a great spot for a snack, and world-class views.

㉝ GOLDEN ROAD 5.11C ★★★

Golden Road is an excellent climb with exhilirating pitches and exposure. Although GR maintains a slightly harder grade, it is certainly attainable for anybody stepping up to HG.

The first pitch leaves a little something to be desired and needs a small rack to properly protect. From P2 onward, it is entirely bolted. Excellent movement and impeccable rock are only slightly marred by the line's position next to a bushy chimney, which detracts from the exposure normally found on upper wall routes. Otherwise, totally classic!

FA: Benjit Hull.

Gear: Single rack to 2", 10+ quickdraws (16+ if linking pitches).

Pitch 1—5.10b/c

This pitch used to be 5.11+ but recent rockfall obliterated the original line, knocking the grade down and deteriorating the quality a bit, partly because the bolts were placed pre-rockfall and clips are currently awkward.

Either begin by clipping two bolts on a slab off the ground (slightly contrived) or simply bypassing this by third-classing the ledge system from the left. Further right, continue past three bolts (awkward) into a dirty crack system. Clip another bolt up and left to meet the arête and the chains.

Leave the gear at this anchor as the rest of the climb is entirely bolted!

Pitch 2—5.11b

Stiff moves off the belay and up the arête ease slightly as you engage the face out left. Steep, excellent, cryptic face climbing through a couple cruxes leads to a cool finish up the arête.

Pitch 3—5.10c

Continue up the arête on what may be one of the finest 5.10 pitches at Index. A steep, glorious, jug-haul that is sure to bring a smile to anyone's face.

(Can be linked with P2 with around 16 quickdraws)

Pitch 4—5.11a

Keep following the awesome arête until it begins to slab out. Bolts lead the way through a tricky bulge, and on up to the next belay.

Pitch 5—5.11c

The heartbreaker finish! Climb up through a steep crux on dark rock with sharp crimpers. After that, gather yourself for a final wild roof maneuver on big holds. Technical climbing above keeps you on your toes all the way to the chains, in an alcove at the top of the wall.

㉞ WILDEST DREAMS 5.12B ★★★★

This is certainly one of the best routes on the Upper Wall, which makes it a contender for one of the best routes at Index. Chris Henson's finest contribution, without a doubt. All the pitches are good, but the bolted second pitch arête is as good as rock climbin can be, and the final pitch is jaw-droppingly aweson Bring a 70m rope, and climb the route in four pitche

Don't be deterred by the first 30' of scruffiness.The rest of the climb is incredible.

Gear: A double rack to #2 Camalot, a single #3, and a smattering of purple and gray C3/TCU-size pieces an RPs for the third pitch seam. You'll also want about 13 quickdraws and slings.

FA: Chris Henson.

Pitch 1—5.10d

Climb a few meters up to a shelf, then traverse the shelf far out right (belayer should belay beneath this point). You'll see two bolt lines emerge—follow the further right one fairly straight up, and into a vertic corner with a splitter crack. Continue up the dihedr to a 2-bolt anchor out right.

Pitch 2—5.11b

This is the best pitch of the route. Enjoy unimaginab good rock, awesome arête laybacking, and a wild sla finish that will grab your attention and hold it until the very end.

May be stiff for 5.11b.

Pitch 3—5.12b

Unless you are an absolute thin-seam crusher, this would be a very difficult onsight. That said, the pitch is really good, and definitely dumbs down. Shorter climbers may be a little flummoxed by the placemen of the first bolt... but it goes. Easily aided at 5.11 C0.

Pitch 4—5.10d

This pitch is incredible! It is steep, long, continuous, pumpy, excellent, and thought-provoking. At 5.10d it is no gimme, but if you keep your cool and shake out where you need to, everything is there.

Climb up two bolts and some funky face moves into the start of the crack. Enjoy big moves between goo locks all the way up a full 35 meters.

z Ca-Honnold taking in the view on Golden Road (5.11c).

TOP 10 ARÊTES

- ❒ Amandla 5.13b/c (p. 76)
- ❒ Slapshot 5.11d (p.50)
- ❒ Spineless 5.10d 5.11a (p.237)
- ❒ The Amphibian 5.10+ (p.214)
- ❒ Golden Road 5.11c (p.152)
- ❒ Tie Me to a Length of That 5.12a (p.55)
- ❒ Biology of Small Appliances 5.12a (p.146)
- ❒ Wildest Dreams (P2) 5.12b (p.152)
- ❒ Everest Without Lycra 5.11b (p.142)
- ❒ Accidental Discharge 5.11b (p.129)

Geologic perfection meets climbing perfection. Sj Lee envisions her Wildest Dreams (5.12b).

·IE SPORT WALL

Sport Wall features some of the most impecca- stone at Index. Most of the routes here are (as name implies) bolted sport routes. Still, this is ordinary sport crag. Expect super-techy, difficult ement, spacey bolting, and some bolts in need eplacement. You won't find tick marks here, or s of chalk, but you won't find lines at the base of routes either. This wall is pure adventure sport bing at it's finest.

roach: Follow the Upper Wall trail to the base of Upper Wall, then continue left. The Sport Wall nmediately left of Davis Holland Area. Many of routes start on a small terrace accessed through ne moderate 5th class, which can be wet at times.

cent: You can rap/TR anything on The Sport l with a single 70.

SCATTERLINGS 5.12B ★★★

previous guidebook claimed the bolts on this te were hard to clip, making *Scatterlings* less than ular. The climbing, however, is quite good. This ne farthest left bolted route on The Sport Wall, ere the ledge meets the trail. Greg Olsen said this y be his favorite route at Index and fully deserves r stars.

r: 11 or so quickdraws.

Andy de Klerk, Randy Farris.

36 QUIETLANDS 5.12B A0 ★★★

The first pitch of this route has been freed at 5.12a, the second pitch has two sections of 5.12b and an A0 move that thwarted Andy de Klerk... AKA stout. The first pitch is very popular, and very, very good.

FA: Andy de Klerk, Randy Farris.

Pitch 1—5.12a

From the left side of the big ledge, make exciting traverse moves left past a low crux. Wild and safe climbing takes you past five more bolts to a 2-bolt anchor.

Pitch 1 5.12b A0

Andy de Klerk got shut down on a move at the second to last bolt... Will you?

37 HEART'S DESIRE 5.12B ★★★★

In spite of a somewhat scary finish, this route is superb. The climbing is typified by difficult edges and challenging high steps. Some of the bolts may be poorly positioned.

Gear: 9 quickdraws.

FA: Keith Lenard, Will Gadd.

Audrea Nolan *climbing splitters with* Jon Masaya Evans *at the belay.* Davis Holland (5.10c, p.158).

Note: Topo for 38-41 on P.155.

38 CALLING WOLFGANG 5.12A ★★★★

This route earned a bad reputation after mixed metal bolts failed due to galvanic corrosion, almost leading to a fatal groundfall. The bolts have since been replaced, and this excellent route deserves to be climbed!

From the right side of the ledge, climb up a somewhat scruffy start with some natural gear to a steep, attractive face. Sustained, spacey climbing leads past three bolts and some gear to a stance. The climbing gets more and more challenging from here until a baffling crux that is pure Index. The crux may feel impossible on hot days.

This is the second line left of *Davis Holland.*

Gear: Cams to 1.5", nuts, and 12 quickdraws should do.

FA: Greg Child, Andy de Klerk.

39 STRAIGHT TO VOICEMAIL 5.12C ★★★

From the anchor of *Calling Wolfgang*, powerful climbing right off the bat leads to a few gear placements, followed by a second crux on small holds.

Gear: A set of cams and quickdraws.

FA: Kevin Newell, Chris Henson, Johnny Goicoechea.

40 CHILD ABUSE 5.12D ★★★

Begin up the first bolted line left of *Davis Holland.* Hang a long draw on the third bolt, and traverse left (*Child's Play* continues up and right). Several cruxes, including an improbable dyno below a fixed pin, bring you to a bolted anchor.

Gear: 12 quickdraws.

FA: Greg Child.

41 CHILD'S PLAY 5.11C ★★

Start up the first route left of *Davis Holland.* At the third bolt, continue up and right. The crux is a height-dependant reach. It is useful to stick-clip the first bolt. At the end, traverse hard right to the anchor of *Davis Holland* P1.

Gear: Cams to 2", nuts, quickdraws.

FA: Greg Child, Sally Oberlin.

DAVIS HOLLAND AREA

This is the most eye-catching, tallest part of the Upper Town Wall. It includes everything from *Davi Holland/Lovin' Arms* over to *Waterway* (which is a waterfall until mid-summer).

Approach: Take the Upper Town Wall trail all the way up to the Upper Town Wall and you're there

42 DAVIS HOLLAND/LOVIN' ARMS 5.10C ★★★★

Two separate routes—*The Davis Holland Route* and *Lovin' Arms*—are now almost always climbed as one four star linkup known as *Davis Holland/Lovin' Arm* (DH/LA).

Hence, we've included this linkup as a single 6-pitc classic. This is one of the most moderate routes up the Upper Wall, and tackles it at its tallest position. Consider this a must-do line.

Rap the route with a single 70, or two 60s. Your best bet is to rap into The Sport Wall, and continue straight down from there à la *Calling Wolfgang* (esp cially if climbing on a single 70). Watch the ends.

Gear: Standard Index Rack.

FA: Dan Davis, John Holland; FFA: Al Givler et al. FA Lovin Arms: Don Brooks; FFA: Dan Lapeska, Larry Kemp (high); Pat Timson (low).

Pitch 1—5.9

Start this classic route by climbing a somewhat dirt broken corner. This quickly turns into steeper crac climbing until a large terraced ledge is reached. Maneuver past slabby steps (out right is easiest) to the belay (then back left) at the base of a right-facin corner. This pitch may seep early season, while the rest of the route is dry.

Pitch 2—5.10b

A great pitch! Get physical and jam your way up the corner. A steep 0.75 crack on great rock provides th business on this pitch. Stop at the bolted belay belo the quartz-dike roof.

Pitch 3—5.10c

Bust tricky moves up and right through a cool roof with quartz features. Above the roof work your way up another right-facing corner to encounter an exciting crux where technique, balance, and good nut craft are sure to leave you feeling invigorated! Conti ue up to a nice belay below an imposing chimney. This is where people climbing just the *Davis Hollan* usually rap, and most parties continue up *Lovin' Arr* If you want to finish up the scruffy, dirty, original Dan's Holland route, continue left and up on the line of least resistance from here.

Pitch 4—5.10b

From the belay, step right through shallow cracks to reach a handcrack that takes you into the chimney. This is better than it looks from below. Fun climbing through the chimney will land you at a semi-hangin belay on the left side.

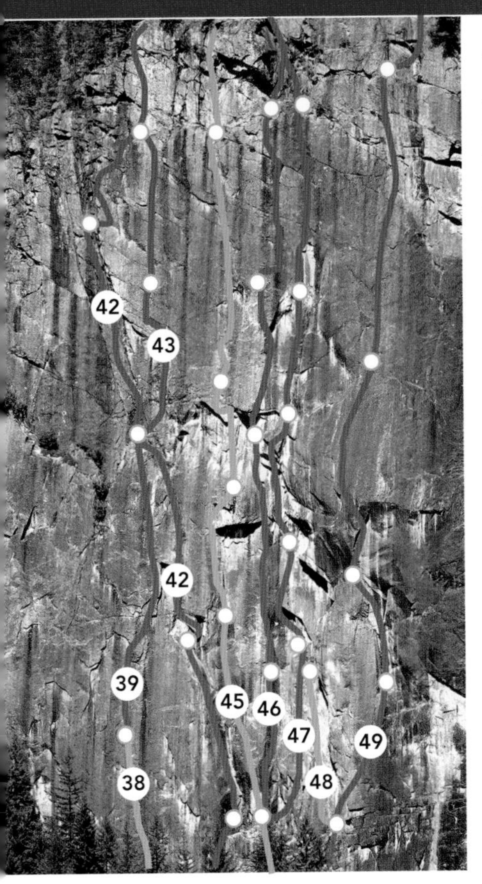

ch 5—5.10c
is pitch has a couple options for the start. For the 0 climber, continue up the chimney for 15-20 ft and en step right to engage the face (5.10c). Trending and right on the face, you will encounter amazing ck/face climbing with good traditional protection d awesome exposure! Mantel onto a ledge below a al short face and belay.

r those looking for a 5.11 challenge, step immediate-right off the belay, balancing your way out a narrow ot rail (pro can be placed at your feet). Tenuous oves right bring you to a much-welcomed bolt. Pull d climb the slabby crux (5.11b) until good holds and acks bring you to where the 5.10 version intersects. om here, continue up. (It is possible to enjoy this ction at 5.10c A0 by simply pulling through on the lt and continuing up).

tch 6—5.9+
om the belay head straight up the short face above. o approaches can be taken, left or right. Both are citing. Right may be easier but is a little runout. Be- atop the wall and soak in the aura of the beautiful y Valley.

43 SENSELESS THOUGHTS OF PARANOIA 5.11C/D ★★★

This climb is basically a variation of *Lovin' Arms*. From the top of P3 of *Davis Holland* you'll notice a line of bolts that traverses enticingly right and up (right of *Lovin' Arms*). Follow the bolts onto the steep slab and up faint dike features (cruxy 5.11+) to a bolted belay. A cool crack pitch follows (this 5.11a can be dirty and needs more traffic!), with amazing position high on the wall, and brings you to the base of the final 5.9 of *Lovin' Arms*.

A variation also exists where you can traverse back into *Lovin' Arms* from the belay atop the slab/dike pitch. Exciting and committing 5.10+ on gear.

Gear: Same as for Davis Holland with plenty of tiny nuts and cams.

FA: David Gunstone, Roger Brown.

44 CRYING DRAGON 5.11D ★★★

Crying Dragon is a fairly recent linkup of various parts of *Davis Holland*, *Rise and Fall*, *Green Drag-on*, and *Town Crier*. The most notable thing about it is that it gives access to some very fine climbing on those routes while keeping the grade below 5.12.

Gear: Triples to 0.4 Camalot. Doubles to #1. Single #2, #3, and #4. 10-12 quickdraws and slings.

FA: Luke Stefurak.

Pitch 1—5.9
Climb *Davis Holland*'s first pitch.

Pitch 2—5.10a
Climb *Davis Holland*'s second pitch.

Pitch 3—5.10c
Look up and right for a bolt with a black hanger. Undercling right out the roof, clip the bolt, and make tricky moves to a #2 cam placement and easier climbing. Continue right to *Rise and Fall*. Pass the belay out right, clip another black bolt and finish up *Rise and Fall*'s excellent second pitch to a 3-bolt anchor.

Pitch 4—5.10d
Start up *Rise and Fall* past a bolt to a finger crack. Move right to a bolt on *Green Drag-on*'s P3, and continue up the steep crack out the right side of the roof and up 5.10 terrain to a 2-bolt anchor.

Pitch 5—5.11+
Climb up the corner to a jug and a bolt out right (the bolts above and left are *Green Drag-on*). Continue right past some hidden holds and powerful moves, clipping bolts to the anchor of P5 of *Town Crier*, 40ft.

Pitch 6—5.11d
Start up the flake, past pins and small gear and layback to establish on a "flexy" flake. After the flake (protected by bolts) traverse left on a horizontal crack for 20 ft back to *Green Drag-on*. Climb a final 50 ft of 5.10 crack to the end of *Green Drag-on*. A #3 is nice on the pitch. Rap *Green Drag-on* back to *Rise and Fall* then straight down.

Note: Full size topo for these routes on p. 159.

45 RISE AND FALL 5.12B ★★★★

This is an excellent climb with recently replaced hardware. Go get it!

Beginning off of Madsen's Ledge, just right of the *Davis Holland* route, this route shares the first four meters or so of *Green Drag-on*. It follows a bolted line that weaves up dikes, amazing pockets, and tricky slabs. The first pitch is exceptionally difficult, but a great variation start (beginning of *Crying Dragon*) is to traverse right from the top of P2 *Davis Holland*, entering the start of P2 *Rise and Fall* making the whole route an exceptional 5.11+ outing. (For this variation bring doubles to 1.5 inches, and singles to 2.5 inches then leave the rack atop P3 and retrieve on rappel).

Gear: Whatever you need to get to Madsen's Ledge (see Davis Holland or Green Drag-on). From Madsen's ledge 16 quickdraws will get you to the top. Bolted anchors the whole way. Some small runouts could be supplemented with a small rack to 1.5". Rap with a single 70m rope.

FA: Greg Child, Andy de Klerk.

Pitch 1—5.9-5.11a

Climb the first pitch of *Davis Holland* or *Green Dragon*.

Pitch 2—5.12b

Begin up the second pitch corner of *Green Drag*-on past four bolts, then move left onto a face. Continue left through challenging climbing, then up a quartz dike to the crux. Follow the dike to an anchor. Sandbag!

Pitch 3—5.10a

Wild climbing continues up another dike past a roof to a belay on a small ledge. This pitch is short and not as runout as previously reported.

Pitch 4—5.11d

This is another short pitch, and may be linked with the previous pitch if rope drag allows. Climb out right and up shallow corners. Trend left over a roof, and onto a slab. A tough mantel and slab (crux) brings you to easier terrain and the belay.

Pitch 5—5.11c

A contender for most amazing 5.11 at Index! Stepping off the ledge leads you into a journey on sticky rock through endless pockets. Mostly sustained with few rests. The moves, the position, the rock... all classic!

Pitch 6—5.10b

Climb overhanging, blocky terrain to an anchor below the top of the Upper Town Wall (5.10b). Loose in places; one of the bolts is in a hanging block stack that vibrates. You can eschew that bolt for gear if you prefer.

From here, you can climb another 20 feet to the top and traverse over to DH/LA to rap; or you can simply rappel the route.

46 GREEN DRAG-ON 5.13A (OR, 5.11 C3) ★★★

This is a popular UTW aid climb that was finally fre in 2008 by Justen Sjong and Ben Gilkison. That said the original belay stances are inconvenient for free climbing purposes. If you plan to free the route, be prepared to make your own belays. If you plan to ai it, please be cognizant of free climbing parties (let them climb through), and don't use a hammer.

Gear: Standard Index Rack or Standard Index Aid Ra

FA: Don Harder, Don Heller; FFA: Justen Sjong, Ben Gilkison.

Pitch 1—5.11a or C2

Free: Climb the funky flared crack past some tricky gear, and tough laybacking to a tenuous finish. This a very cool pitch.

Aid: Aid the crack. Some free climbing may be nece sary.

Pitch 2—5.12a or C2/3

Free: Climb past three bolts (low crux), three pins, a up the flare, protecting the upper crux with RPs.

Aid: Aid up the right-facing corner/flare.

NOTE: If free climbing, it may be better to continue past the 2-bolt anchor and build a belay in a better stance with small cams and nuts.

Pitch 3—5.11a or C2

Free: Climb past hollow flakes and large blocks to a face climbing finish protected by a thin crack. Belay a 2-bolt anchor beneath a roof.

Aid: Aid the pitch.

NOTE: If you built the higher belay on P2 you can s the hanging belay at the end of this pitch. Pull the roof, and keep climbing the 5.10 corner to a stance a bolt below the crux of P4. Belay there.

Pitch 4—5.12c or C1/2

Free: If you didn't climb the 5.10 corner on the last pitch, climb it. Keep an eye out for bolts traversing out left. Follow those bolts past a hard face move continuing left, and follow bolts to the top.

Aid: Do not move left. Climb up the corner to a bolt ladder which brings you to a small belay ledge.

Pitch 5—5.13a or C1

Free: Sustained face climbing immediately off the anchor past the last three bolts of the original route aid ladder provides the crux of the route. This is followed by a 5.10 corner.

Aid: Continue up the end of the bolt ladder, and aid the corner.

Pitch 6—5.6

Climb a dirty nasty gully grovel pitch to the top... or don't, and just rap the route from here.

Jesse Heineman on the impeccable stone of Rise and Fall (5.12b) | Photo by Ben Gilkison

See full size topo on p. 159.

47 TOWN CRIER 5.12D (OR 5.10 C2/3) ★★★★

This is one of Index's most classic Upper Wall routes, either free or aid. As one of the longest lines at Index, it achieves great position and exposure. This is also probably the most popular route to aid on the Upper Town Wall. If you are planning to jump on this as a free route, have beta for some neighboring lines as well, just in case of slow aid climbers.

Gear: Standard Index aid or free rack, pick your poison. No hammers!

FA: Fred Beckey, Dave Beckstead; FFA: Justen Sjong.

Pitch 1–5.9 or 5.11a

Climb the first pitch of *Davis Holland* or *Green Drag-on* to Madsen's Ledge. If you climb *DH*, belay at the bolted anchor far right (not at the base of *DH* P2).

Pitch 2–5.10 or C2

Free: From the bolted belay on Madsen's Ledge, head up and right climbing broken flakes into an obvious chimney. Squeeze on through and top out on a small slab. To the right are a set of chains (stop here if free climbing).

Aid: Continue up broken cracks on the left then make a hard traverse right across a small ledge to a cozy belay below a seam to a roof.

Pitch 3–5.11c or C2+

Free: From the chain anchor where you stopped on P2, climb the broken cracks out left and continue straight up the hollow flake. Thin, steep climbing and a cool position bring you to the imposingly steep Triple Overhangs pitch.

Aid: Continue up the seam with tricky gear and head out left under the roof. There is an anchor soon after pulling around the lip, but it is possible and may be desirable to link into the next pitch.

Pitch 4–5.12b/c or C2+

Free: Turn on the power and follow the aid line out the wild roofs (boulder problem), then keep it together as you exit the corner out left for some fa climbing, and then back right to the belay. Phew!

Aid: Blast on up through the infamous Triple Over-hangs (Beckey called it, following the FA, "one of th most difficult problems I have seen"), following the obvious seam system. Fixed pins will get you throug most of the way. Wildly steep with great exposure. Make sure and take in the view!

Pitch 5–5.11b or C2+

Free: Continue up the pin-scarred seam into a smal flare. The first 10 feet are cruxy, and tricky to prote Thin pieces that excel at protecting pin scars are w you want. Finish through the flare and up at the bel

Aid: Aid up, then free 5.8 to the base of the upper flare.

Pitch 6–5.12d or C2+

Free: Another flare leads to fixed pins through an overhang. This deposits you on a steep, almost fea-tureless slab with a bolt ladder for upward progress Free climbing this pitch will require a solid grasp of Index friction trickery. Not all bolts can be clipped while freeing through the faint seam on upward. Co tinue past the visible anchor and onto the second.

Aid: Head up the flare, then the bolt ladder, then a little tough-to-protect 5.8 to a 2-bolt anchor.

Pitch 7–5.6

Rappel the route from where you are or continue up *Green Drag-on* for a dirty romp to the top of the wa At that point it would probably be easiest to descen *Davis Holland.*

ns Holsten high on Green Drag-on (5.13a, p.160) | Photo by Ben Gilkison

Matty Van Biene perhaps wishing he better lived up to the name of Good Girls Like Bad Boys (5.12a).

TOP 10 MULTIPITCH

- ❒ Davis Holland - Lovin' Arms 5.10c (p.158)
- ❒ Godzilla - City Park - Slow Children - Tommy's Sandbox 5.10d (p.88)
- ❒ Free at Last 5.10d (p.94)
- ❒ Technicians of the Sacred 5.12b (p.168)
- ❒ Good Girls Like Bad Boys 5.12a (p.172)
- ❒ Wildest Dreams 5.12b (or 5.11 C1) (p. 152)
- ❒ Japanese Gardens 5.11c (p.84)
- ❒ Zoom - KFB - Over Orcsposed 5.12a (p.112)
- ❒ A National Acrobat 5.12 (p.206)
- ❒ An Act of Strange Boar 5.10c (p.230)

48 12 ANGRY BEES 5.11C ★★★

This is a fine line that may serve as an alternative to *Swim's* P2. From the anchors of *Swim* P1 (or you can traverse to this point from P1 of *Green Drag-on* or *Davis Holland*), climb up the beautiful, bolted, golden face left of the large, left-facing corner. The crux is short-lived, and easily aided.

Gear: *12 quickdraws.*

FA: Larry Kemp, Greg Olsen, Darryl Cramer.

49 SWIM 5.12C (OR 5.12A C0) ★★★

This is an excellent route, and one of the first ones on the UTW to dry. It was finally freed in 2011 by Mikey Schaefer. In standard Index fashion, the first pitch is said to go at 5.11+/solid 5.12. The latter is likely closer to the truth. You can avoid the first pitch and climb *Green Drag-on's* P1 instead for a mostly 5.11 outing.

Note: Topo for this route is on page 157.

Gear: *Gear to 3", 14 quickdraws. Only the 3rd and 7th pitches require cams.*

FA: Darryl Cramer, Larry Kemp, Doug Teague, Greg Olsen. FFA: Mikey Schaefer, via P4 variation.

Pitch 1–5.12a

Difficult edging past two small roofs leads to a corner. Climb the cruxy corner to the ledge and a 2-bolt anchor. Significantly harder than the rest of the route (minus the 5.12c free variation).

There's also a direct start to the left which goes at roughly the same grade.

Pitch 2–5.11+

Enjoyable face climbing through two cruxes leads to another belay stance. Hard, but not as challenging as the first pitch.

Pitch 3–5.9+

Much easier crack climbing in a right-facing dihedral brings you to Big Honker Ledge. If 5.9+ fists give you fits, you may want to bring a #4 for the last few feet of this pitch. A very short pitch.

Pitch 4–5.12c

Free: Begin climbing to the right of the bolt ladder, and cross the ladder at the second or third bolt. A low crux brings you to a poor stance. From there, summon up some wizardry and ascend out of a left-arching corner to easier terrain above.

Aid: A short bolt ladder leads to easier and interesting face climbing to a 2-bolt anchor. 5.10 A0.

Pitch 5–5.11b/c

Continuous thin edging and face climbing past bolts leads to a belay.

Pitch 6–5.11c

More of the same style as P5–bolt protected thin face.

Pitch 7–5.9+

A short scruffy pitch to the top with bolts and gear. Most choose to avoid this pitch and rap the route from here.

50 NON-LOCAL BARK HOUSE 5.11D ★★★

Right of the start of *Swim* is a bit of a 3rd class ledge. On the left side of that ledge is an obvious crack/overlap feature that diagonals up and left. Climb this crack. This is a very good pitch, and a decent alternative to *Swim* P1. The jams can be rather sharp.

Gear: *Standard Index Rack–emphasis on thin gear.*

FA: Terry Lien, Jon Nelson, Greg Olsen.

51 STEEL POLE BATHTUB 5.11A A3+ ★★

This route begins just right of *Non-Local Bark House* on the third class ledge. The first pitch is a decent alternative to the start of *Waterway Left*.

Gear: *Standard Index Rack. Emphasis on thin gear.*

FA: Jon Nelson, Terry Lien, Greg Olsen.

Pitch 1–5.11a

Climb up from the right side of the ledge to a difficult bolt-protected move at the roof. Continue up a flaring and diagonaling crack to the ledge.

Pitch 2–A3+

This pitch is purportedly very, very good. Whether that is only as an aid pitch, or whether that means excellent free climbing potential is not disclosed.

Climb the right side of a flake, then up and left to a big ledge (and the anchor of *Swim* P2).

Pitch 3–5.9

Climb *Swim's* 5.9 P3–a right-facing dihedral crack. Gear to 3 inches, or 4 if you are carrying a #4.

Pitch 4–A2

Aid up and right out an arch to a bolted anchor. *Swim* goes straight up.

Greg Olsen questing up the incredible edges of 12 Angry Bees (5.11c) | Photo by Larry Kemp

MADSEN'S LEDGE

This is the area between the *Waterway* route (which is a huge obvious waterfall until about August), and the East terminus of the UTW. Some of the finest multi-pitch routes here. Named for the famous Washington climber, Jim Madsen

Approach: From the Davis Holland Area, traverse climber's right to the base of the waterfall. There are many options from here to access Madsen's Ledge, including a via ferrata on the far right side of the wall.

Descent: Bring a single 70 or two 60s for the routes here.

52 WATERWAY 5.11D (OR 5.8 A3) ★★★

Surprisingly clean given its location, the first two pitches will most likely need a light scrubbing after the waterfall has dried up for the season. Do not nail this route if you are aid climbing.

Gear Aid: Offset nuts (brass and aluminum), offset cams, cams (TCU-#3) hooks, ballnuts. No hammer.

Gear Free: Standard Index Rack. Emphasis on thin cams and nuts.

FA: Les Davenport, Jim Stoddard–1968; FFA: Mikey Schaefer, the late, great, Sean Leary.

Pitch 1–5.11+ or A3

Free: Climb difficult terrain left of the left-facing corner (and left of the bolted first pitch of *Technicians*). Improbable moves and a crux near the top make this pitch a bit of a heartbreaker.

Aid: Thin cracks bring you to a left-facing corner. Climb the corner to Madsen's Ledge. There are many variations possible. A3 or C2+ with ball nuts.

Pitch 2–5.11b or A3

Free: Face climbing on good holds leads to a bolt, and a move down and left to a mantel. Lieback up a small roof, and pass it on it's left side via good side pulls. Pull the crux, then continue up to the anchor.

Aid: Aid up the right-facing corner to a crack in the face and a good stance. From here, a short 5.5 section brings you to the anchor.

Pitch 3–5.10 or A1

Free: Climb a right-facing corner almost to the bolt, but traverse left before it. Climb the nice, left-facing corner to a 2-bolt anchor.

Aid: Aid up to the bolt, tension traverse left to the left-facing corner, aid it to the anchor.

* An aid climbing variation (*Waterway Right*) traverses right from the P2 anchor to a left-facing dihedral, and climbs that feature to the top (A2).

Pitch 4–5.10+ or 5.8 A3

Free: Traverse right into *The Golden Arch*. Then climb up and left (5.10+) to the top.

Aid: Traverse right into *The Golden Arch*. Short pitch. 5.8. If aiding, there is a final pitch climbing *The Golden Arch* to the top (5.5).

53 TECHNICIANS OF THE SACRED 5.12B/C ★★★★

One of Andy de Klerk's finest contributions to Index–this route is absolutely stellar. The final pitch has some gear on it, but it is 5.8, short, and rarely climbed. Otherwise, the whole thing goes on bolts. *Technicians* climbs left of the impressive *Golden Arch*, then improbably crosses it at a high and very exposed arête. Not to be missed.

There are a number of easier ways to reach Madsen's Ledge (*The Ave* P1 or the via ferrata) which, if done instead of the first pitch, makes this route a fantastic 5.12a.

Gear: Quickdraws.

FA: Andy de Klerk.

Pitch 1–5.12b/c

This pitch climbs the attractive black and white corner to the right of *Waterway*. It is the first bolted pitch encountered on the right side of the wall. A crux down low leads to continuous steep climbing through bulges and corners to Madsen's Ledge, and a 2-bolt anchor.

Pitch 2–5.11a

Two variations exist. The original second pitch climbs out left of the anchor through some 5.10, then back up and right along a bolted ramp (5.11a, 10 bolts). A variation (*Fetch* 5.11a, Collum-Kerns) heads right from the ledge to a bolted line below a leftward arching corner, then climbs that to a 2-bolt anchor below the ramp (6 bolts to the ramp). Don't stop here (unless your rope drag is horrible); continue up the rightward diagonaling ramp to the next anchor.

Pitch 3–5.12a

This is a fine pitch with a distinct crux. The bolts are somewhat spacey, and the climbing brings you to the top of *The Golden Arch*.

Pitch 4–5.11b or 5.12b/c

This pitch is wild, steep, and exposed! Climb up the somewhat dirty and chossy corner until it is possible to traverse right to the super steep arête on improbable and possibly friable face holds. Continue up easier terrain to a 2-bolt anchor (5.11b, 9 bolts).

The low variation is better, harder, and even more impressive. Make a very challenging low traverse, and then power your way up the crazy arête. Continue up easier terrain to a 2-bolt anchor (5.12b/c, 9 bolts).

Pitch 5–5.11b

Another incredible four star pitch! Climb the V-slot to a wild exit move out right at its top with a ton of air beneath you. Though rated 5.11b, this pitch feels somewhat like the slot on *Natural Log Cabin* (5.11d), but twice as long. Bring your tech. Best to rap at the end of this pitch.

Pitch 6–5.8

Chossy cracks and blocky ledgy climbing brings you to the top.

g Teague trying not to sink on Swim (5.12, p.166) | Photo by Larry Kemp.

54 ABRAXAS 5.11D A3/4 ★★

Cramer called this a "difficult and rarely done aid route." If that was true then, it's certainly true now. Can it be freed? Time alone will tell.

Gear: Standard Index aid rack.

FA: Bob Crawford, Pat Timson.

Pitch 1–A2/3

Begin just right of *Technician's* bolted first pitch beneath a left-facing corner. Climb the thin crack just right of the large block until below the first roof. Continue up the right-handcrack, then traverse left before the second roof. Low-angle cracks lead to a belay with five bolts: one good, two probably good, one probably bad, and one definitely bad–none with chains or rap rings.

Pitch 2–A3

Climb the short, low-angle, thin crack with many fixed copperheads to Madsen's Ledge.

Pitch 3–5.10a A1

Move the belay right to the base of a pillar right of *Golden Arch*. Climb the pillar, and move right to a bolt anchor.

Pitch 4–A3+

Aid up and left to another anchor past many hooks.

Pitch 5–A3/4

Traverse up and right to where *Good Girls, the Ave*, and *Sisu* meet. Choose your own adventure from there.

55 CHICKEN McNUGGETS 5.10 A4 ★

Two pitches of aid that climb off of Madsen's Ledge between *Technicians* and *The Golden Arch*. Not popular, rarely climbed. The first pitch climbs up to the 2-bolt anchor at the top of *Technician's* bolted ramp. Pitch two ascends up and left of *Technicians* P3, and shares the same anchor.

Gear: Standard Index aid rack.

FA: Randy Stout, Pete Doorish.

56 THE GOLDEN ARCH 5.7 A3- ★★★

This was once considered the best aid route at the UTW. Now it is rarely climbed. Only the first pitch has been freed. This climbs up to and out the obvious huge golden arch. Potential for an epic free climb.

Gear: Standard Index aid rack.

FA: Ron Burgner, Jim Madsen; FFA P1: Kjell Swedin, Erik Winkelman.

Pitch 1–5.11b

Climb directly up beneath the bottom of the arch on manky bolts that need replacing. Plenty of better P1 options to access Madsen's Ledge exist.

Pitch 2–C1

Climb up the arch to a bolted belay. This pitch has almost been freed.

Pitch 3–A3+

Continue out the arch hooking on flakes. Belay at the top of the arch.

Pitch 4–A1

50 feet of easy aid brings you to a wet 5.5 chimney, and the top.

57 KLEWIN'S ROUTE A4★★

On the fifth pitch of *Abraxas*, do not move right on *The Ave*. Instead, traverse left under the huge roof until it is possible to surmount it. Traverse left agai under another roof until it, too, can be breached. Continue left to a left-facing corner, and follow thi the top. Beta on this route is sketchy at best, and it anyone's guess whether this thing has been repeat

Gear: Standard Index aid rack.

FA: Doug Klewin.

58 STARFISH ENTERPRISE 5.11D ★★★★

What began as a retro-bolting effort on *Good Girls Like Bad Boys* turned into a new route that shares t exceptional 3rd pitch.

These new pitches are fantastic and provides a gre albiet slightly easier, compliment to GGLBB.

Gear: 16-18 quickdraws, small rack of thin gear to 0.7

FA: Tom Ramier.

Pitch 1–5.11d

Climb a face and arête past three bolts to a steep corner with a crack at the far left side of Madsen's Ledge. Stem and jam up the corner using cams for pro. Tricky arête and stemming above leads to a semi-hanging belay.

Pitch 2–5.11a

Head left from the belay and join the second pitch GGLBB above the crux of that pitch. 5.11a (P1 and P2 can be linked with minimal rope drag).

Pitch 3–5.11+

Climb the amazing 3rd pitch of GGLBB to the belay a corner.

Pitch 4–5.11c

Leave the corner and head left onto the exposed fa to start this long and varied pitch. Pull through the crux passing a bizarre and questionable brass starfi and cross P4 of GGLBB, for a direct finish on enjoyable knobs. Excellent.

Pitch 5–5.10

After a tenuous move above the belay (crux) climb t broken face passing bolts where needed. A few smal cams can be used to supplement the easier climbing between the bolts.

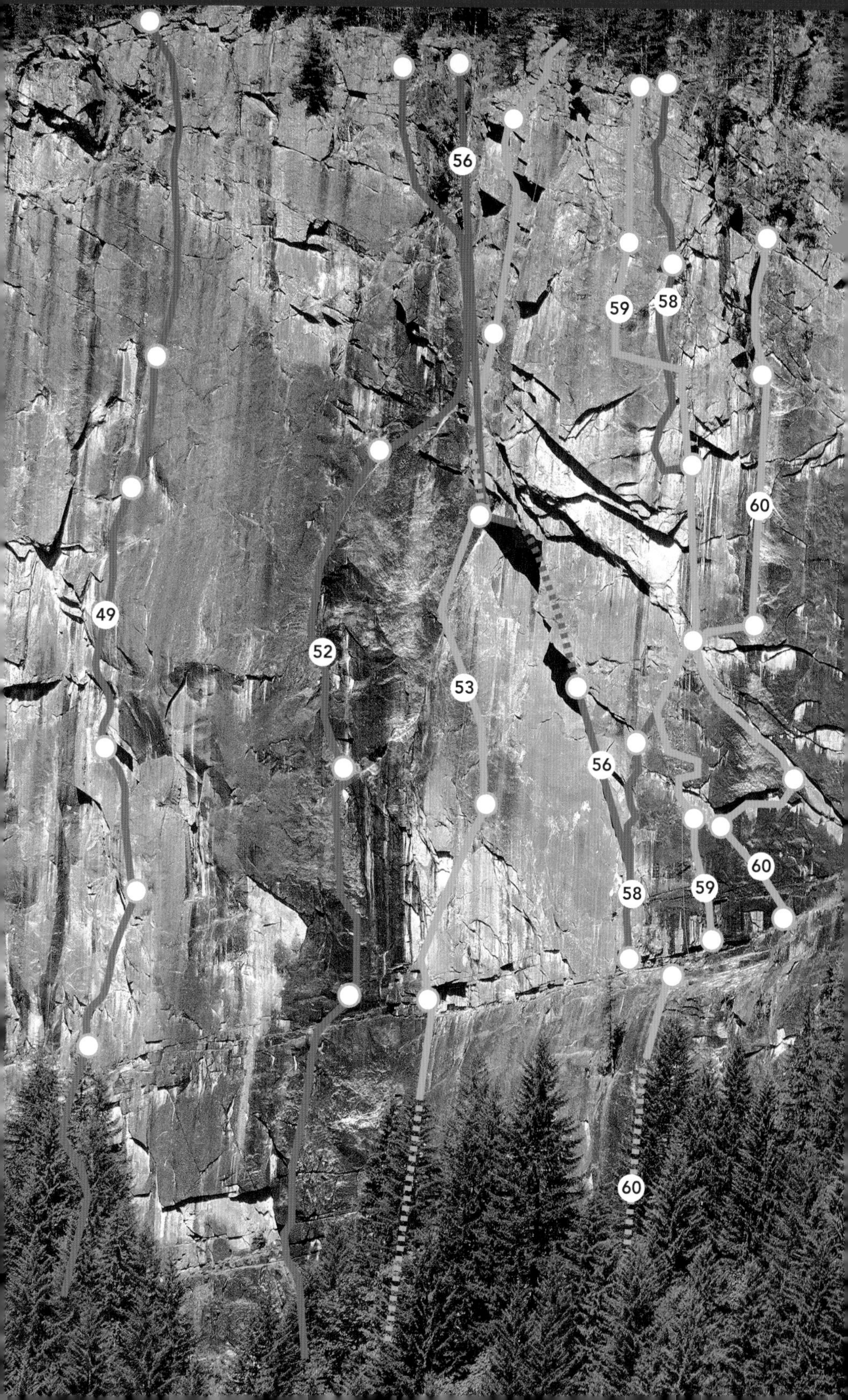
56
59
58
60
49
52
53
56
60
58
59
60

59 GOOD GIRLS LIKE BAD BOYS 5.12A ★★★★

Absolutely stellar. Combined with *Sisu* P1, this is one of the best routes on the UTW. The only thing that can mar this route is a bizarre fifth pitch, and a questionable piece of "tasteful aid" found there.

The route starts directly above *Sisu* P1 on Madsen's Ledge. The best way to reach it is by climbing *Sisu's* four star first pitch; but you can also access the ledge from the via ferrata.

Finishing on the final two pitches of *Starfish Enterprise* is highly recommended. Rap the route.

Gear: 16-18 quickdraws.

FA: Karl Kaiyala, Darryl Cramer.

Pitch 1–5.11c
From Madsen's Ledge start up either the right side of a flake or a thin crack. Pass a low roof, and a couple more bolts, to a 2-bolt anchor.

Pitch 2–5.12a
An incredible pitch. Climb up to the roof, and pass it (cruxy). Then make a traverse out left (crux) and keep it together through more moderate, but still challenging, climbing to the anchor. The rock on this pitch is unique and excellent.

Pitch 3–5.11+
The changing corners pitch—possibly the best pitch of the route. Climb up the left-facing corner until you can step right into the right-facing corner. Fire up the strenuous climbing to a corner belay. From here one can choose to finish on *Starfish Enterprise* or continue on GGLBB proper.

Pitch 4–5.11+
This is the funky pitch. Climb straight up on moves that feel somewhere between improbable and impossible. Follow the shallow corner until knobs provide a hard traverse left. Follow the traverse, crossing *Starfish Enterprise*. Keep questing left until your reach a 2-bolt anchor.

Pitch 5–5.11c
Excellent knob climbing leads up an ever-steepening wave-shaped headwall, and continually hard face climbing above. A stupendous pitch.

Pitch 6–5.10b
Easier climbing leads to the top. Best to combine with P5.

60 SISU 5.11B/C ★★★

Sisu is a fun and varied route, and was eye-opening for the area when Karl Kaiyala & Co. established it in 1989. The name is a Finnish word for "a stubborn refusal to capitulate" which Kaiyala said "is basically the Finnish national motto."

It may be a bit challenging for the grade, but what isn't at Index? At 5.11b/c, it's probably the easiest ri side free route.

The first pitch offers absolutely spectacular four st knob climbing. It climbs the first excellent looking bolt line right of *Technicians'* P1. After Madsen's Ledge, make a 4th-class exposed traverse right. Fro there, the route weaves its way up the right side of the buttress.

The first pitch is a bit longer, and may require a 70 rap. Otherwise, descend the whole route with a 60. (It's easy to downclimb the via ferrata from Madsen Ledge if your rope is too short for the 1st pitch).

Gear: 16 quickdraws.

FA: Karl Kaiyala, Karl Heiss, Marianna Hviding, Sand Nagy.

Pitch 1–5.11b/c
Climb past a low roof through super-cool knobs to Madsen's Ledge.

Pitch 2–5.10d
Make an exposed but easy traverse out right to a slight ledge. Climb out left to a 2-bolt anchor benea the left side of the roof.

Pitch 3–5.10d
Traverse right under the roof past a reachy move to the anchor.

Pitch 4–5.11a
Face climb up and left to the top of the prominent arch of *The Ave*, and a 2-bolt belay.

Pitch 5–5.11c
Move up and then make a difficult and cerebral traverse right to a step-down to the anchor. This is the crux of the route.

Pitch 6–5.11a
Climb straight up the airy and exposed face to a 2-bolt anchor beside the final corner. This pitch ma be dirty and/or wet early season.

Pitch 7–5.8
Easy dirty munge climbing takes you to the top. Mo opt to rap instead of climbing this final pitch.

61 GERITOL 5.12B ★

Climb the bolted line right of *Sisu* P1. The upper par climbs very close to *The Ave*, and is slightly contrive Belay just beneath Madsen's Ledge. Rarely climbed. May need rebolting. The crux is dirty 5.12b.

Gear: 13 quickdraws.

FA: Dave Tower, Steve Risse.

›VER FORTY 5.11C ★

veen *Geritol* and *The Ave* P1. Climb past 11 bolts ıtly left, then right towards *The Ave*, then parallel *Ave* before continuing hard left past the last five s of *Geritol*. Not recommended.

r: 14 quickdraws.

Steve Risse, Dave Tower, Keith Hartel.

'HE AVE (AND VIA FERRATA) 5.11D A2 ★★

first pitch is a reasonable way to access Mad-s Ledge if you don't want to climb *Sisu*, or the via ata. Beyond that, this climb is rarely done. Two of pitches are shared with the excellent free climb, *d Girls Like Bad Boys*. Do not use a hammer on se pitches.

ind this route, and the via ferrata, hike almost to *man's Walkabout* at the Upper Cheeks. Just before buttress, switchback left up a scruffy trail to the e of the left-trending corner/ramp. *The Ave* goes ight up, the via ferrata ascends fixed lines and les on the wall up and right.

r: Standard Index aid rack.

Mark Weigelt, Jim Langdon.

Pitch 1–5.8
Climb the left leaning ramp/chimney to Madsen's Ledge. Then move the belay right to the bottom of a prominent arch.

Pitch 2–A1/2
A mostly clean aid pitch. Aid up the left-trending arch to a belay that is shared with *Sisu*.

Pitch 3–5.11d
This is the excellent changing-corners pitch of *Good Girls*. Belay above the roofs.

Pitch 4–5.11d A2
Continue straight up three more bolts (5.11d) then get out the aiders for A2 climbing straight up to the top. Can be done in one long pitch, or in two.

64 ELECTROMATIC MARK IV 5.12A ★★★

As of 2017, this was an almost unrecognizable route due to forest reclamation. Michal Rynkiewicz intends to retrobolt and clean this line during the summer of 2017, and promises it will be a three star route. Up and right of *The Ave*, fight your way through thick vegetation to reach the base. Climb up the dirty face, left of the gully and the via ferrata, past bolts and a right-facing corner.

Gear: A few handsize pieces, and 8 quickdraws.

FA: Max Dufford, Greg Olsen.

This species is the most recent of human relatives to go extinct; it coexisted with humans for the duration of its known time range. Evidence to date indicates it is the smallest species in our genus, *Homo*, with a brain a third the size of ours. Its small size earned it the nickname "hobbit" and may have been due to the scarcity of resources on its island habitat.
Homo heidelbergensis
700,000 to 200,000 YEARS AGO
Europe; possibly China; eastern and southern Africa
The first early humans to venture into the cold latitudes of Europe, *Homo heidelbergensis* were also the first to build shelters and hunt big game animals with wooden spears. European populations of this species were the direct ancestors of the Neanderthals, while African populations likely gave rise to our species.

GREG CHILD

THE STORY BEHIND RISE AND FALL

Rise and Fall came at the zenith of my wire brushing days, and it was almost my demise. I installed ropes from top to bottom, and spent long days scrubbing to find the holds, and the route. One day while I was a hundred feet below the rim I heard shooting of all kinds from above. Local gun heads on maneuver, I assumed, so I kept scrubbing. Hearing voices, I looked to a point of rock jutting overhead to see three men in camo. “There he is.” One of them aimed a weapon at me, eyeing me through his scope. I would have made a fun target, but they were friendlies and they waved me on to keep scrubbing while they went back to spatter the forest with lead.

The day the route was ready to go, I was pulling all my ropes down, and drilling the last few bolts. On the final rappel I was covered in gear, and so much moss clung to my sweaty skin that I looked like I was wearing a Ghillie suit. I got distracted by sweeping moss particles off the holds of that first pitch, and I failed to notice I had neglected to equalize my ropes. Forty feet above the ground an end of rope whipped through my rappel device, and I dropped toward a spike of rock poking out of the ground.

That arse-reaming point passed swiftly between my legs. I hit the deck, bounced downhill, and came to rest in a mess of brush. Taking stock of the situation, and fancying myself relatively unscathed, I stood up. It was then that I felt the searing pain in my ankle, and I fell over. Then, I noticed blood trickling into my eyes.

Panic. I must have a hole in my head.

I started to pass out, then remembered the first rule of freaking out, which is, Stay Calm. No one else was at the cliff, so I crawled down the trail, and drove home using a stick to operate the clutch in my Subaru. At the hospital I told the staff I fell off a trail while hiking. The nurse was a climber who recognized me from the Vertical Club (now known as Vertical World), and she muttered and laughed under her breath at this lie. A few months later, after having my talus bone surgically repaired, I returned to *Rise and Fall* with Andy de Klerk. We had one of the finest days on rock I can recall.

THE CHEEKS

The Cheeks are the large, cheeky-looking, white walls between the Upper Town Walls and The Diamond. Just like everywhere else at Index, you can expect to find mindblowingly good routes here. The Upper Cheeks (Wilman's Walkabout Area, The Black Sea, and The Beach) feature stunning vistas, severe exposure, and often Index's best temperatures and rain cover. The Lower Cheeks (Black Planet, Clay Area, Lower Zipper, and Wizard Area), meanwhile, are nearly as good as The Upper Cheeks, also tend to stay dry in a light rain, and are better to visit if you are traveling with dogs or children. Either way, up or down, The Cheeks are as good as climbing gets.

Approach: Follow the Upper Wall trail almost all the way to the base of the Upper Wall. Continue right on the trail along the base, then back into the woods. Shortly after, you will see a slight trail branch–follow the uphill trending branch for The Upper Cheeks, and the downhill trending branch for the The Lower Cheeks. In just a minute or two, you are deposited at the first routes of either zone.

Brad Lignoski channeling his madness on A Wisdom That Is Woe (5.13-).

WILMAN'S WALK-ABOUT AREA

Wilman's Walkabout Area is the first wall you come to at The Upper Cheeks, and ends at the boulder at the start of the Perverse Traverse. It is not as popular as The Black Sea or The Beach, but has some excellent routes and a great free climbing project.

Approach: Hike up to The Upper Cheeks, and this is the first wall you reach.

Descent: Most routes can be done with a single 60.

1 JESTERS OF CHAOS 5.11D ★★

This route has largely been forgotten, but the first pitch is actually quite good. Around the corner left of *The Incision*, this is the furthest left route on The Upper Cheeks.

Climb up a strenuous crack past laybacks and jams to a belay (anchor may need replacing, 5.10d). The second pitch continues up a crack, traverses under a roof, and then climbs flakes to the anchor (5.11d). The traverse under the roof may or may not have a pin, and may or may not be C0.

Gear: Standard Index Rack.

FA: Max Dufford, Jeff Baird.

2 THE INCISION 5.9 A2 ★★★

About 15 yards left of *Wilman's Walkabout*, you'll see this incredible looking thin crack—or perhaps it is an incredibly thin-looking crack. Cramer called it "a lower-angle, thinner version of *City Park*," which sounds about right. This thing is just begging for a free ascent—and probably a new anchor.

Gear: Standard Index Aid Rack.

3 SEDAN DELIVERY 5.11D ★★★★

This is such a good pitch, it's amazing how infrequently it gets climbed. Climb *Wilman's Walkabout* past a low crux, then traverse left to the obvious splitter finger crack on the face. Expect challenging jams, difficult laybacks, and a burly, bouldery finish.

The variation, *Direct Delivery*, is three stars, and features a mindboggling slab dyno if you are short. It apparently also goes at 5.11d...which may be a sandbag

Gear: Doubles or triples to 1", with a good variety of different sizes. RPs. 5 quickdraws and a handful of slings.

FA: Terry Lien, Darryl Cramer. Direct Delivery: Darryl Cramer, Greg Olsen, Max Dufford, Jeff Baird.

The Perverse Traverse

Chris Tirrell straining to see on Echolocation (5.11d, p.181).

❹ WILMAN'S WALKABOUT 5.11C A3 ★★★

Wilman's Walkabout is an excellent 3-pitch route that has yet to see a full free ascent. The first pitch is the only one commonly done, in spite of continuous quality climbing. P1, taken on its own, is verging on four stars.

Gear: Doubles to 1", and a couple hand size pieces. Small nuts.

FA: Terry Lien, Darryl Cramer, Max Dufford, Nicola Masciandaro.

Pitch 1–5.11c
Climb past three bolts in the corner to thought-provoking moves up and left through cracks on the face. Some thin gear and wild moves get you to a no-hands rest. From here, head back into the corner, and follows more awesome climbing to the anchor.

Pitch 2–5.10c
Climb a procession of awkward corners to a spacious ledge. This is a two star pitch.

It is also possible to step right off the anchor and attempt the Quadruple Cracks (P2 of *Lions Tigers and Bears*). This should make for a stellar (minimum three stars) free pitch in the solid 5.12 range or harder.

Pitch 3–A3
Aid the cracks to the top. This is also a two star pitch. It might be three stars if it goes free. It can probably be freed in the 5.12+ range.

❺ LIONS, TIGERS, & BEARS 5.8 A2 ★★

This route has a LOT of potential. The first pitch could go free with a hard boulder problem in the V8+ range. The second pitch–the Quadruple Cracks–could go free at hard 5.12 or low 5.13, and is very striking. This route starts up *Wilman's Walkabout* and cuts right through a seam and a roof.

Gear: Standard Index aid rack.

FA: Darryl Cramer, David Gunstone.

Pitch 1–5.8 A1
After the first few meters of *Wilman's Walkabout*, cut right through some cool terrain to a roof, and a dirty slot. Climb the slot to the ledge and an old anchor that needs replacing. Probably can go on clean aid. Probably can also go free.

Pitch 2–A2
Aid up the attractive looking Quad Cracks. Can also likely go clean, and free.

TOP 10 CRACK CLIMBS

❒ Slow Children 5.10d (p.88)
❒ Bobcat Cringe 5.12b (p.227)
❒ Japanese Gardens (P1-3) 5.11c (p.84)
❒ Stern Farmer 5.12 (p.83)
❒ Master of Reality 5.11 (p.206)
❒ Iron Horse 5.11d (p.78)
❒ I Am In Top A Shader 5.11c (p.233)
❒ Thin Fingers 5.11a (p.92)
❒ Sedan Delivery 5.11d (p.178)
❒ Earwax 5.11c (p.146)

Adam Butterfield recieves the goods post-haste via Sedan Delivery (5.11c).

THE BLACK SEA

The Black Sea is stacked to the brim with excellent climbs, all of which have Tom Ramier's name on them. The namesake of the wall is exceptionally good, and is the access point for all the other routes here.

Approach: Just past Wilman's Walkabout, a large boulder forms a cave with the main wall. The Black Sea starts atop that boulder, via a short 4th class climb.

Descent: A 70 is requisite to climb on this wall. Many of the routes also require maintaining a healthy swing while descending.

6 DEAD MAN'S REACH 5.11+ ★★★

From the anchor on *The Black Sea* P1, climb a corner up and left to a large ledge at the base of a left-facing corner (5.10). Either belay here, or continue up the steep corner past a tricky crux (Dead Man's Reach), and make your way to the anchor.

Gear: Same rack as The Black Sea.

FA: Tom Ramier, Brad Lignoski.

7 A TURTLE TOO FAR 5.12A ★★★

A good route, with an absurd piece of aid: a brass turtle bolted to the wall. Jury's still out on what to think of that one...

From the anchors of *The Black Sea*'s first pitch, climb a short pitch up and left to a 2-bolt anchor on a grassy ledge. From here, climb the steep arête past bolts and a turtle and then keep your try-hard face o[n un]til the end.

Gear: 14-16 quickdraws, 70 meter rope.

FA: Tom Ramier.

8 THE BLACK SEA 5.11D ★★★★

The Black Sea begins atop the large boulder at the beginning of the Perverse Traverse. Climb up the cav[e] side of the boulder, and belay from a 2-bolt anchor.

This two pitch route features stunning face climbing on knobs and wild features. Both pitches are high quality, and not to be missed. This is also the access route for other classics such as *Echolocation* and *God's Bones*.

NOTE: You can descend in two raps with a single 70, but make sure to continually kick off the wall maintaining a large swing on the lower rappel. Otherwise, it will be difficult to return to the Perverse Traverse and you may get stuck in space.

Gear: 14-16 quickdraws, single set of cams to #1. #2, # nice for P2. 70 meter rope is mandatory.

FA: Tom Ramier, Derek Pearson, Jon Nelson.

Pitch 1–5.11d

Pre-clip the initial bolt, then start from an undercling out right. Follow bolts, a few small cams and a fixed half-inch rod behind a flake to a decent rest. Climb u[p] and right for more bolts, multiple short cruxes, and a short layback up an arête past a few good cams. A fe[w] more bolts and a heartbreaker finish brings you to th[e] anchor.

itch 2–5.11b
ontinue up the corner, then step left past a bolt to ain another corner/arête. Climb past some huge 1obs, and head left past two more bolts through a eep bulge, then up a corner to the belay. A short, irty third pitch can be led to gain the summit, and a olted rap station about five meters right of the top it. Most will simply rap back down the route from ere.

corner crack called *Squid Ink* (Ramier, 5.11a) can be imbed directly left of P2 returning back right to the me anchors.

ECHOLOCATION 5.11D ★★★★
mazing endless knobs in the middle of The Black ea! This is a fantastic route, and may be the quintes- ential Index knob climb. From the top of P1 of *Black ea*, clip a bolt then step down and right around the orner. Follow amazing knobs up and right to a chain 1chor.

OTE: Like *Black Sea*, make sure to continually kick f the wall while rappeling, maintaining a large swing, you'll be unable to return to the Perverse Traverse.

ear: 12-14 quickdraws, 70 meter rope.

A: Tom Ramier.

ADMIRAL HERRINGTON, HIS JOLLY BOYS, AND THE CODE OF THE SEA 5.11A ★★★
eally a link up more than an independent line, it al- ws quick and easy access to the quality second pitch *God's Bones*. Climb the first half of *Echolocation*, en sail up and right to the top of *God's Bones*.

ear: 12-14 quickdraws, 70 meter rope.

A: Tom Ramier, Micah Faville.

GOD'S BONES 5.11D ★★★
his is an excellent line, and unique for Index. It fea- res strange overhanging compression moves, funk emming, and unusually steep laybacking. Overall, is is not the best route in The Black Sea–but it's etty darn good.

access, climb either the second pitch of *Black Sea* *Echolocation*, then rap down and right to a narrow dge in the middle of the wall called the Poop Deck.

apping from the Poop Deck requires maintaining a ll swing to back to the Perverse Traverse. Knot your pe ends to be safe.

ear: 12-14 quickdraws. 70 meter rope is mandatory.

A: Tom Ramier, Micah Faville.

itch 1–5.11b
imb the frighteningly thin flake straight up to cool 1obs, and a traverse out left. When the line of bolts verges into two, go straight up instead of farther ght.

itch 2–5.11d
his is the namesake pitch–the route from here looks e the spinal column of G-O-D him(her)self. Work our way up the steep overhang, and stave off the mp as long as you can!

THE BEACH

The Beach is accessed via the Perverse Traverse, and includes everything from the end of that traverse to the right end of The Upper Cheeks.

Approach: Hike the trail to The Upper Cheeks, rack up, clip in through the Perverse Traverse via ferrata, and you're there.

Descent: Some of the routes here require a 70, but most can be done with a 60.

12 NORMANDY 5.12B ★★★★
Another Tom Ramier classic. This one was originally called 5.12- but 5.12d may be more appropriate. For now, as this IS Index, let's just call it 5.12b. Whatever you call it, this thing is safe and unforgettable.

Climb the overhanging, leftward-trending sport route at the end of the Perverse Traverse on clean white stone through two roofs.

Gear: 12-14 quickdraws and an optional #2.

FA: Tom Ramier.

13 HEAVEN'S REAR ENTRY VEHICLE–PARKED OUT BACK, TOW AWAY ZONE (HREV-POB-TAZ) 5.10 ★★
HREV-POB-TAZ is as good as its name. This route climbs the steep chimney system about 20 feet right of *Normandy* and 20 feet left of *Between the Cheeks*. This is a 3-pitch route, and the easiest line to ascend the cheeks. Gear belays!

The more it gets climbed, the better it will be.

Gear: Cams to 4", emphasis on hand sizes.

FA HREV: Isao Fujita & Jon Nelson; FA POBTAZ: Nicola Masciandaro & Jon Nelson.

Pitch 1–5.10a
A short steep pitch climbing out the chimney. Pull the bulge with awkward hand jams.

Pitch 2–5.10
Continue up and through the chimney. When you exit above, follow the fist-to wide-hands crack (crux) to a ledge in a corner system.

P1 and P2 can be combined.

Pitch 3–5.10
Climb the corner to the top. Either rap back down the route (may need tat for anchors) or walk left and rap *God's Bones*.

14 BETWEEN THE CHEEKS 5.10C ★★★
This is the best warm-up for The Beach, and is a pretty good climb. Ascend the bolted line on the left side of a large, often wet, chimney right in the middle of the cheeks.

Note: Keep a swing going on the descent or you may end up in space.

Gear: 12-14 quickdraws.

FA: Matt Kerns, Mike Massey.

⑮ THE ZIPPER (P3-6) **5.11B ★★★★**

The first two pitches of *The Zipper* (located on The Lower Cheeks) are pretty good, but not as classic as these upper pitches. Starting from The Beach, this route features high quality crack and face climbing–not to be missed.

Gear: *A double set of cams up to #3 is plenty, along with a variety of quickdraws. A single #4 protects the crux after the first chains.*

FA: Dennis Fenstermaker, Brent Hoffman, Karl Kaiyala; FFA: Thomas Ramier, Derek Pearson, Jon Nelson, Bradley Lignoski.

Pitch 3–5.11b

A strenuous layback start leads to fun climbing on flakes and knobs. If you are gassed at the first chains, you can stop there. That said, you can avoid a hanging belay by continuing to a ledge and making a gear anchor up above the wide-hands crux at the start of P2. You will need to save some cams for the anchor if you choose this option. Alternately, you can link P1 and P2 for one kick-ass long pitch with a tough finish.

Pitch 4–5.11a/b

If you stopped at the chains, climb up past the cruxy start. Bring a #4. Follow great crack climbing through a dihedral to a tricky thin section at the finish. This pitch is full value, and amazing.

Pitch 5-6–5.10a

Though technically two pitches, these last two are both 5.10a, short, and better linked. That said, there IS a memorable cave belay at the top of P5, if you feel like breaking it up.

Continue up the same crack past stemming and a steep rib. Belay in the "luscious cove" or continue right up a bolted face to the summit.

⑯ ALBINESTONE **5.11D ★★★**

An appealing bolted line on fine, white rock. Start up shallow left-facing groove/arch and climb directly up to the chains. Shallow stemming and balancy moves characterize this quality route.

Gear: *8 quickdraws.*

FA: Jens Klubberud, Eric Gratz.

⑰ APES AND BALLERINAS **5.10B ★★★**

This route, also known as *Stock Options*, is better than it looks, and climbs the wide crack just right of the upper *Zipper*. P1 (*Apes*) climbs a steep blocky fist crack and overhanging corner. P2 (*Ballerinas*) heads up and right to a leftward-trending thin crack through a knobby face. Both pitches are good. If you manage your rope-drag right you can climb this in a single long pitch. Rap with a 70.

Gear: *Doubles to 4". Ditch the wide gear after P1.*

FA: Mark Bebie, Jim Ruch.

⑱ CRACK IN THE COSMIC EGG **5.12C ★★★**

Crack in the Cosmic Egg is the obvious short thin crack, just right of *Apes and Ballerinas*. It was sent to the anchor at the top of the crack by Tom Ramier, who later added bolts and extended the route. The extension is currently an open project.

Gear: *Thin gear.*

FA: Tom Ramier.

m Ramier deep into the battle for Normandy (5.12)

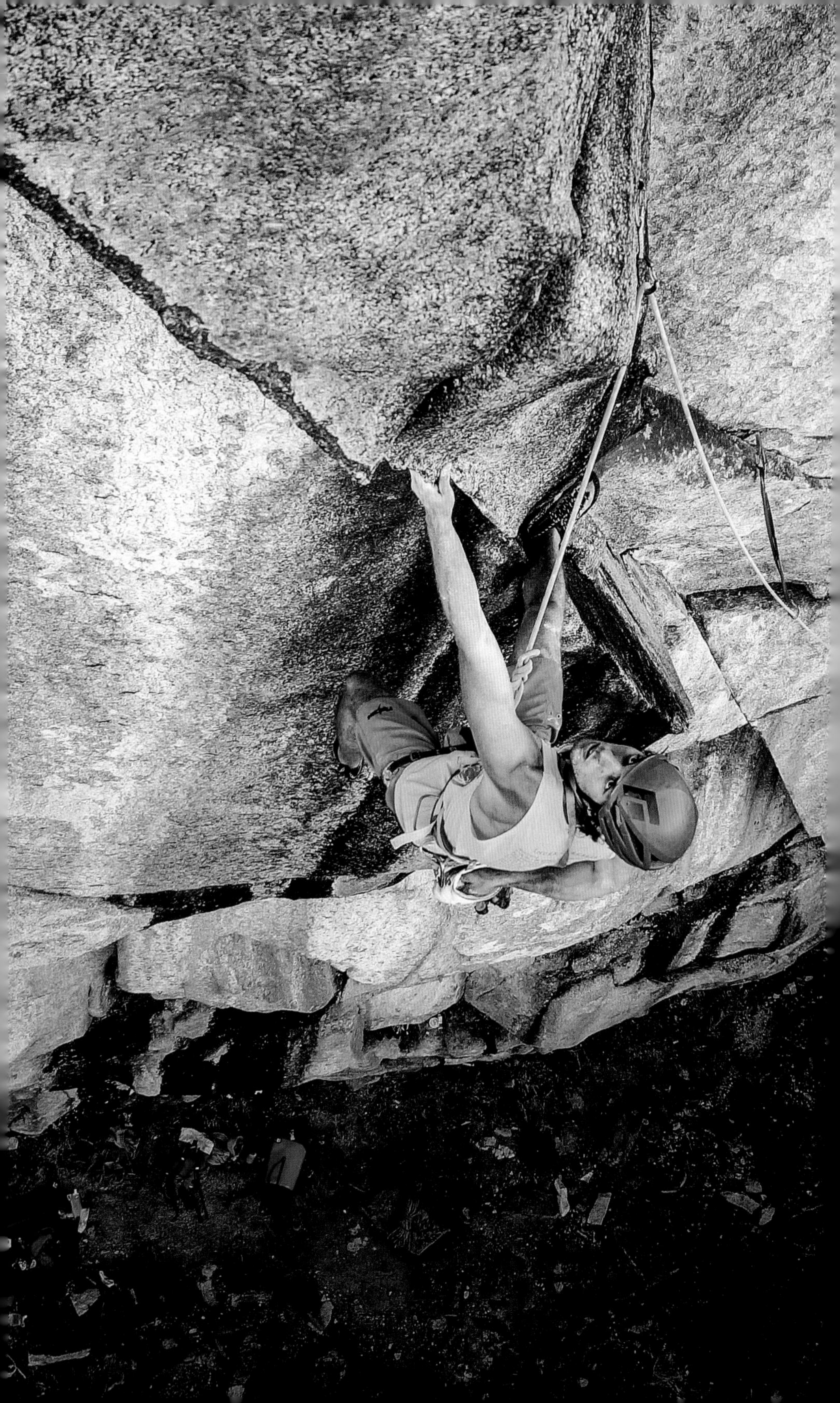

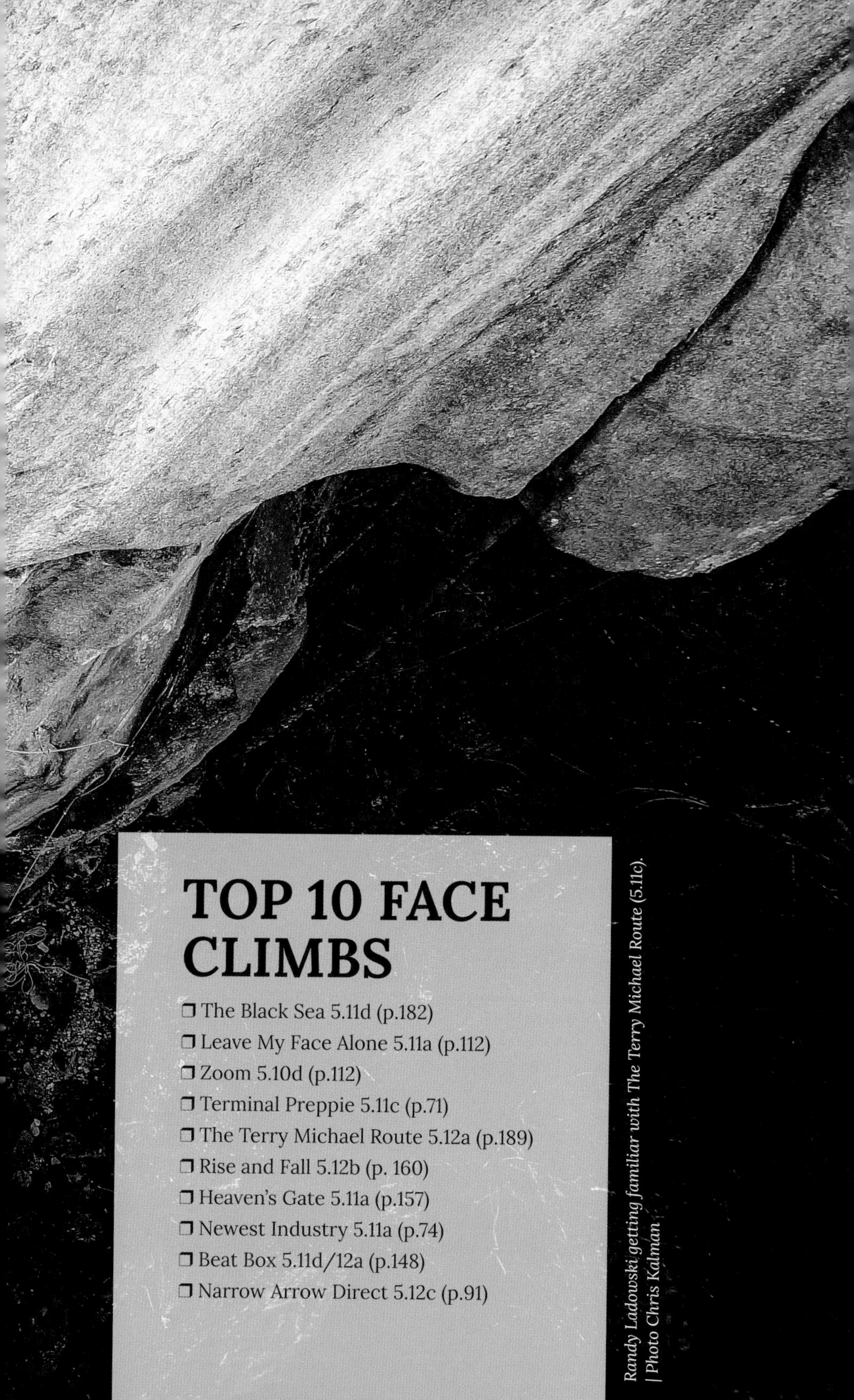

TOP 10 FACE CLIMBS

- ❒ The Black Sea 5.11d (p.182)
- ❒ Leave My Face Alone 5.11a (p.112)
- ❒ Zoom 5.10d (p.112)
- ❒ Terminal Preppie 5.11c (p.71)
- ❒ The Terry Michael Route 5.12a (p.189)
- ❒ Rise and Fall 5.12b (p. 160)
- ❒ Heaven's Gate 5.11a (p.157)
- ❒ Newest Industry 5.11a (p.74)
- ❒ Beat Box 5.11d/12a (p.148)
- ❒ Narrow Arrow Direct 5.12c (p.91)

Randy Ladowski getting familiar with The Terry Michael Route (5.11c). | Photo Chris Kalman

Greg Horvath feeling no need to sew up The Zipper (5.11, p.184).

9 A WISDOM THAT IS WOE 5.13A ★★★

: is said that infamous Index climber, "7 Topropes" rad, projected this thing for longer than it took Ahab o find Moby Dick. Sitting in prime real estate just be-ween *Crack in the Cosmic Egg* and *The Terry Michael oute*, this impressive line pulls through a low bulge, akes a move back left to a layback arête (crux), and ontinues past one more crux to the chains. There also a challenging second pitch (redtagged) that rad is presumably rope-soloing this very moment. arness your inner Catskill eagle, and Melville your ay up this white whale of a pitch.

ear: Quickdraws and optional purple TCU.

A: Brad Lignoski.

0 HASSELHOFF 5.12A ★★

tarting just right of *A Wisdom that is Woe*, the scruff-r, dirtier pitch that shares the same finish.

ear: Quickdraws.

A: Tom Ramier.

) THE TERRY MICHAEL ROUTE (AKA, DEAD RECKONING) 5.12A ★★★★

his is as good as it gets. Spectacular rock, unfathom-ole features, dizzying exposure, and varied climbing ake this one of the best routes at Index. Originally, omehow, this route was called 5.11c. According to erry Lien, they went ground-up, placing one bolt n lead on the first pitch after tying off the low knob. 'ow. Later on, Tom Ramier established this as a more cessible free route by putting in more bolts.

ear: Single set of cams to #2, optional #3 for the cond pitch. Two purple Camalots for pitch one.

A: Terry Lien, Tom Michael.

Pitch 1–5.11c

Sooo good! The starting crux may feel impossible if you can't reach the crucial knob hold. Traverse up and left on wild moves into some of the craziest granite holds you've ever seen.

Pitch 2–5.12a

Wow. It's hard to say much else. Stellar position, stel-lar moves, and stellar rock make this as good a pitch as any, anywhere. Climb past bolts and gear up and right from the anchor.

22 SOULFINGER (OPEN PROJECT) 5.11 A2 ★★★

At the top of the first bolted section on P1 of *The Terry Michael Route*, a thin crack leads through a roof and continues above it. This is *Soulfinger*. It looks hard. It likely goes in the high 5.13 range.

Gear: Standard Index Rack.

FA: Terry Lien, Tom Michael.

23 UNDER THE SUN 5.11 ★★★

From the bolt at the base of the *The Terry Michael Route*, lower down to a 2-bolt anchor at the lip of The Beach. Rappel to another 2-bolt anchor. Outrageously positive 5.9+ chickenheads lead to a boulder problem on slopey knobs; an undercling-flake traverses left then up toward the anchor. Consider leaving a fixed line if you can't climb solid 5.11.

Gear: Standard Index Rack.

FA: Michal Rynkiewicz.

Chris Kalman setting sail on *The Black Sea* (5.11d)

BLACK PLANET AREA

This is the first wall encountered along The Lower Cheeks. Most of the routes are short, steep, sport climbing affairs. The last four routes (*Heat Seeker* to *Engines*) are accessed by climbing onto a steep jumble of boulders at the base of the wall. All of the Black Planet routes can be easily topropped, or accessed for toproping, via anchors along the Perverse Traverse.

Approach: Hike up to The Upper Walls, then continue right. At the break between The Upper Cheeks and Lower Cheeks, continue downhill towards the lower cheeks—then sharply uphill to the base of the short wall.

Descent: A single 60 should be sufficient for everything here.

24 BLACK PLANET 5.9 ★★

Cool knobs lead to a nice right-facing corner, and an exciting traverse at the top. A variety of peculiar belay options (including granite V-threads) exist on the boulder at the start of *The Black Sea*, above.

A dirty 5.11 toprope pitch exists just left called *Ted, Ted Nugent* (Nelson, Masciandaro), and could make for an interesting pitch with some bolts and cleaning.

Gear: Standard Index Rack to 3" and some slings.

FA: Darryl Cramer, Jeff Baird.

25 THE GERBERDING ROUTE 5.9+ ★★

At the start of *Black Planet*, a left-facing corner rises to the right. Climb that corner to a rightward traverse under a roof. Cleaned/retro'd for leading in 2013, this is actually a pretty good route.

Gear: Standard Index Rack to 2.5".

FA: Darryl Cramer, Terry Lien; FFA: Steve Gerberding.

26 THE GREEN ROOM 5.11C ★★

This route would be three stars if it were cleaned up and climbed more. Begin just right of *The Gerberding Route* on a large and charismatic knob. Climb up a left-facing corner. Belay on two bolts along the Perverse Traverse.

Gear: Quickdraws and an optional small cam for the end.

FA: Terry Lien, Darryl Cramer; FFA: Tom Ramier.

27 HEAT SEEKER 5.12A ★★★

A short, good route that packs a punch. Climb up the cool featured rock just right of *The Green Room*, employing compression technique through steep roc to the anchors.

Gear: Quickdraws and a single set of cams to 2".

FA: Dick Cilley, Andy Cairns (on TR); FFA: Tom Ramier

28 INFINITE JEST 5.12+ ★★★★

This is the excellent bolted line between *Heat Seeker* and *Friendly Fire*. Mikey Schaefer called it "one of the best fully-bolted pitches at Index." Don't miss this climb.

Gear: Quickdraws.

FA: Tom Ramier.

29 FRIENDLY FIRE 5.10B ★★★

Climb up the right-facing bolted corner between *Infinite Jest* and *Engines of Archimedes*, starting with an easy but unprotected flake. This is a very nice line which deserves more attention, and serves as a good warm-up for neighboring routes.

Gear: Quickdraws.

FA: Max Dufford, Fred Grafton.

30 ENGINES OF ARCHIMEDES 5.12A ★★★

Archimedes was one of the greatest of ancient math ematicians. He is said to have designed one machine that was capable of lifting attacking ships out of the water, and another that could set ships on fire using an array of mirrors.

You may need an Archimedian intellect to deduce th sequences necessary to climb this stellar pitch. If yo are planning to onsight, having the draws pre-hung would be pretty nice.

Gear: 10-12 quickdraws.

FA: Max Dufford, Fred Grafton.

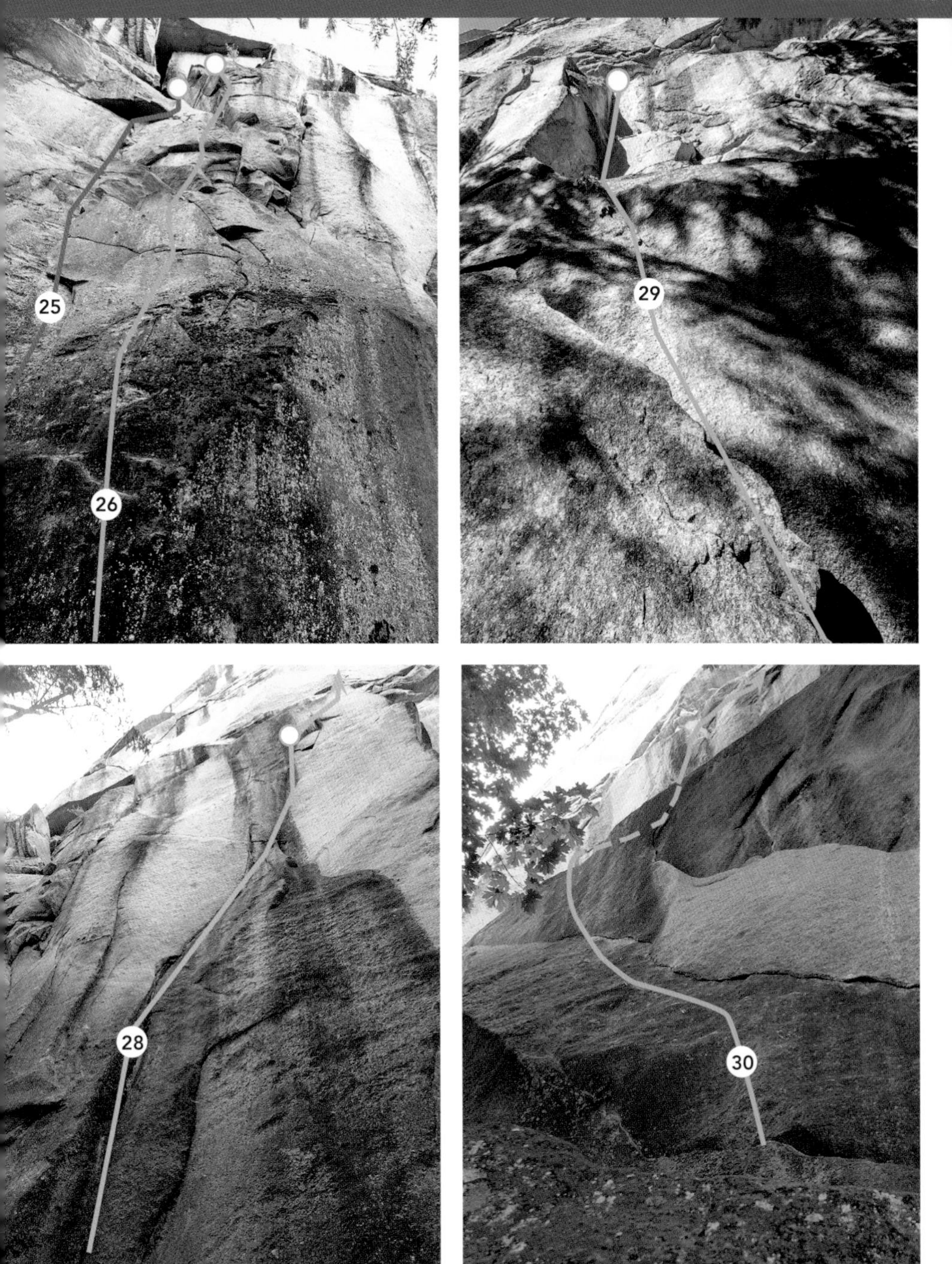
25
26
29
28
30

Ali Patz firing on all four cylinders on Engines of Archimedes (5.12a, p.192).

:LAY AREA

is is the area that includes *Clay*, and the various ıtes surrounding it. It is tall, steep, and awesome. ' also a great hang for kids and/or dogs, and just a nerally beautiful zone. Many of the routes here re- ıin dry even in a downpour, as they climb beneath e enormous roof of *The Zipper*.

proach: After keeping right at The Upper Cheeks/ wer Cheeks split, pass by the jumble of boulders neath Black Planet area. Continue along the trail til *Clay's* obvious and impressive left-facing cor- r—that is *Clay*. Routes in this area are described m left to right, beginning just left of *Clay*.

scent: A 60 meter rope may be sufficient here, t keep a close eye on your ends on longer routes ch as *Clay*.

THE LITTLE DUTCH CUP 5.12B TR ★★

is toprope breaks off of *The Boneyard* at the second p, and climbs up and left to a 2-bolt anchor at mid- ight. Someone should just slap a couple more bolts this thing and make it a three star leadable pitch.

: Unknown.

ar: Toprope from anchor of Boneyard.

THE BONEYARD 5.12B ★★

is bolted line sits about 20 yards left of *Clay*. The lts may need replacing, and could possibly be miss- g hangers. If this got cleaned up, it would be a three ır route. Climb through a techy low crux to a steep d pumpy finish by a very difficult clip.

ar: 11 quickdraws.

: Andy de Klerk.

OPEN PROJECT ★★★

ght of *Boneyard* is an impossible-ish looking project. meone super strong should put it together.

CLAY 5.11D ★★★★

is left-facing corner is absolutely stellar. Jam, stem, back, undercling, deadpoint, and do anything se you have in your arsenal to reach an amazingly posed jug rest (friable rock, hopefully this doesn't eak!) near the end of the pitch. Regain steam, and e cruxy moves to the top.

e second pitch is a rarely-climbed slab that goes at 10+R. This could clean up and retro-bolt nicely.

ıother stellar variation is to traverse left under the of laybacking up to a 2-bolt anchor—may be dirty d require new bolts or tat at anchor.

you climb *Clay* on a 60 meter rope, watch your ıds.

ear: A single set of cams to #3, double up on finger zes and #2 Camalot, minimum six quickdraws.

 P1: Darryl Cramer, Jon Nelson, Terry Lien; FA P2: n Nelson, Terry Lien.

35 ALL DOGS GO TO HEAVEN 5.12C ★★

This is the sport route right of *Clay*. The bottom is often wet, and the holds are often dirty, but the climbing is good. Climb up and turn the crux roof, then keep it together through the steep and pumpy finish.

May be a bit of a de Klerk sandbag.

Gear: 8 quickdraws.

FA: Andy de Klerk.

Max Dufford and classic old school stemming on Clay (5.11d) | Photo by Larry Kemp

LOWER ZIPPER / OUTDOOR HANGBOARD AREA

This is the area clearly defined by The Lower Zipper's, huge "ice cream scoop" roofs, and the steep wall immediately right: the Outdoor Hangboard. Not Index's best wall, but the site of some of Index's steepest terrain. If some climbing mutant like Megos or Ondra came to check out the Zipper roof, who knows what could go down?

Approach: Continue along The Lower Cheeks trail until the huge-roof-capped slab, and the steep right wall.

Descent: Everything can be done with a single 60.

36 FICTION — 5.11B PG13 ★★

This was originally a TR, then led by Greg Child, now rarely climbed in any way at all. For some reason, it has just enough bolts to almost be a reasonably safe rock climb. The four bolts that remain are ancient and shouldn't be expected to hold a fall. This would be a nice three star slab climb if someone gave it a proper bolting, and cleaned it up.

: doubt that Mr. Child would mind.

Climb the bottom part of *The Zipper*, then bust out eft to the slab.

Gear: *4 quickdraws, a solid head.*

FA: Greg Child.

37 THE ZIPPER (P1-2) — 5.10B A2 ★★★

This is the original start to the 6-pitch route, *The Zipper*, which is now most commonly done as a 3-4 pitch route starting at The Beach. Taken alone, the irst pitch is a three star warm-up. The second pitch ackles a wild overhanging wall–one of the steepest t Index. This pitch is just screaming for some super trong climber to give it an FFA and make it the hardst pitch at Index. There is also an A2+ variation going hrough the roof that would be equally interesting to onsider for free climbing... for mutants... maybe.

Gear: *Standard Index Rack (free and aid).*

A: Mark Weigelt, Dennis Fenstermaker, Brent Hoffıan, Karl Kaiyala.

itch 1–5.10b

his is a spectacular pitch. Climb the crack in the corer up to the slab, then follow the thin face crack all ıe way up the slab to the anchors. This pitch is super ın, and probably the best warmup on The Cheeks.

itch 2–A2

d out the imposing roof. Belay on the terrace above, ıd do one more short section of A1 to The Beach. an break into two pitches if necessary.

38 TANGO FOR TWO — 5.10 ★★

Begin up the arching left-facing corner just right of *The Zipper's* starting alcove. Climb up the corner until it is possible to traverse left onto the face, clipping two bolts, and continuing up to *The Zipper* anchor. It is also possible to start *The Zipper* P1, then traverse right into the bolts of this pitch (*Active Boys Puke a Lot*, one star, 5.10b, Manchego).

Gear: *Standard Index Rack.*

FA: Randy Stout, Greg Nelson; FFA: Dan Lapeska, Kjell Swedin.

39 ATTRACTIVE NUISANCE — 5.12C ★

This route is on the overhanging wall just past *The Zipper* known as the Outdoor Hangboard. Thuggy more than juggy, the holds were sadly created with a Bosch making it a completely unnatural route. Three star climbing on a one star route.

This and the next two routes stay dry in a complete downpour.

Gear: *8-9 quickdraws.*

FA: Jeff Baird, Max Dufford.

40 EXTENDED PLAY 5.13A ★★
Begin up *La Bomba Roof* but at the end traverse back left to the anchor for *Attractive Nuisance.*

Gear: 7 quickdraws.

FA: Max Dufford.

41 LA BOMBA ROOF 5.12B ★★
Climb the bolted line just right of *Attractive Nuisance*, turning a crux roof at the fourth bolt, then continuing to anchors up and right.

Gear: 6 quickdraws.

FA: Max Dufford, Jeff Baird.

THE ROOF / WIZARD AREA

This is the last (farthest east) wall on The Lower Cheeks. The Roof is characterized by clean, short, bouldery, overhanging climbing, and is not much to write home about. Just past The Roof, The Wizard area is a taller buttress with some very high quality lines, and potential for at least one incredibly hard pitch.

Approach: Continue along The Lower Cheeks trail past The Zipper and Outdoor Hangboard, until the short, steep, heavily bolted roof-capped face. Everything on the roof can probably be done with a single 30m rope.

Descent: For The Wizard Area, a single 70 is advised (especially if exploring the upper terrain).

42 BENT 5.11+ ★★
A fairly contrived route. Begin on the left side of the roof, climb up to the second bolt, then traverse hard right clipping bolts all the way to the right end of the roof and a late crux.

Gear: Stick-clip, or a couple small pieces for the start.

FA: Greg Collum, Paul Gonzales.

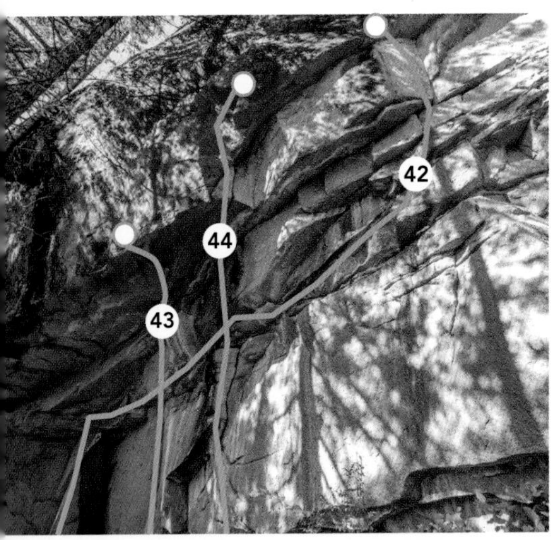

43 DANNY BOY 5.11A ★
Often wet, even though it's under a roof. Climb the middle bolted line up three bolts to an anchor.

FA: Max Dufford, Jeff Walker.

44 PEDAL TO THE METAL 5.12A ★
Often wet, chossy rock, and spacey bolting (may want to supplement with gear) make this a less than popular 30-foot-tall route.

Gear: 3 quickdraws, perhaps some supplementary cams.

FA: Max Dufford.

45 FAERIES WEAR BOOTS 5.11A ★★★★
This wonderful addition to the area from 2016 begins at the right end of the roof. Initial juggy climbing leads to a boulder problem, throwing to knobs. Continue up the slab to a shallow, knob-studded corner. Stem and press your way up to a small roof, face climb to another corner and finish on a sloper mantel.

Gear: Standard Index Rack.

FA: Michal Rynkiewicz, Chandler Davis, Ryan Hoover.

46 LESS THAN ZERO 5.11C ★★
Between *Faeries* and *The Wizard* is a wet V-slot. Begin in that slot, and climb up through some excellent cracks until a roof. Climb up and left into a right-facing corner, and follow that all the way to The Beach.

Gear: Standard Index Rack.

FA: Terry Lien, Jeff Walker.

THE WIZARD 5.10C ★★★

ıis pitch climbs the clean bolted pillar just left of ss *than Zero*, employing interesting compression oves and double-arête slapping. Begin by walkg your feet up the groove of *Less Than Zero* and ʼbacking the left arête of the pillar. When you are ·le, transition onto the face, and slap and compress › the awesome knob studded pillar. An exciting quence guards the anchor.

the anchor, a number of options for more climbing ist. You can traverse left into either of two bolted utes that may need new bolts, and may have never ·en freed. Or, if you're really feeling your oats, you n try to climb the difficult-to-protect tippytips ,back straight up and left, which becomes a finger ack eventually.

:ar: Quickdraws.

: Michal Rynkiewicz, Chandler Davis, Ryan Hoover.

PROJECTS ★★★

ound the corner from *The Wizard* is a tall, goodoking buttress with a few nice looking pitches. ıere's a bolted arête, a thin face crack that leads to ır more bolts and an anchor, and a scruffy corner. ıese pitches were listed in the Cummins guide as ojects, and omitted from the Cramer guide. They ay never have been freed, or named. They look like eat routes, and deserve to be climbed. Current bolts :ely need to be replaced.

49 BRAVO JEAN MARC 5.11A ★★

Beyond the projects, this route climbs a left-leaning thin finger crack just left of an arête. It may be scruffy/dirty, but is supposed to be a pretty good route.

Would the arête to the right go? Only one way to find out.

There may be a few other scruffy pitches in the woods farther right not fully worth climbing or mentioning.

Gear: Gear to 2", focus on small cams.

FA: Cal Folsom, Mark Bebie.

Terry Lien on the first ascent of Non-Local Bark House (5.11d, p.164) | Photo by Greg Olsen.

TERRY LIEN

THE ORIGINS OF THE MYTHICAL INDEX 5.11B

I've been asked what the deal is with Index 5.11b many times over the years. It's hard to answer, but I'll try. Back in the day, if a climb broke the 5.10 barrier it was considered pretty hard, even cutting edge for the majority of climbers. For years the hardest routes at Index's Lower Wall were *Sagittarius*, *Godzilla*, and *Breakfast of Champions*, all stiff 5.9s that many consider 5.10 today. Although 5.12 had been established in places such as Yosemite, this was the early 80s and with the exception of probably Pat Timson, there sure weren't any climbers in Washington that were that good.

When *Slow Children* was first climbed, its rating was discussed. The consensus was *Slow Children*'s difficulty was similar to that of Thin Fingers. It, therefore, became the second 5.11a established on the cliff.

The next significant route, and I believe the third 5.11 on the Lower Town Wall, was the first pitch of *Japanese Gardens*. This climb was noticeably more difficult than both *Slow Children* and *Thin Fingers*. It therefore seemed reasonable to rate *Japanese Gardens* (5.11b). After all, there were no established 5.11c's in the area. The closest route to compare to *Japanese Gardens* would have been *Iron Horse*, which at the time had not had a true second free ascent.

Once established, the first pitch of *Japanese Gardens* became the standard for the 5.11b grade. Shortly thereafter and reinforcing the grade, came *Earwax* and *Domestic Violence*. Both of these climbs were of similar difficulty to *Japanese Gardens*. Thus, this standard perpetuated itself for quite some time. If the 5.11b category is a little wide at Index, that's because, in those early years, none of us had the confidence to rate anything 5.11c.

Since there wasn't a current guidebook for Index, and information in the guides that were available contained mostly information on aid climbs, none of the new 80s free routes got much attention nor did they see much traffic. The majority of the free climbing in Washington was centered around Leavenworth where there were more climbs and climbers. Although we did occasionally climb in Leavenworth we spent 95% of our time at Index. As such, the Index ratings evolved sort of on their own. At the time no one cared, and no one complained.

As the early 90s came around, more and more climbers were showing up at the cliff. Whereas before it was easy for us to rate climbs because we'd done them all, it now became more and more difficult. Ratings were all over the board, and of course, everyone had their own opinion on the subject. As such, rating controversies erupted just like they always do at emerging climbing areas.

Were the early climbs underrated, or did the standard come down? Decide for yourself. Were climbs intentionally under rated? No way. We did the best we could with what we had.

Does it really matter? Maybe at the time, but not in the long run. Respect the past, push the future, and remember it's about the climbing, the friends, and most importantly, the beer at the end of the day.

Route Name	Terry's Grade	Modern Grade
Godzilla	5.9	5.9+
Sagittarius	5.9	5.11b
Breakfast of Champions	5.9	5.10a
Slow Children	5.11a	5.10d
Thin Fingers	5.11a	5.11a
Japanese Gardens	5.11b	5.11c

Route Name	Terry's Grade	Modern Grade
Earwax	5.11b	5.11c
Domestic Violence	5.11b	5.11d
Clay	5.11b/c	5.11d
Natural Log Cabin	5.11b/c	5.11d
The Terry Michael Route	5.11b/c	5.12b
Stern Farmer	5.11d	5.12b

We all know why Chris Kalman wrote this book: he's Hell Bent For Glory (5.10, p.205)

THE DIAMOND

The Diamond is the beautiful diamond-shaped wall rising between the Upper Town Walls and Lookout Point. Over the past few years the upper half of the wall, which was previously almost entirely unclimbed, has been filled in with a smattering of excellent routes. In the past, The Diamond has been closed for much of the summer due to peregrine falcon nesting. This is one of Index's least visited areas, along with the Lower Lump and The Quarry.

Approach: A number of approaches exist. The most direct and obvious begins on the trail to Lookout Point. Park at the Bush House, or in town along the park. Walk west along the train tracks, towards the Lower Town Walls, and after a few minutes duck into the woods along an inconspicuous, but well-worn trail. At the first junction go right (left takes you to *Rattletale*). At the second junction go left (right takes you to Private Idaho). At the third junction continue left (right takes you to Lookout Point proper). Continue past Wall of Ten Thousand Insects (the short wall with a few moderates) and enter the large gully beneath The Diamond, with the Duck Wall on your right. This is The Diamond Gully. All The Diamond crags start here.

Any number of Lookout Point trail variations can also get you there. Another option is to hike all the way up to the end of The Lower Cheeks (using the UTW trail). From the end of The Lower Cheeks, The Diamond is a short hike to the east.

THE DARK CRYSTAL AREA

The Dark Crystal Area doesn't look like much from the base, but it is the jumping off point for two of Index's longest routes, both of which are modern classics. There are plenty of other fine climbs here as well. Don't expect these routes to be spic and span; but on the other hand, you won't have to wait in line for them either.

Approach: Follow the Lookout Point trail to WOTI, then up and left in The Diamond Gully until the huge cave/boulder. A variety of routes start there, while others begin above it, after exiting the cave.

Descent: A 60 is probably fine, but bring a 70 to be safe, especially for the newer routes.

❶ NOTHING BUT NET 5.11C ★★

This is a sport route at the far left end of The Diamond wall after you pass through the tunnel, up and left of *Dark Crystal*. It is often wet.

Gear: 12 quickdraws.

FA: Chris Henson.

❷ SWEET LEAF 5.11+ ★★★

A challenging thin face climb on a faint dike. Small edges to a perplexing blank crux. Good footwork and fresh skin help make the climb more enjoyable.

Gear: Quickdraws.

FA: Michal Rynkiewicz, Ryan Hoover.

❸ THE DARK CRYSTAL 5.11B ★★★

To the left of the huge dihedral above the cave is a smaller left-facing corner that arches up and left, and then back right. The first pitch climbs this feature. Originally, this route was accessed by hiking through the cave, up on top of the cave boulder, and over to the base. Now there is a nice first pitch starting in the cave (R.O.U.S.) that takes you straight to the base of *The Dark Crystal's* first pitch. Doesn't dry out till late June.

Gear: Standard Index Rack to #4 Camalot, optional

FA: Carla Firey, Kjell Swedin.

Pitch 1—5.11b

Climb the steep corner. When possible at the top o the pitch, traverse left past difficult protection (5.1 to a ledge and a bolted anchor.

Pitch 2—5.7

An easy short pitch continuing up the rampy dihed to another bolted anchor. If rope drag allows, you c combine P2 and P3.

Pitch 3—5.11b

Technical climbing up a series of layback cruxes finishes the route at another 2-bolt anchor.

❹ DREAMWEAVER 5.11D ★★

This short sport pitch climbs the overhanging side the boulder that forms the tunnel beneath The Diamond. To reach the base, go through the tunnel, th emerge on the ledge above it up and right.

Gear: Quickdraws.

FA: Chris Henson.

❺ WICKED WORLD 5.10 ★★

This very short climb is located in the cave beneath *Dreamweaver*. Stick clip the first bolt. A slightly overhung powerful crux off the ground leads to eas terrain, and the top.

Gear: Quickdraws.

FA: Michal Rynkiewicz.

❻ WAR PIGS 5.10 ★★★

Crawl through the hole in The Diamond Gully and start on top of a huge block. Funky underclings and gastons trend leftwards to a slightly overhung alcov A surprisingly physical crux leads to slopers and crimps, eventually hitting a horizontal crack that yo climb right to the anchor. Make sure your belayer is attentive on the fourth clip, with zero unnecessary slack out.

Gear: Quickdraws, couple finger sized cams.

FA: Michal Rynkiewicz.

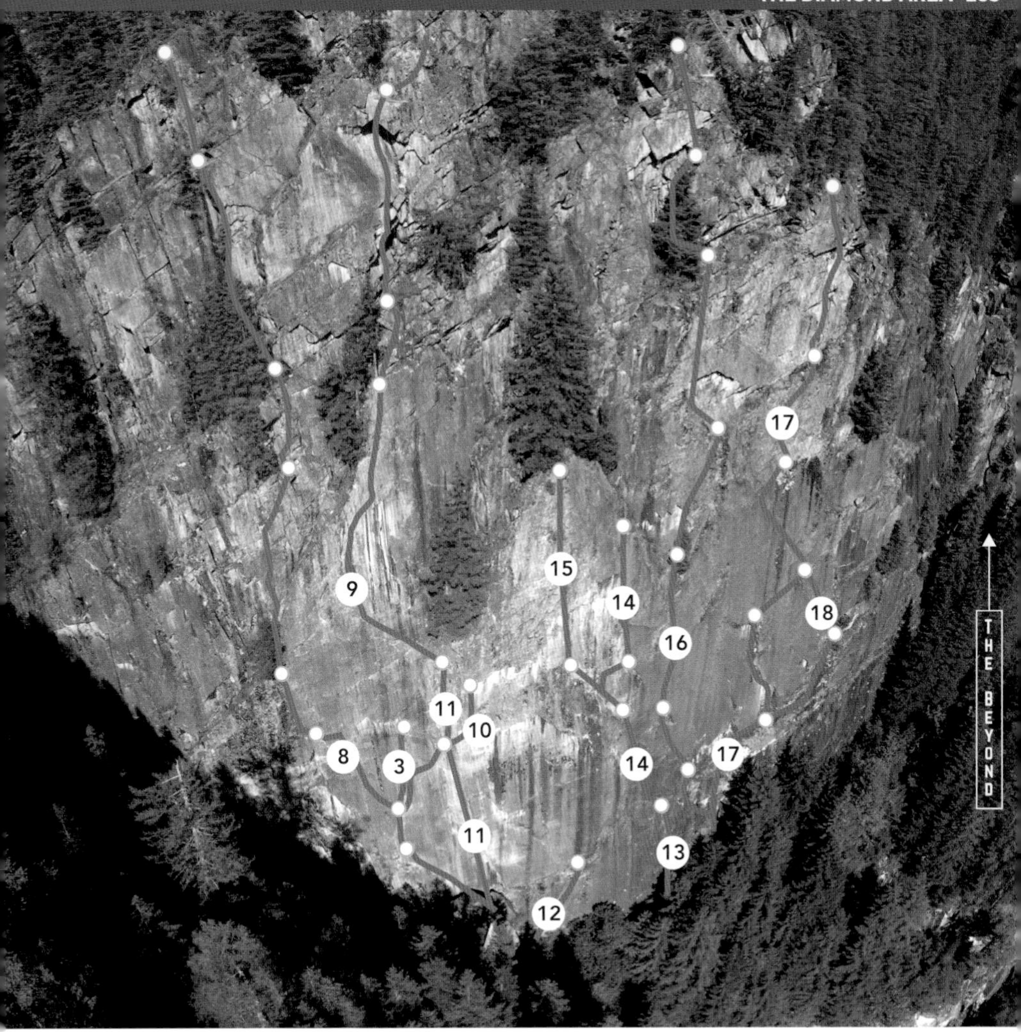

R.O.U.S. 5.9 ★★★

ɪs short sport pitch climbs the slab side of the nel up to the ledge beneath *The Dark Crystal*. It is ool way to start that route.

ar: Quickdraws.

: Chris Henson, Ron Cotman.

NATIVITY IN BLACK 5.11+ ★★★

is line follows a unique dike system that was eyed years and only recently established. Well-featured ne and good belay stances will likely make this a dern classic.

ar: Doubles to 3", single #4, optional #5.

: Michal Rynkiewicz, Ryan Hoover.

:ch 1–5.9
mb R.O.U.S.

:ch 2–5.11
mb the *Dark Crystal* to where the original route eaks left and instead, climb straight up to a small of. Boulder past a few bolts into a traversing crack d on to the belay.

Pitch 3–5.10
A short balancy pitch leads to good ledge.

Pitch 4–5.11+
Follow a bolted rail out left. Campusy climbing leads to a dike. Really fun.

Pitch 5–5.10-
Follow the dike to the large ledge.

Pitch 6–5.10-
Start up the chimney and break into steep, juggy dike climbing. Fun Pitch.

Pitch 7–5.7
A short pitch brings you to a ledge.

Pitch 8–5.10
Climb the striking corner into a slightly overhung handcrack. This beautiful feature continues to the anchor.

Pitch 9– 5.8
Follow bolts up an arête to the top.

9 A NATIONAL ACROBAT 5.12 ★★★★

Physical cracks, blank faces, roofs, and steep jugs define this modern classic that tackles the most striking features on The Diamond. Although a sustained free climb the cruxes can be aided at 5.11- A0. Bring two ropes for rappel. This is the longest route at Index.

Gear: Standard Index Rack to #4 Camalot, optional #5 (leave 3-5" at top of P2).

FA: Michal Rynkiewicz, Ryan Hoover.

Pitch 1–5.9
Climb R.O.U.S.

Pitch 2–5.11
Climb P2 of *Nativity in Black.*

Pitch 3–5.10
Climb P3 of *Nativity in Black.*

Pitch 4–5.12-
Clip a bolt out right and layback the shallow right-facing rail. A short crux leads to the dihedral.

Pitch 5–5.11
This golden left-facing dihedral is absolutely stunning.

Pitch 6–5.11+
Traverse left on jugs to discontinuous cracks. A mixture of gear and bolts leads you up a steep and memorable pitch.

Pitch 7–5.0
Move the belay past one bolt to a 2-bolt anchor on Squamish Ledge.

Pitch 8–5.11+
Climb up featured, slightly overhung jugs leading to a slab move. Climb straight through the roof.

Pitch 9–5.9
Easy, fun climbing leads to the top of the wall.

10 MASTER OF REALITY 5.11 ★★★

One of the most attractive splitters at Index. From the top of pitch four of *National Acrobat* step right and clip a bolt. A tricky move leads to the base of the crack. Airy climbing out of the roof crack pulls over the lip on thin locks. Break left into the bomb-bay which quickly turns to OW.

Gear: A full set of cams to #6 Camalot, doubles in #3 and #4.

FA: Michal Rynkiewicz, Ryan Hoover.

11 THE DIHEDRAL ROUTE 5.11 A4 ★★

This route climbs the obvious huge left-facing dihe dral on the left side of The Diamond Wall above the cave. So far it has repelled free climbing efforts. Th said, if freed, it would be a most excellent route.

In Cramer's 2000 guide, he wrote that this route probably hasn't seen a complete ascent in the 80s c 90s. You can likely add another decade and a half tc that now.

P3 & 4 of this route are four star free climbs, best a cessed by climbing the first half of *A National Acrob* and rapping into the belay. They were recently free by Michal Rynkiewicz and Ryan Hoover.

Gear: Standard Index Aid Rack.

FA: Dana Dudley, Jim Langdon.

Pitch 1–5.8
Hike along the ramp past *Dark Crystal*, and climb tl steep and thin left-facing corner to a 2-bolt anchor

Pitch 2–A3
Aid up the corner to an anchor out left.

Pitch 3–5.11
Continue up the corner, and make a belay where th angle eases and cracks head up the dihedral's right wall.

Pitch 4–5.11
Continue up the brilliant dihedral (P5 of *A National Acrobat* goes left). *Master of Reality* goes right here.

Pitch 5–4th class
Fourth class leads up a forested ledge. Most parties rappel from here straight down the extremely steep face past roofs.

Pitch 6-7–5.8
Another two pitches of loose, dirty, blocky, easy climbing lead to the top of the wall. These pitches may not have been climbed in 30 years. Bring tat, a brush, a nut tool, and maybe a shovel.

12 ASTERISK 5.8 ★★★

Near the start of the ledge to Centerfold Area, climb up to a ledge and up the open book corner passing a thin section down low that eventually turns to perfe locks. One of the better routes of its grade. It's close to 35 meters so tie knots and be careful while lower ing. Should become popular.

Gear: Standard Index Rack.

FA: Nina Friedman, Alysse Hotz, Michal Rynkiewicz, Ryan Hoover.

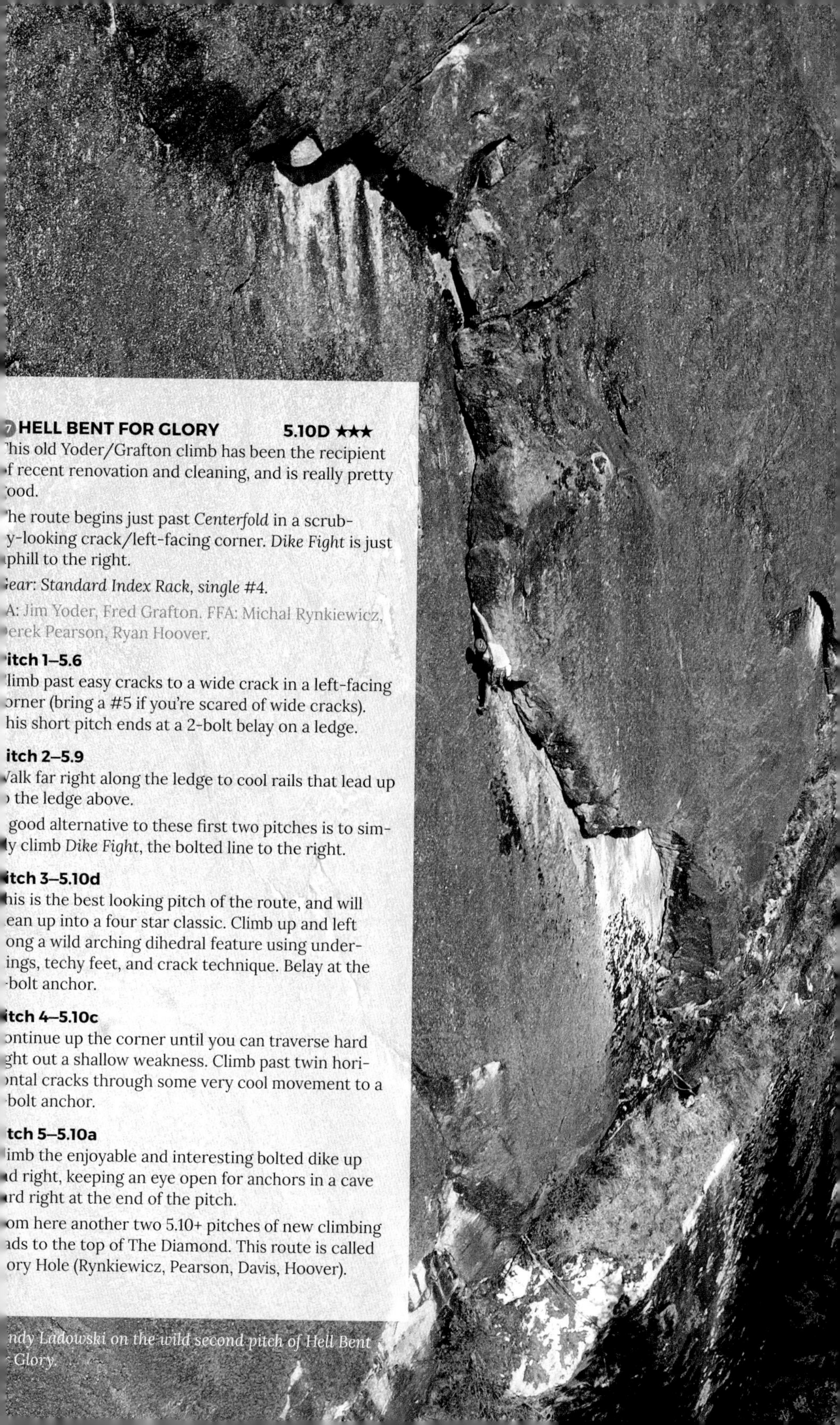

HELL BENT FOR GLORY 5.10D ★★★

'his old Yoder/Grafton climb has been the recipient ·f recent renovation and cleaning, and is really pretty :ood.

'he route begins just past *Centerfold* in a scrub-y-looking crack/left-facing corner. *Dike Fight* is just ıphill to the right.

ear: Standard Index Rack, single #4.

A: Jim Yoder, Fred Grafton. FFA: Michal Rynkiewicz, erek Pearson, Ryan Hoover.

'itch 1–5.6

limb past easy cracks to a wide crack in a left-facing orner (bring a #5 if you're scared of wide cracks). his short pitch ends at a 2-bolt belay on a ledge.

itch 2–5.9

Valk far right along the ledge to cool rails that lead up) the ledge above.

good alternative to these first two pitches is to sim-ly climb *Dike Fight*, the bolted line to the right.

itch 3–5.10d

his is the best looking pitch of the route, and will ean up into a four star classic. Climb up and left ong a wild arching dihedral feature using under-ings, techy feet, and crack technique. Belay at the -bolt anchor.

itch 4–5.10c

ontinue up the corner until you can traverse hard ght out a shallow weakness. Climb past twin hori-ontal cracks through some very cool movement to a -bolt anchor.

tch 5–5.10a

imb the enjoyable and interesting bolted dike up ıd right, keeping an eye open for anchors in a cave ırd right at the end of the pitch.

om here another two 5.10+ pitches of new climbing ads to the top of The Diamond. This route is called ory Hole (Rynkiewicz, Pearson, Davis, Hoover).

ndy Ladowski on the wild second pitch of Hell Bent Glory.

TOP 10 CORNERS, STEMS, AND SLOTS

- ❒ Natural Log Cabin 5.11d (p.91)
- ❒ Clay 5.11d (p.195)
- ❒ Technicians of the Scared P4 5.12b/c (p.168)
- ❒ An Act of Strange Boar 5.10c (p.230)
- ❒ Shirley 5.11c (p.92)
- ❒ Iron Horse 5.11d (p.78)
- ❒ Numbah 10 5.12b (p.76)
- ❒ Narrow Arrow Overhang (to 2nd anchors) 5.12c (p.91)
- ❒ Voyage of the Majestic Glass-Eyed Tuna (P4 of VOT-MGET) 5.10d (p.94)
- ❒ A National Acrobat P5 5.12 (p.206)

Matt Upton breaking the mold on Clay (5.11d, p.195)

ENTERFOLD AREA

e routes at Centerfold Area climb some of the anest, most continuous rock at The Diamond. is wall includes everything along the ramp before e cave, up to *The Beyond*. The site of recent de-opment, surely this zone could host a few more ssic lines.

proach: Follow the Lookout Point trail to WOTI, en up and left in The Diamond Gully until the ed ledge and trail that leads up and right along e base of The Diamond Wall.

scent: Bring a single 70 to rap any route on this ll, a 60 will give you fewer options.

SLIDING INTO FIRST 5.11A ★★

is is an alternate first pitch to *Centerfold*'s often wet rting corner. Climb the first line of bolts encoun-red as you hike up the treed ramp along the base of e Diamond. At the fourth bolt you can either cross ht over the standard route, or continue left up the ndard route. Either way is 5.11a and passes three ore bolts to the anchor.

ar: Standard Index Rack.

.: Cal Folsom.

CENTERFOLD 5.11A ★★★

fore 2016 this was the most popular route on The amond, and one of the easiest big multi-pitch utes at Index. It can be a little dirty from time to ne, but is not to be missed.

gin in an often wet left-facing flake/dihedral.

ar: Standard Index Rack. Single 70 to rap.

.: Cal Folsom, Andy Tuthill.

tch 1–5.11a

imb *Sliding into First*, or the regular first pitch, or y combination of the two. Either way, it's 5.11a past lts to a 2-bolt anchor.

tch 2–5.10d

imb face moves to a white corner with flakes and acks to a belay. Small cams are useful.

tch 3–5.10d

short pitch past two bolts to a ledge at the base the big dihedral. *Jack o' Diamonds* heads out left ortly after the second bolt.

tch 4–5.10d

imb the thin right-facing corner to a 2-bolt anchor. is possible to continue to the top of the wall from re, but not advisable.

JACK O' DIAMONDS 5.11B ★★

is route is accessed via the first two and a half tches of *Centerfold*. It climbs the beautiful golden amond headwall.

ar: Standard Index Rack.

: Greg Child, Andy Tuthill.

Pitch 1–5.9

Begin up the third pitch of *Centerfold*, but at soon as you can, move left to a ramp and continue left to anchors.

Pitch 2–5.11b

Climb up past two bolts and a roof to splitter headwall cracks. Follow these to the top.

16 SABBRA CADABRA 5.11- ★★★

The newest climb in the book and an impressive feat considering it was established during the winter. This great climb weaves its way through fun face climbing and natural features. Rappel the route with a single 70.

Gear: Standard Index Rack and a single #4, 12 quick-draws and plenty of slings.

FA: Ryan Hoover, Chandler Davis, Derek Pearson, Michal Rynkiewicz.

Pitch 1–5.6

Climb P1 of *Hell Bent*.

Pitch 2–5.10

Continue the first 15 ft of *Hell Bent*'s second pitch then break left at the bolt line.

Pitch 3–5.11-

Above the belay, climb straight up to a traversing pitch. Technical, yet powerful climbing leads to the base of a finger crack.

Pitch 4–5.11-

Follow the long striking finger crack.

Pitch 5–5.10-

Start up the corner system and break right onto face climbing past bolts to Eyelid Roof.

Pitch 6–5.10+

From the belay, follow a ramp and break through the left side of Eyelid Roof. Fun climbing on highly featured stone. Skip the rap anchor, and belay at the base of the corner on Lovely Lady Ledge.

Pitch 7–5.9

Climb the corner. Break right at the roof and belay atop the slab.

Pitch 8–5.10

Climb the overhanging hand crack and step onto the ledge. Place small cams and move out left to a rail. Press out on the rail and climb straight up on small gear.

⑰ HELL BENT FOR GLORY 5.10D ★★★
See page 207.

⑱ HELL BENT FOR LEATHER 5.10+ ★★★
Another recent addition to The Diamond. This is a quality variation to *Hell Bent For Glory* that substitutes thought-provoking face climbing for the burly crack climbing of the original line. By the time of printing, this climb may have its own direct start from the ground.

Gear: Standard Index Rack, (for HBFGlory pitches), quickdraws for HBFLeather.

FA: Derek Pearson.

⑲ DIKE FIGHT 5.11C ★★★
To the right of the start of *Hell Bent for Glory*, next to a tree is a bolted line on a mostly clean part of a mostly vegetated face. *Dike Fight* climbs the rippled face up to chains at the lip of a large ledge, beneath the third pitch of *Hell Bent for Glory*.

Gear: 10 quickdraws, plus a finger cam or two for the start.

FA: Danny Diamond, Mike Massey.

THE BEYOND

The Beyond is a small, rarely visited formation that abuts The Diamond Wall at its eastern terminus. There are a few good single pitches here, which may need new bolts, and scrubbing.

Approach: Follow the Lookout Point trail to WOTI, then up and left in The Diamond Gully until the treed ledge and trail that leads up and right along the base of The Diamond Wall. Continue up this ledge til it ends at a steep white wall.

Descent: A single 60 will get you off these climbs.

⑳ PORK CHOP TORPEDO 5.10B ★★★
This route climbs the excellent handcrack in a left-facing corner.

Gear: Double set of hand size cams.

FA: Bryan Burdo, Kevin Cadigan.

㉑ JUST GIVE 'EM WHISKEY 5.12A ★★★
Climb up the left-leaning thin crack (bring RPs) to the bolt-protected face. The crux comes at the end–right where it should.

Gear: RPs, cams to 1", 4 quickdraws.

FA: Bryan Burdo, Greg White, Erik Winkelman.

㉒ NEARLY NAKED NOW 5.10D ★★
This route climbs the left side of the right arête of the wall. It may be missing the first bolt hanger. If cleaned, it would be a better climb.

Gear: Single rack of cams, quickdraws.

FA: Greg White, Bryan Burdo.

㉓ THE CAD-BURD SEAT 5.10A ★
A short and dirty handcrack right of the arête.

Gear: Hand-size pieces.

FA: Kevin Cadigan, Bryan Burdo.

㉔ THE LAST BARSTOOL IN MECCA 5.10D ★
Short, and unimpressive. Climbs the far arête at the right end of the wall.

Gear: 3 quickdraws.

FA: Bryan Burdo, Kevin Cadigan, Pete Doorish.

Mount Index in all it's glory.

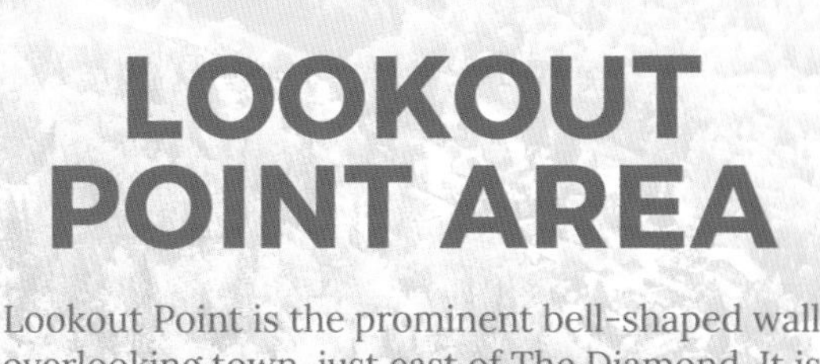

LOOKOUT POINT AREA

Lookout Point is the prominent bell-shaped wall overlooking town, just east of The Diamond. It is a beautiful and mystical-feeling zone, with many hidden gems. From short knob climbs to multi-pitch adventure routes, there's a bit of everything at Lookout Point. Rattletale and Private Idaho, though not exactly part of Lookout Point, per se, are included in this general area. Some of Index's best moderates are here, as well as one of the best finger cracks in Washington. It's a bit more of a hike than the Lower Walls, but the tradeoff for that, commonly, is solitude, and first dibs at anything you'd like to climb.

Approach: Park at the Bush House, or in town by the park. Walk west along the train tracks, towards the Lower Town Walls, and after a few minutes, duck into the woods along an inconspicuous, but well-worn trail. All the Lookout Point crags are accessed via this trail.

Derek Pearson on the first ascent of Little Fire (5.10d).

RATTLETALE WALL

Rattletale Wall is the steepest, and perhaps most striking wall in the Lookout Point area. The site of extensive recent route development, this crag has gone from a sleepy obscurity to a fantastic wall brimming with fine lines.. Beneath the wall, there is a recently-discovered bouldering traverse of nearly 70 feet, which purportedly stays dry in the rain.

Approach: Follow the Lookout Point trail to the first branch, and go left. Follow this trail uphill and then left and down a little to the base of the wall.

Descent: You may be able to descend most climbs here with a 60, but if you have a 70, bring it.

1 THE AARDVARK/ANTEATER 5.10+/5.11 ★★

To the left of *The Amphibian*, a 5-10 minute hike brings you to another wall with two established routes, and much more potential. The two established lines are both 5.10+/5.11, both two stars, both established by Logan Fusso and Evan Larsell, and both named either *Aardvark*, or *Anteater*. The first asentionists can't recall which is which.

FA: Logan Fusso, Evan Larsell.

New route alert! See page 226.

2 THE AMPHIBIAN 5.10+ ★★★★

This is one of the best new routes at Index, and is an absolute classic. The first bolt or two may feel slightly contrived, as you can walk up the muddy hill to the right, but just get on the rock and start climbing. It's actually really good, and the upper part is a full-on doozy. If you don't keep cool, you could catch a lot of air at the finish–but not to worry, the fall is safe. Named after the newt who helped discover the line.

Gear: *Quickdraws.*

FA: Michal Rynkiewicz.

3 AVENGING THE GODDESS KRING 5.12A ★★★

This route is rumored to be quite good, but doesn't (a of 2017) see much traffic. The bolts up high are plated but good. If you want to rap in to have a look, you car do so by topping out *Rattletale*.

Climb three short pitches on the far left side of Rattletale Wall. It is best to link 1 and 2, or 2 and 3, depending on rope drag. You can rap the route with a single 70. For those wanting to avoid the 5.12 climbin the first two pitches can be toproped with a single 70 with some trickery, and some knots tied in the ends the rope. It's a rope stretcher.

Gear: *Standard Index Rack to #4 (#5 if you struggle o wide cracks).*

FA: David Gunstone, Darryl Cramer.

Pitch 1–5.10b

Climb up the left of two converging cracks (the right is *Chasing the Lizard*) past two bolts. Make a short traverse left, just below the chimney to a 2-bolt anchor.

Pitch 2–5.9

Climb up the short, left-facing corner to a large ledg and a 2-bolt anchor. The chimney to the right goes at 5.8.

Pitch 3–5.12a

Cross right over the chimney, and climb the steep bolted face to a 2-bolt anchor. Very good climbing. Rumored to be only 5.11b/c.

To the left, three bolts lead you up a dirty 5.7 variatic and a different anchor.

Michal Rynkiewicz establishing The Amphibian (5.11a) | Photo by Ryan Hoover

❹ CHASING THE LIZARD 5.9 ★★★

Climb the crack just right of *Avenging*, continuing up the corner system all the way to a step out right to the top of *Avenging*'s second pitch. Make one long rap from here with a 70 and some trickery (watch rope ends), or two short raps to the ground (using the anchor atop *Avenging*'s P1). You can also climb a final dirty 5.7 to the top, if you want.

This route is said to be a really nice crack climb, but like its neighbor, doesn't see much traffic.

Gear: Standard Index Rack to #4 (#5 if you struggle on wide cracks).

FA: David Gunstone, Darryl Cramer.

❺ NON-STOP EROTIC CABARET 5.12A ★★

This route is likely dirty, and the bolts may be suspect. That said, there was some interest in cleaning it in September 2016, so it may be in great shape. Either way, it would probably clean up (with new bolts if necessary) into a three star route.

Climb the face and arête left of *Rattletale*.

Gear: Standard Index Rack.

FA: Greg Child, Darryl Cramer, Sally Oberlin, Greg Collum.

Pitch 1–5.11c
Climb several short corners then up the arête left of *Rattletale*. You can skip this pitch altogether by doing *Rattletale*'s first pitch (recommended).

Pitch 2–5.10b
Climb around the arête to the left of *Rattletale* past some cool features, and runout terrain, to a natural belay on a ledge. It is recommended to link P2 and P3.

Pitch 3–5.12a
This is the best pitch of the route—difficult bolt-protected climbing up the right side of the arête.

❻ RATTLETALE 5.10B ★★★★

This is a fantastic splitter, and great for practicing hand jams. Two ledges make it better to pitch out than link the short pitches. This route got two stars i the old guidebook—a testament to what can happen when routes stay clean from regular traffic.

Gear: Doubles or triples of hand-size cams, and a few smaller pieces.

FA: Dave Anderson, Cal Folsom, Phil McCrudden.

Pitch 1–5.9
Easy and somewhat dirty climbing leads to a right-facing splitter corner. Climb this to the ledge and anchor.

Pitch 2–5.10b
Continue up the obvious splitter corner another 50 feet to the anchor (optional #4).

Pitch 3–5.10a
A wide chimney can be climbed via stemming, lay-backing, or straight in jamming. Pick your poison. Tw raps get you to the ground.

Note: There is a new 5.11- sport climb right of Rattletal called Jane Goodall (three stars, Anagnostou, Hoover, Rankiewicz)

elene Blair snaking her way up Rattletale (5.10b) | Photo by Truc Nguyen Allen

⑦ THE ORANGUTAN 5.11 ★★★★

The Orangutan is a sustained face climb on quintessential Index knobs. A powerful boulder problem off the ground leads to a right-leaning crack. Some small cams and a rightward traverse take you up to bolted knob climbing. The chains are guarded by an exasperatingly difficult crux.

Gear: Draws, small cams, offset brassy RPs.

FA: Michal Rynkiewicz, Ryan Hoover.

⑧ THE BONOBO 5.11 PG13 ★★★

This route ascends *Arch Enemy* until it steps left to the first bolt you can clip on *The Orangutan.*

A couple good placements on easy climbing thin out to a nest of offset stoppers and ballnuts. Make committing, difficult moves to side-pulls out right, finally clipping a bolt. From here, finish up on *The Orangutan.* Be solid at the grade. The end is the crux, but the start would be a tough and spicy onsight.

Gear: Draws, small cams, DMM brass offsets, ballnuts.

FA: Stamati Anagnostou.

⑨ ARCH ENEMY A4 ★★★

This is a terrifying aid line, and one of the most aesthetic at Index. Very psychologically demanding, this route has likely never been repeated.

We have not climbed it so our description of the two-pitch route is rather short. Climb through seams and knobs to a series of left-trending expanding flakes and roofs, then climb a rightfacing corner to the top.

Gear: Standard Index Aid Rack.

FA: Paul Gonzales, Greg Collum.

⑩ WITH MAN GONE WILL THERE BE HOPE FOR GORILLA A2 ★★★

This two-pitch route is probably the first intentiona aid climbing first ascent in Index in the last ten year

Clean aid leads out a prominent, long, left/downward-facing arch just right of *Arch Enemy*, then ascends briefly to a bolted anchor. Expect some excitement with tiny gear off the ground, followed by som good pieces at the apex of the arch, and then the cr as the crack becomes shallow and flaring. C2+.

Be aware that a boulder pad or three is probably better protection than any of the gear you're going to g until the apex of the arch.

From the bolted anchor at the top of P1, bat-hook right to a series of upward-facing flakes, then head up the thin seam from the bolt to a bolted anchor. This pitch would likely go clean at C3-4, but is A2, currently.

Gear: Standard Index Aid Rack, ballnuts.

FA: Jacob Smith.

⑪ THE CLAW 5.11- ★★

This route and the others after it lie just uphill and right from the main wall of *Rattletale*. You'll walk pas them on your way here.

Juggy moves starting on the right side of the arête lead leftward. A bolt-protected perplexing barndoo move busts left on slopey knobs. Continue left past a couple small cams to a no-hands rest, then climb straight up the short slab.

There's a really nice highball splitter under this pitc *The Millipede* (V2, Rynkiewicz, Nesselquist).

Gear: Bolts, singles to #2 Camalot.

FA: Michal Rynkiewicz, Ryan Hoover.

Chandler Davis taming The Shrew (5.10, p.218) | Photo by Ryan Hoover

⑫ THE SNAKE 5.10- ★★★

Climb *The Claw* or *The Cricket* to access this pitch–the best in the general vicinity. Start up knobs, and move left to a mantel past the first bolt. Continue up a thin crack and another mantel to a ledge.

Gear: Doubles to 0.5, offset RPs, optional ballnuts.

FA: Ryan Hoover, Michal Rynkiewicz.

⑬ THE CRICKET 5.5 ★★

Behold Index's easiest climb–a little bugger that loves to collect muck from the ledge above. Originally climbed as a solo. Ascend the twin cracks to a ledge 30 feet up with an anchor on the left.

Gear: Singles to #2 Camalot.

FA: Chandler Davis.

⑭ THE SHREW 5.10 ★★★

Accessed via *The Cricket* or *The Claw*. Gorgeous knobs lead past twin fins of rock to a no-hands rest. Slap up the bouldery, slightly overhanging arête. Airy climbing leads to a friction move getting to the anchor.

Gear: Quickdraws.

FA: Michal Rynkiewicz.

⑮ ZE SQUID 5.10 ★★★

Start up *The Cricket* and move right past an offset crack to a ledge. Face climb up to a slabby crux, clip the bolt and boulder through to a jug. Make a short runout to the obvious, left-facing corner, and continue to the top.

Gear: Two quickdraws, singles to 0.75 Camalot, doubles 0.5 Camalot.

FA: Logan Fusso.

⑯ THE SOURCE 5.10- ★★

A slab climb that has a tricky little section at the middle breaking left to the arête. Above the roof at the top head slightly right and up to a spacious bela ledge, located right of the buttress.

Gear: Quickdraws.

FA: Chandler Davis.

THE DUCK WALL

The Duck Wall is an attractive formation of steep white rock that rises beneath the forested ramp leading to the right half of The Diamond, and The Beyond. The Duck Wall is actually a collection of three walls: The Wall of Ten Thousand Insects (WOTI), The Diamond Gully, and The Duck Wall proper. Although some very good and steep rock ca be found here, this area is mostly overlooked.

Approach: Take the trail toward Lookout Point and Private Idaho. At the first junction, go right (left goes to *Rattletale*). At the second junction, veer left (right goes to Private Idaho). At the third junction, travel left again (right goes to Lookout Point proper) Shortly after crossing a narrow gully, you'll see a short, clean wall right on the trail. This is WOTI. Pas WOTI are the routes in The Diamond Gully. Betweer WOTI and The Diamond Gully routes, there is a narrow, treed ledge. Hiking up this trail will take you to Duck Wall proper, and a few longer routes, which are accessed by a succession of fixed hand lines.

Descent: A 60 will be sufficient for most routes, but bring the 70 to be safe.

INGUS FLING 5.11B ★★

s route starts on the right side of The Diamond ly uphill and left of Wall of Ten Thousand Insects, is the more uphill of the two routes obvious from gully. It climbs the clean splitter thin handcrack ough a roof.

r: *Standard Index Rack.*

Bryan Burdo, Pete Doorish, Kevin Cadigan.

SWEETS FOR MANUEL 5.10B ★★

t downhill of *Jingus Fling, Sweets for Manuel* climbs nooth right-facing corner. The thin crack changes ners about 30 feet up.

r: *Standard Index Rack.*

Jeff Kelly, Matt Arksey.

MESSAGE OF LOVE 5.11A ★★★

hort but physical climb, located at the toe of The ck Wall (right of *Sweets for M*). Start with slop- off the ground (an optional finger-size cam can placed between the 1st and 2nd bolt). Climb the htly overhung left-leaning rail, leading to com- ssion moves and powerful laybacks. Well bolted oughout. Although somewhat short, it provides a asant pump. Named after the classic Jimi Hendrix ng. Stout.

ar: *Quickdraws.*

Michal Rynkiewicz.

PLANET CARAVAN 5.10+★★★

ecently-finished climb that features a low-angle hnical stemming corner, a true squeeze flair, and airy final hanging corner. The pitches are short, e to good belay stances, and can easily be linked. is is a great climb to add to *Rattletail* and *Little Fire* a great "first time at Yosemite" training day.

ar: *Cams to 3", RPs, 6-12 quickdraws and runners.*

: Michal Rynkiewicz, Stamati Anagnostou, Ryan over, Jon Nelson.

tch 1–5.4

om the spot where the trail meets The Duck Wall, mb up and right on a low-angle ramp to a very ort layback accessing the ledge at the base of the vious corner.

tch 2–5.11a

ew technical moves off the belay start this short t sustained corner. Make sure you have a good lay for the first three bolts. Sandbag.

tch 3–5.9

imb out right into the womb eventually maneuver- g into a beautiful left-facing squeeze chimney at the p of the flair. Do not continue straight up toward e dirty blocky section, instead stem out right and ll through the roof on a diagonal rail, clipping a lt at its terminus, and climb up to the anchor. (For *dless Skies*, move the belay 30 feet to the right).

itch 4–5.10-

imb the final pitch up and slightly left to a treed dge.

21 ENDLESS SKIES 5.12 ★★★★

Approach via *Planet Caravan. Endless Skies* is the righthand of the two alcove belays. This quality route is atypical for Index–it feels a lot like something you'd find at Equinox or in a climbing gym.

Gear: *Quickdraws.*

FA: Michal Rynkiewicz, Stamati Anagnostou.

22 MAKING THE LITTLE DUCKS QUACK
5.11A ★★

A straight-up, vertical layback crack in a shallow corner which starts with a few fist jams, but quickly narrows to fingers.

Follow the trail along the base of the wall. After the first rope ladder, and before the second, walk right to the obvious ledge with the 2-bolt anchor at the top of this route. Rap in to climb.

Gear: *Standard Index Rack.*

FA: Jon Nelson, Darryl Cramer.

23 LITTLE FIRE 5.10D ★★

This is the longest route on the The Duck Wall. It starts as *Meadow and Spicer* does, at the top of the second fixed hand line on the treed ledge above WOTI. The route was named for Derek's daughter. Cute, Derek.

Gear: *Single rack to 4", including a selection of nuts. Double-up on Camalots #1 & #2.*

FA: Derek Pearson.

Pitch 1–5.5

At the top of the second hand line walk out a ledge to two bolts and belay from there.

Pitch 2–5.10

Climb the clean, left-facing corner. Traverse out the roof to a rest, then climb the wide crack to the anchor.

Pitch 3–5.8

Head right from the belay. May be a bit dirty.

Pitch 4–5.10d

This is the best pitch of the route. Traverse left past five bolts, and one optional .75 Camalot.

Pitch 5–5.9

A finger crack leads to a mantle and a nice ledge.

24 MEADOW AND SPICER 5.11B ★★

After passing WOTI, at the start of The Diamond Gully, hike up the treed ledge. *Meadow and Spicer* and *Little Fire* both start at the top of the second handline.

Gear: Cams to 4", RPs, 6-12 quickdraws and runners.

FA: Darryl Cramer, Nicola Masciandaro, Jon Nelson.

Pitch 1–5.11b

Stick clip the high first bolt, and tackle a short (hard) boulder problem to get established on the ledge. From the ledge, follow the corner and surmount the roof. Face climb up to the crack, and ascend the wide crack to a large ledge with a 2-bolt anchor. Can be climbed at 5.10 C1.

Pitch 2–5.8

Start up the corner just above the anchor, and follow the enjoyable headwall crack to a ledge with a 2-bolt anchor.

Pitch 3–5.6

Climb the short flake/corner system to the top.

25 INDEX AIR FORCE 5.10A ★★

IAF and the following route are located on WOTI. This is the left-facing crack on the left. It is 5.8 to the roof where a 5.10a crux brings you to the anchor.

There is a variation, a right-facing corner start which goes at the same grade.

Gear: Standard Index Rack.

FA: Cal Folsom, Don Brooks.

26 THEM 5.9 ★★

The right-facing layback flake on the right side of WOTI. This climb is good, and clean. If it were not so short, it would be a three star route for sure.

Gear: Standard Index Rack.

FA: Cal Folsom, Don Brooks.

LOOKOUT POINT

Lookout Point has some stellar lines, including *Bobcat Cringe, Peanuts to Serve You, Steel Pulse,* and *An Act of Strange Boar*. The routes here tend to be multi-pitch affairs, but this is certainly an easy place to simply crag out the first pitches, a la LTW. It should be noted that Derek Pearson in particular has put in a ton of work keeping this crag climbable over the years. He is the man. Thank him if you meet him.

Approach: Take the Lookout Point trail from the railroad through the woods, and pass an awesome boulder. Stay right at the first fork (avoiding *Rattle-tale*), and left at the second fork (avoiding Private Idaho). The trail will deposit you at the wall near Bobcat Cringe area. Alternately, you can top out a variety of routes in Private Idaho and walk uphill, or walk past Private Idaho right, then up a steep trail and back left.

Descent: A 60 is fine for some routes. Just bring a 70.

27 VELVET PEDESTAL 5.10A ★★★

On the far left side of Lookout Point is a short fixed line. Everything from *Velvet Pedestal* to *Bobcat Cringe* are accessed via that fixed line. This route is the furthest left in the area.

Gear: Standard Index Rack, bring a #4.

FA: Derek Pearson, Jon Nelson.

Pitch 1–5.9
Start in the blocky corner. Pass an intermediate chain anchor, and continue up a right-leaning crack to some hand jams behind a flake. At the top of the flake, traverse left on the sloping ledge to a 2-bolt anchor.

Pitch 2–5.10a
Walk left past the tree then traverse left on the slab past the bolt. Face climb up the minor roof to a left-trending layback crack, and a 2-bolt anchor on the ledge above.

Pitch 3–5.8
When cleaned, this will rival the classic second pitch. But if dirty, this pitch is not recommendable. Beware of enormous loose flakes.

28 AND SAY 5.12 ★★★

This 5-pitch route starts left and uphill of *Bowling for Biscuits*. It was a new climb in 2015 and may still be dirty in places. The second pitch is splitter.

Gear: Standard Index Rack to #4.

FA: Derek Pearson.

Pitch 1–5.8
Climb the obvious corner to the wide crack finish. May be dirty.

Pitch 2–5.11a
This pitch is money. Begin by climbing on top of a block then make an off-balance move to some hand jams and a stance at the base of the finger crack. Climb the finger crack to some knobs and a tricky crux.

Pitch 3–5.10a
Begin with some easy laybacking from fingers to hand sizes, then finish with a short traverse through two crystal pockets.

Pitch 4–5.12
Hard slab. This pitch may still be a project.

Pitch 5–5.11
This pitch ascends a tips crack to face climbing up the steep wall. May still be a project.

29 BOWLING FOR BISCUITS 5.10D ★★

This two-pitch route is located 30 feet left of *Peanu to Serve You*. If it got cleaned up and climbed more, it'd be three stars for sure.

Bring two ropes to rap, or you may be able to swing back to the first anchor chains to rap the route wit single 60 meter rope.

Gear: Standard Index Rack to #4.

FA: Jon Nelson, Dave Toler, Derek Pearson, Nicola Masciandaro.

Pitch 1–5.10a
Climb a short crack on a pedestal. At the top of the pedestal layback up and right past two bolts to a le below a handcrack. Climb the crack then traverse l to the 2-bolt anchor.

Pitch 2–5.10d
Surmount the roof on the right side on flakes and cracks. Follow the corner to a ledge and 3-bolt bela

30 BOBCAT REALITY PROJECT ★★★

This obvious and imposing roof crack has yet to fin suitor. It certainly isn't low-hanging fruit, but is wo the effort if you can climb Index 5.13. Good luck!

Gear: Standard Index Rack, emphasis on hands and f

³² SOLITUDE 5.11D ★★★

'his five-pitch route is a fairly recent addition to .ookout Point (2011) and is definitely worth the outing.

Gear: Standard Index Rack.

'A: Jon Nelson, Derek Pearson.

'itch 1—5.9
:limb *Peanuts to Serve You (p.225).*

'itch 2—5.10d
:ontinue up the corner, then take the fin-ger-to-handcrack up and left to a 3-bolt belay on nice ledge. Combine with pitch one if rope drag ermits.

'itch 3—5.11d
:limb up right in a wide crack that quickly narrows o fingers. Pass an overlap with a hand pod, continue ft up tips for about 25 feet, then jam straight up to a orested ledge.

'itch 4—5.9
lead up and right through the forest to a cave, and ike the short chimney on the left past two bolts to a omfortable, grassy belay stance below a large corner.

itch 5—5.11a
limb up and right past corners to a final corner back ft. Mantel the ledge, continue up and left, clip a final olt, and dyno for the finish jug!

Jeremy Park finding Solitude.

Ollie looking oily on The Wasp. | Photo by Ryan Hoover.

NEW ROUTE!

Just before we sent this book off to the printer, we caught wind of a brand new route.

The Wasp is a three star 5.10 just left of The Amphibian. It takes gear to 0.5 Camalot and two quickdraws.

FA: Ryan Hoover, Michal Rynkiewicz.

PEANUTS TO SERVE YOU 5.9 ★★★

is is a nice crack climb, an excellent beginner's ıte, and a good opportunity to learn to place gear. ou are pushing your grade with this one, you'll ely want the #5.

ntinuing above this fun pitch is the route *Solitude*. ere is a one star 5.10a variation called *Purple Kool* l (Olsen, Mirande), which traverse right 15 feet to a ping ledge, and then follows a flair back left to the chor.

ar: Doubles of hand-size cams to #3, and a #5 can nice as well.

: Greg Olsen, Jon Nelson.

SOLITUDE 5.11C ★★★

e page 225.

BOBCAT CRINGE 5.12B ★★★★

is is one of the best finger cracks in Washington. It ves like a snake, is completely splitter, and sepaes the walls above and below into black and white k like a yin-yang.

rt as for *Peanuts to Serve You*, then bust right on sy ground to reach a 2-bolt belay. Your best bet is solo this entrance pitch, and clip the anchor for ur first piece. Otherwise, tackle the route in two ches.

arely-done second pitch exists called *He is Truly a eat Airplane*. It's 5.10d, and takes gear to 2".

ar: Single set to #2 if you want to protect the start, ples in tips to finger sizes. A handful of slings and ckdraws.

Terry Lien, Darryl Cramer.

34 CATTALK AND OTHER PROJECTS ★★★

Up and left of the second pitch of *Lookout Point Direct* lie a couple of unsent projects that are rumored to be quite good, steep, and hard 5.12 or 5.13.

35 LOOKOUT POINT DIRECT 5.11A ★★

LPD begins on the trail about 100 feet right of *Bobcat Cringe*, and just left of *House of the 7th Bobcat*. There are a variety of shrubby one star methods to start. None is worth climbing in its own right, but the rest of the route is quality.

Gear: A single rack to 4", nuts, and 6-12 quickdraws and slings.

FA: Derek Pearson, Jeff Mizenko, Jon Nelson.

Pitch 1–5.9

Climb any of the various starts–the bolted mossy slab is probably the best. Climb up and left, passing three bolts. Can be linked with P2.

Pitch 2–5.10b

A 5.10 traverse leads to a 5.9 layback. Continue up a flare/chimney.

Pitch 3–5.11a

Head up a finger to hand-sized crack in a corner, turning into a right-leaning tips crack below an arching roof. The finish is a wild layback in a shallow, right-facing corner.

36 HOUSE OF THE 7TH BOBCAT 5.11D ★★★

This climb starts just right of *Lookout Point Direct*. Often climbed in two pitches, it can also be linked with sparse gear and slings on the first pitch. The first pitch can also be climbed and toproped on its own as a 5.9.

A 70 meter rope might just barely get you to the ground from the top anchor. Watch the rope ends.

Gear: Single rack to 3", doubles in the 0.5" to 1" range. RPs, nuts.

FA: Eric Hirst, Derek Pearson.

Pitch 1–5.9

Start on a short handcrack up a trailside block, then continue up moderate ground to a bolt and a final short splitter. Belay at a comfortable ledge with a chain anchor.

Pitch 2–5.11d

Bouldery tips laybacking (crux) past two closely spaced bolts leads to a rest, followed by 5.10 crack climbing to a chain anchor.

37 BABY TAPIR 5.11A ★★

This route and the following two start in the middle of Lookout Point at some interesting bubbly rock, a slight overhang, and good cracks.

Baby Tapir climbs the leftmost finger crack, through a small roof. It is short, but good. It may be wise to stick clip the first bolt at the low roof.

Gear: Light rack to 1", two quickdraws.

FA: Eric Hirst, Derek Pearson, Jon Nelson.

JON NELSON

GOODNIGHT G: A BOBCAT TALE

ting: Typical boy's bedroom. Late evening. Nightlights illuminate wall posters of The Banana Splits, baby bob-s, Mt. Index, and Jim Whittaker.

ng G– in bed, but awake. His grandfather walks by.

UNG G–I can't sleep grandpa. Please tell me a story.

ANDPA: (Inwardly elated, but not showing it.) OK, but it's gonna be a short one.

UNG G–Will it have mountaineers? I like the ones with mountaineers.

ANDPA: (Now sitting by the bed.) I don't know. It has bobcats. It might also have a mountie.

(Grandpa then starts his story.)

ture three bobcats. Holding handbags, they are walking upright into a bar.

e doors close behind them. They see Ted (Ted Nugent) sitting on a barstool. He briefly glances their way n pipes out to no one in particular:

nph. My housecat is bigger than those guys."

e bobcat in front says: "Nugent, you don't even have a housecat. And get off my stool."

d, gravely insulted and shaking with rage, whips out his blowgun, and takes aim. Time stops. Then suddenly bar doors fly open and Brad Driscol with a badge appears.

t down that blowgun Mr. Ted Nugent."

body moves a muscle. Then, the second bobcat steps forward, holds up a paw, pans the room, and sets down bag. The other two follow his lead, putting down their bags. They simultaneously pull out very large horns. ne chuckles come from the far stools.

a sound emerges, a crescendoing sound both mesmerizing and antagonizing, that soon sends everyone o a mass panic attack. Pandemonium all over the place. But before anyone realizes what was happening, a ge earthquake levels the entire bar, burying everyone. (At this point *young* G– interrupts.)

UNG G–Hey! That's too short.

ANDPA: (Feigning dissapointment.) Do I look like I'm done?

UNG G–Was Mr. Ted, Ted Nugent a mountaineer?

ANDPA: I don't know. Some might think so.

UNG G–How about Brad Driscol?

ANDPA: Nobody knows. Now pipe down, let me finish the story. (Grandpa continues his story.)

ew weeks later, while digging through the rubble, someone discovers a manuscript. The thing goes viral, and on the "Bobcat Manifesto (tm)" takes the whole world by storm. Translated into all languages, everyone starts ding it. The book, though, cast a slow-evolving spell on each reader. An errant whisker would appear here, a all patch of hair there, ears would get a little more pointed, the eyes a little more golden.

ll happened so slowly as to be nearly imperceptible. But there was no mistaking it: the manifesto was gradu- y turning Earth-people into upright, tuft-eared bobcats.

ns pass. A small spaceship lands. Aliens emerge from their ship to find very large bobcats, who they imme- tely attempt to destroy by blasting Ted Nugent Comes Alive (c) through humungous holographic horns. ndemonium ensues. Yet the bobcat people actually seem to be enjoying the sounds. Sensing danger, the ens start to escape. But just as they are taking off, rogue members of a different race of aliens, who had been biting a safe distance away, blasts the Earth to smithereens with their giant moon-shooting blowgun.

rth rubble spreads far and wide through space in all directions.

UNG G– (As wide awake as ever.) Is that the end?

ANDPA: It is for now. Goodnight Greg. (Pats him on the head, gets up, and leaves the room.)

The End

Logan Fusso goofing his way up An Act of Strange Boar (5.10C

38 AN ACT OF STRANGE BOAR 5.10C ★★★★

An Act of Strange Boar climbs up the blocky bubbly rock just right of *Baby Tapir*, to an obvious finger crack in a curving slot.

This is really a 4-pitch route, and a very good one at that. All four pitches are fantastic, and all but the final pitch (5.12a) are under 5.11.

Technically, the route's full name is a paragraph long, as Jon Nelson et al saw to it that each pitch would have its own bizarre appelation. For the sake of convenience, we're calling it *An Act of Strange Boar*, and listing it as 5.10c. Get on it, enjoy it, and climb the whole thing if you can handle *The Hatch*...

Gear: Doubles or triples to .5, single rack to #2, RPs, draws and runners

FA: Derek Pearson, Carolyn Marquardt, Eric Hirst, & Jon Nelson.

Pitch 1–5.10c

This is an excellent pitch, quite reminiscent of *Slow Children*. Climb easy terrain up to the obvious V-slot, and then ascend through an overlap to chains above.

It is possible to link P1 and P2 without much rope drag if you find yourself at this anchor with plenty of gear.

Pitch 2–5.9

Another nice pitch of crack climbing, much easier than the first. Continue straight up, climbing cracks and stemming to a 2-bolt anchor on a small ledge. This pitch is called A *Group of Mysteries of French Women*.

Pitch 3–5.10c

A *Ship Called Black Rock* is an excellent and devious pitch–completely safe, but a bit more psychologically engaging than the average sew-up.

From the anchor of P2, scramble up and right to a good stance at the base of a clean left-leaning dihedral. Move the belay here, and then climb your way up the cool dihedral with some thought provoking moves and gear placements.

Pitch 4–5.12a

Traverse left along the forested ledge until you see the obvious bolt line right of a large roof/dihedral.

Climb through those bolts to the start of an impressive left-diagonaling crack. Getting established in the crack is the crux, but it stays with you the whole way. Continue left, groping for slopers and bad footholds, until the splitter handcrack finish. Either rap the route, or walk off Lookout Point via the access trail.

This pitch may be easier for taller climbers.

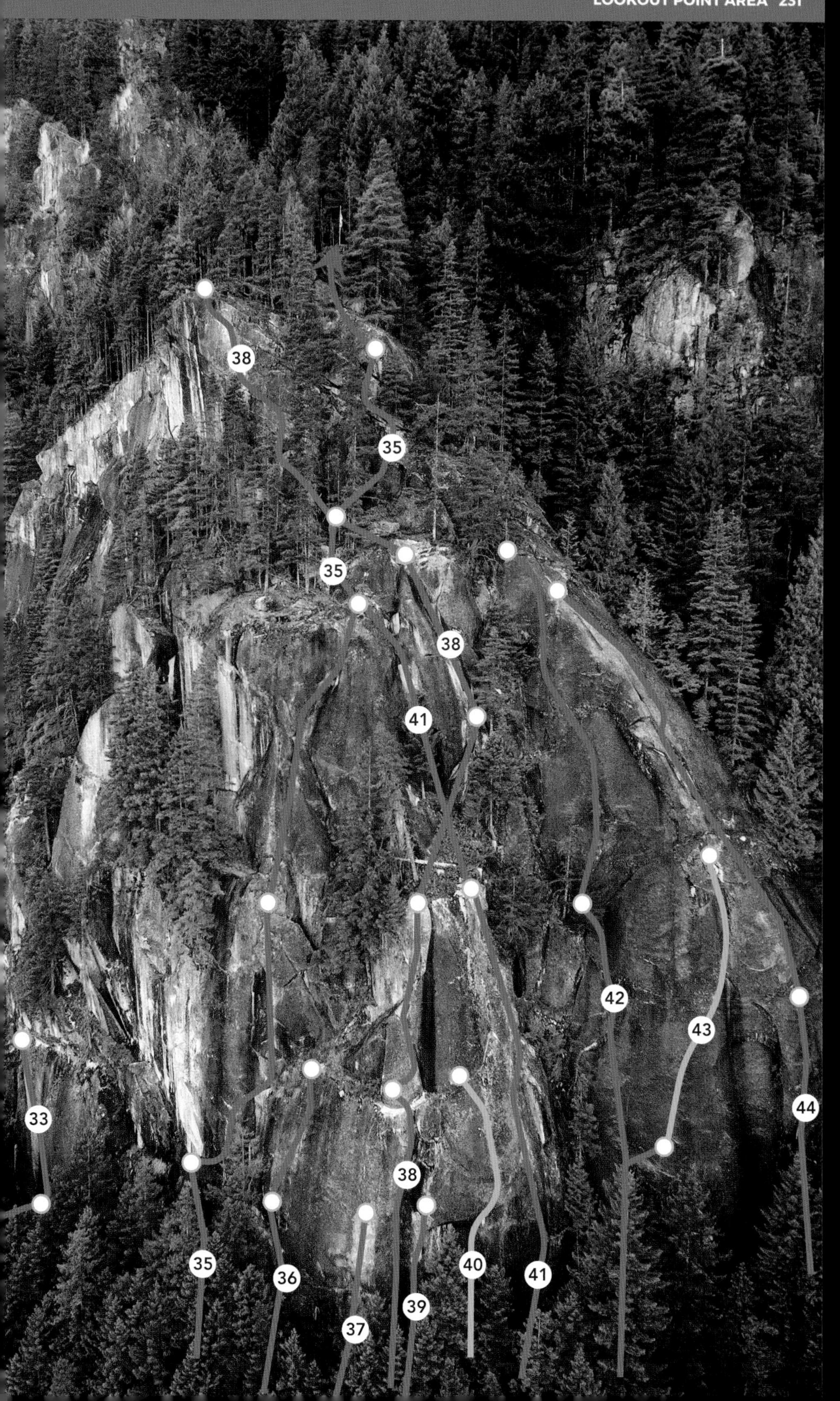
38
35
35
38
41
33
42
43
44
35
36
37
38
39
40
41

39 RICE KRISPIES 5.10B ★★★

This route climbs the flake just right of *Strange Boar*, sharing its start. The flake is somewhat hollow, and may give pause to leaders likely to fall. Place the gear as deep as you can (without losing it).

An even better variation called *Pork Fried Rice* (5.10c) continues past the anchors to rejoin *Act of Strange Boar* at its anchor.

Gear: *Cams to 3", including thin cams for the start.*

FA: Jon Nelson, Mark McKillup.

40 SPIT 5.11D ★★★

Right of *Act of Strange Boar* and *Rice Krispies*, it is possible to scramble up and right to the base of a bolted face beneath a roof.

Climb up to the roof (crux), clip the bolt above it, then traverse right till you can surmount it on the right side. Clip another bolt (watch for drag), and continue up and left to the anchor.

Good hardware, but could use a scrubbing. Don't let the vegetated start deter you—this is an excellent climb. The crux is short, and can be aided at C0 to make the rest of the climb a nice 5.10 slab.

Gear: *Quickdraws, and a few runners.*

FA: Erik Thixton, Greg Olsen, Steve Strong, Tom Michael.

41 LAW AND ORDER 5.10A ★★★

This route starts just right of *Spit*, and is very good. Don't be deterred by the dirty start.

Gear: *Nuts and cams to 2", 5-6 quickdraws for bolts.*

FA: Jeff Kelley, Matt Arksey.

Pitch 1—5.10a

Face climbing on large holds leads to a bolt-protected, left-facing corner. About 30 feet up, the corner system splits into two. The left corner is 5.10a, the right corner is 5.9. Where the corners merge, continue up a slot to the top of the pedestal with a three bolt anchor and chains.

Pitch 2—5.9

Continue up the next corner on the left. It is fun climbing, but may be dirty. As an alternative, you can climb the pitch to the right, which is the third pitch of *An Act of Strange Boar* (5.10c).

42 THE DUKES OF STRATOSPHERE 5.11D ★★★

The Cramer guide called this the best multi-pitch route at Lookout Point. It has since fallen into obscurity, and is currently difficult to recommend due to vegetation and poor hardware. A great candidate for an upgrade.

Begin on the far right side of Lookout Point above the trail between Private Idaho and Hag Crag. It is the furthest left line in that immediate area. Look for trees choking the starting crack above an aging bolt.

Gear: *Standard Index Rack.*

FA: Jeff Kelly, Matt Arksey.

Pitch 1—5.11b

Climb the corner with a crack that peters out past five bolts. Keep climbing up and left (out right is *Barking Bobcat*), to an anchor on a ledge.

Some of the bolts may be slightly challenging to clip as the climbing does not follow them precisely.

Pitch 2—5.11d

Difficult moves arrive right off the bat as you pass two bolts headed right. The crux comes at three closely spaced bolts. Easier climbing brings you to the top.

43 THE BARKING BOBCAT 5.11A ★★★

This is an excellent pitch linking *Dukes* with *Steel Pulse*. Start up *Dukes*, then bust right at the fifth bolt to a 2-bolt anchor. Belay here, or continue upwards passing five more bolts and a right-facing corner with a killer finger crack to a 2-bolt anchor. As of September 2016, it sorely needed new hardware just like *Dukes*. From the anchor, it is easy to join *Steel Pulse*.

Gear: *A couple pieces from 1"-1.5" and quickdraws.*

FA: Darryl Cramer, Erik Thixton.

TEEL PULSE 5.10C ★★★

riety of options for the start are mostly dirty and The best is a steep handcrack through a bulge off ground that gains the bolt line. The first pitch is y but is still climbable and enjoyable. The climbing ve is classic 5.10 Index slab.

r: *Standard Index Rack.*

Jeff Kelly, Dan Klimke, Gary Buckham. FFA: Jeff y, Jeff Boucher, Matt Arksey.

ch 1–5.10b

best start is to climb up to a short roof and pass bolts trending right. Continue past three more s to a right-facing corner, then another bolt to anchor. Supplement bolts with gear. If the first 20 look dirty don't be deterred, the rest of the route 's clean.

ch 2–5.10a

s short pitch has a dirty, bolted slab crossing, with 10a move.

ch 3–5.10c

nb the groove to the top. This pitch once was rath- unout, but some recent bolts have made it a little re friendly for the budding 5.10 climber.

BAD REPUTATION / BONE DADDY 5.11A ★

nill of *Steel Pulse* are two rarely done and not very active climbs: *Bad Reputation*, and *Bone Daddy*. h are 5.11a and require significant cleaning. Both the same FA team.

ır: *Standard Index Rack.*

Jeff Kelly, Matt Arksey.

PRIVATE IDAHO

If 5.10 is a little above your head, you are looking to break into crack climbing with some lower grades, or you just want to do some fantastic moderates, Private Idaho is the crag for you. While there are not a ton of routes here, there is a good concentration of high quality crack climbs under 5.10. Most are well protected, clean, and excellent.

Approach: Take the Lookout Point trail, veering right at the first branch, and right again at the second branch. The first routes you encounter are difficult to comprehend, and exceptionally mungey. Just a touch further are the money pitches.

Descent: All routes can be climbed with a single 70.

46 BRAD DRISCOLL, ET AL. 5.11C ★

There are a few routes left of *Top A Shader* which barely justify noting. They are short, desperate slab climbs which have long ago been reclaimed by the forest.

These are *Brad Driscoll Outnumbered His Guests, but a Good Time Was Had by All* (5.10d); *Three Trucks Stacked on Top of Each Other* (5.11c); and *Tea Bag* (5.12d).

According to Greg Child, "By stacking the syllables on top of each other, the first ascentionists found they could bypass the crux entirely."

According to Jon Nelson, regarding the recommended rack: "Doesn't matter, nobody does the route anyway." And regarding the first ascentionists, "There were four first ascentionists, though it is possible that it has been climbed less than four times."

While the commentary is certainly four stars, we can't in good faith give these routes more than one.

Gear: *Doesn't matter.*

FA: Greg Olsen, Jon Nelson, Duck Novikoff, Rob Knudson.

47 I AM IN TOP A SHADER 5.11C ★★★★

This climb is exceptional. The slab moves to access the crack are difficult, mind-blowing, awesome and quintessentially Index. Just when you think you're on the best slab climb ever, the wall kicks back with an incredible finger crack. Bring a full toolbox of tricks for this super-classic pitch.

Worthy of an honest ground-up attempt, but one can also easily set up a toprope by traversing along the fixed chain below the *Bobcat Cringe* area. What the name means, not even Jon Nelson knows (literally, we asked him).

Gear: *3-4 quickdraws, 3-4 runners, an assortment of nuts and doubles of cams from purple TCU to 0.4. Single 0.5.*

FA: Jon Nelson, Darryl Cramer.

Chris Kalman, through the crux and entering the... crux. I Am in Top A Shader (5.11c)

BECKEY-STANLEY 5.11B ★★★

imb to the fourth bolt on 900 *Oil Stricken Water-wl*, then traverse hard left passing three more bolts. nish on the excellent upper finger crack of *Top A ader*.

ear: About 10 draws and runners, and finger size gear.

: Darryl Cramer Beckey, Jon Nelson Stanley.

BRAVE THE SUPPRESSED LAUGHTER OF THE TWEENY MAID 5.11B ★★

gin on the first four bolts of *900 Oil Stricken aterfowl*, then head left on *Beckey-Stanley*. After ree more bolts and a crux, head straight up a short, ft-facing corner. Not as good as the finger crack nish of *Beckey-Stanley*.

ear: Quickdraws and an optional medium-sized nut the corner.

: Tom Michael, Jon Nelson.

900 OIL STRICKEN WATERFOWL TAKEN TO OCEAN SHORES 5.10C ★★★

art up the bolts right of *Top A Shader* on a slight edestal. Ascend past four bolts, and a small ght-facing flake, to a steep, sustained, bolted head-all. three stars when clean.

ear: Five quickdraws, a #3 for the flake, and small uts.

: Greg Olsen, Jon Nelson.

51 THE PRAIRIE FIRE THAT WANDERS 5.10D ★★

Commence up the shallow corner just right of *900 Oil Stricken Waterfowl*.

Clip a bolt over the left side of the roof, then layback the left side (crux). Pull a small bulge, then continue up face and crack features to a nice finger crack, which ends at a large ledge.

Gear: Standard Index Rack.

FA: Jon Nelson.

52 IMAGINE YOUR BEST STUDENT HERE 5.11A ★★

Starts as per *Prairie Fire*, but moves right around the hanging pillar. Tricky slab moves past the roof provide a crux before the anchors.

Gear: A couple small cams, five quickdraws.

FA: Darryl Cramer, Jeff Walker, Greg Olsen.

53 SHORT AND STUPID / FISHING NET 5.8 ★

Just right of *Prairie Fire* is a scruffy right-facing corner. To climb that corner is, as the name suggests, *Short and Stupid*.

Conversely, to head hard left traversing through all the other routes and finishing at the anchor for *Tweeny Maid*, is to cast a *Fishing Net Large Enough to Swallow the Statue of Liberty*.

Both routes are possible, neither is recommendable.

Gear: Standard Index Rack.

FA: Darryl Cramer, Greg Olsen.

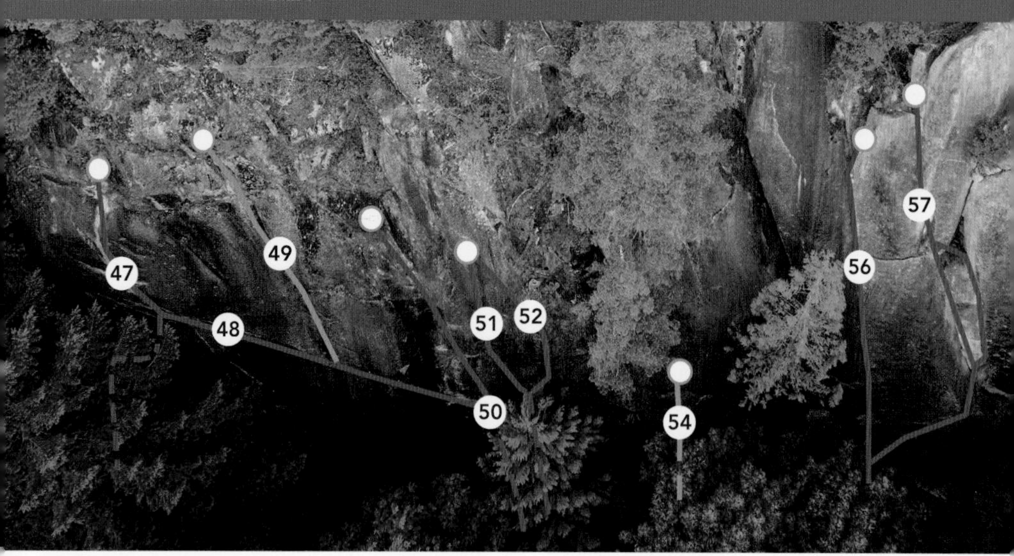

54 ERASERHEAD 5.11B ★★★

This route goes up the short, bolted, shallow groove in the middle of the wall. Hard if you're short, hard if you're tall.

Eraserhead is a much better route than it would appear–though it is currently protected by 1/4 inch SMC bolts. Expect fantastic friction slab climbing, with a contemplative crux.

Welcome to Index 5.11b, boys and girls.

Gear: *Four quickdraws.*

FA: Greg Collum, Dan Cauthorn.

55 UNNAMED 7 5.7 ★★

Just next to the obvious left-facing corner of *Wet Dream* is a dirty vegetated series of ramps that goes at 5.7. If these were cleaned up, and climbed often, they would be a worthwhile addition to the cliff. May need tat or new bolts for anchor.

Gear: *Standard Index Rack.*

FA: Unknown.

56 WET DREAM 5.9+ ★★★

This route is a fun and sustained splitter, but it does not climb like a straight-in crack. It helps to have some crack trickery for this one. Still, it is easily aidable, and fun to climb. As the name would imply, i can be slippery.

Gear: *Single set of cams up to #1, doubles #1-3.*

FA: Tish Nakaya, Jon Fisk.

57 CURIOUS POSES / MAGIC FERN 5.10D ★★

These two routes begin just right of *Wet Dream* on t thin crack that angles up and right through the face and into a corner.

Climb the corner to a ledge. Belay here, or continue upwards if drag permits.

Curious Poses is the thin crack on the left side of the arête. *Magic Fern* is the wide crack on the right belo the ledge. After the ledge, *CP* goes right through a roof while *MF* goes left through a cruxy hand jam. Either variation is good, both share an anchor.

Gear: *Double set of cams, 5-10 slings and draws.*

FA: Cal Folsom, Dave Anderson, Don Brooks.

58 ISTANBUL 5.9 ★

This short steep dirty offwidth crack goes up just lef of *Wild Turkey*, and *Battered Sandwich*. It is rarely climbed.

Gear: *Gear to 5".*

FA: Cal Folsom, Don Brooks.

59 WILD TURKEY 5.7 ★★★

This recently cleaned and renovated route is an exce lent addition to the crag. Climb the widening crack i the corner to an anchor. Stop here, or continue right and up the finish for *Battered Sandwich*.

Gear: *Cams to 5". Double up in mid sizes for Battered's finish.*

FA: Cal Folsom, Don Brooks.

BATTERED SANDWICH 5.9 ★★★★

his route is unique, fun, interesting, and may feel a it stiff for the grade if you are not used to offwidth/ queeze trickery. Not a bad training pitch for those osemite squeeze-flares.

ote: Shares anchors with *Senior Citizens in Space*, ut uses a directional bolt to keep the rope in a good osition, bring an extra long sling for this purpose.

ear: Two #3s, two #4s, and a #5 will not go unused you are climbing at your limit. Otherwise a Standard ıdex Rack is fine.

A: Ed Gibson, Steve Barnett; FFA: Lindi McIlwaine, ale Nelson.

61 I CAN SEE YOUR HOUSE FROM HERE 5.12+ ★★★

This was a project for some time, but was finally freed by Brent Kertzmann in 1998. It appears quite despa-rate, and probably could use new bolts. If the bolts are shiny when you see this pitch, climb it right away! It's sure to be good.

Gear: 10-12 quickdraws ought to do.

FA: Greg Olsen, Greg Collum (TR); FFA: Brent Kertz-mann.

62 SENIOR CITIZENS IN SPACE 5.7+ ★★★★

See page 239.

63 SPINELESS 5.11A ★★★★

This bolted route just right of *Senior Citizens* is a fantastic Gritstone-esque arête on very sticky rock. Place a premium on balance and technique, and enjoy! Some may wish to pre-hang draws on the route from *Senior Citizens*... a clip near the crux is hard to reach if you are short.

Right of Spineless are two low-quality forest routes that have probably never been repeated (*Noodle* 5.11a, Cramer,Baird; and *Little Buttress* 5.11a, Olsen,Cram-er,Baird). To identify them, alone, would be a feat.

Gear: About 10 quickdraws.

FA: Greg Collum, Greg Olsen.

HAG CRAG

Hag Crag is the slabby wall just beyond (east of) Private Idaho. Some very nice routes will appear here once regular traffic cleans them up. For now, there is a fantastic 5.6 crack that is clean and safe to lead, and which deserves a lot more attention from beginning climbers.

Approach: Just past Private Idaho, continue along the trail a short way to this wall.

Descent: Everything can be done with a 60.

64 END RUN — 5.10A ★★

When you first approach Hag Crag you may notice a couple bolt hangers poking out of thick moss. These are routes.

Without moss they are certainly worth climbing. *End Run* starts the furthest left, traversing hard right at the start into a bolted slab.

Gear: *Quickdraws.*

FA: Don Brooks, Chris Syrjala.

65 RUN-IN — 5.11D ★★

This is the direct start to *End Run*. The first couple clips are very difficult.

Gear: *A single 1" piece at the start of the crack is helpful, otherwise quickdraws.*

FA: Greg Olsen, Darryl Cramer, Jeff Baird, Susan Cordery.

66 ON THE REBOUND — 5.10A ★★

Hag Crag is split by an impressive widening crack. This crack is accessed either via *Run-In*, or by climbing the start of *Regular Route*, and reaching around left (crux) as soon as possible to step up on the slab. Bring your big cams.

Gear: *Cams to 6".*

FA: Jon Nelson, Dan Lapeska.

67 REGULAR ROUTE — 5.7 ★

RR climbs the cool, roofed right-facing corner beneath *On the Rebound*. If cleaned up, it would be a nice beginner trad lead to complement *Hag Crack*.

It may need a new anchor, and probably needs cleaning.

A variation (*Telephone and Rubber Band*, 5.10a, Crame Olsen) exists to avoid the dirty finish, traversing har right on bolts.

There is also a bolted A0 going up directly to the sta of *Telephone*.

Gear: *Cams to 4".*

FA: Unknown.

68 FREE CAT — 5.10D ★★

The bolted slab just left of *Hag Crack* is really good climbing, and worth cleaning up if it's dirty.

FA: Greg Olsen, Darryl Cramer.

69 HAG CRACK — 5.6 ★★★

An excellent first trad lead, and one of the easiest routes at Index. It is low-angle, so pine duff can tend to clog up some parts of the crack. Still, if this route got climbed regularly, and cleaned as regularly, it would be a four star classic. Just imagine it in Leavenworth.

Gear: *Double set of cams from purple TCU to .5, a rack of nuts.*

⑥② SENIOR CITIZENS IN SPACE 5.7+ ★★★★

This is the one of the best routes at Private Idaho, and possibly the best 5.7 at Index.

Around the corner from the arching offwidth slot of *Battered Sandwhich* lies this incredible V-slot with a crack in the corner, and one on the left wall. Stem jam, and layback your way to the top (save some small cams for up here). This is a great route to learn to place gear on, and an awesome first trad lead.

Gear: Doubles from .3 to #1, possibly a single #2.

FA: Peter and David Gunstone.

Young Zen getting council from the elders on Senior Citizens In Space (5.8). | Photo by Chris Kalman

Michal Rynkewicz bears down on Spooner (5.11d)

MICHAL RYNKIEWICZ

THE BIRTH OF THE AMPHIBIAN

"*Inclination of direction, walk the turned and twisted rift*
With the children of creation futuristic dreams we sift
Clutching violently we whisper with a liquefying cry
Any deadly final answers that are surely doomed to die"

Black Sabbath wails through my scrappy Honda CRV speakers as I cross the bridge over the North Fork of the Skykomish for the umpteenth time. A familiar view brings a smile to my face. Slug, Falcon, Salmon, Shrew all call this place home. Although I am not a true local of the valley, still, every time I leave Index I am thinking of Index. The amount of climbable featured stone is sacred. In the past three years I have been fortunate enough to indulge in the untouched granite delicacies that are as fresh as the huckleberries that bless the trails.

After climbing the same timeless classics year after year, the realization of potential awakened one rainy afternoon at *Rattletail*. A sleek prow left of the main wall begged to be climbed. Drill? Check. Brush? Check. Bolts? Check. Hoppy beverage? Of course, check. I am greeted by a Salamander at the base of the prow. She grants me access to establish the route. Like a squab, I feed from what Index has provided. Bass frequencies and flute notes open my eyes. So The Amphibian was born.

***

One may think Index only provides rock, but its yield is much deeper. Chanterelle, Boletus, Oyster Mushroom, Cauliflower Mushroom all feed off the fertile forest groves. But one shall not shrug off the flow of the North Fork. Just like the Salmon I appreciate the melt of the high peaks.

Like the glow of a small squirrel discovering a field of acorns, the upper wall shown most bright. Granite, Quartzite, Calcite, Epidote minerals grow on the vertical walls, hidden for years. Earth Mother blesses Index. The Autumn leaves weave their ways through the fractal trees. Another season passes.

Happiness, Sadness, Darkness, Light. Croak, croak the frog's words resonate. The fortress crumbles. Index, Index, I thank you.

ALPHABETICAL

SYMBOLS

A

B

C

D

E

F

G

T

U

V

W

Y

Z

BY GRADE

5.6

5.7

5.8

5.9

5.10

5.11

5.12

5.13

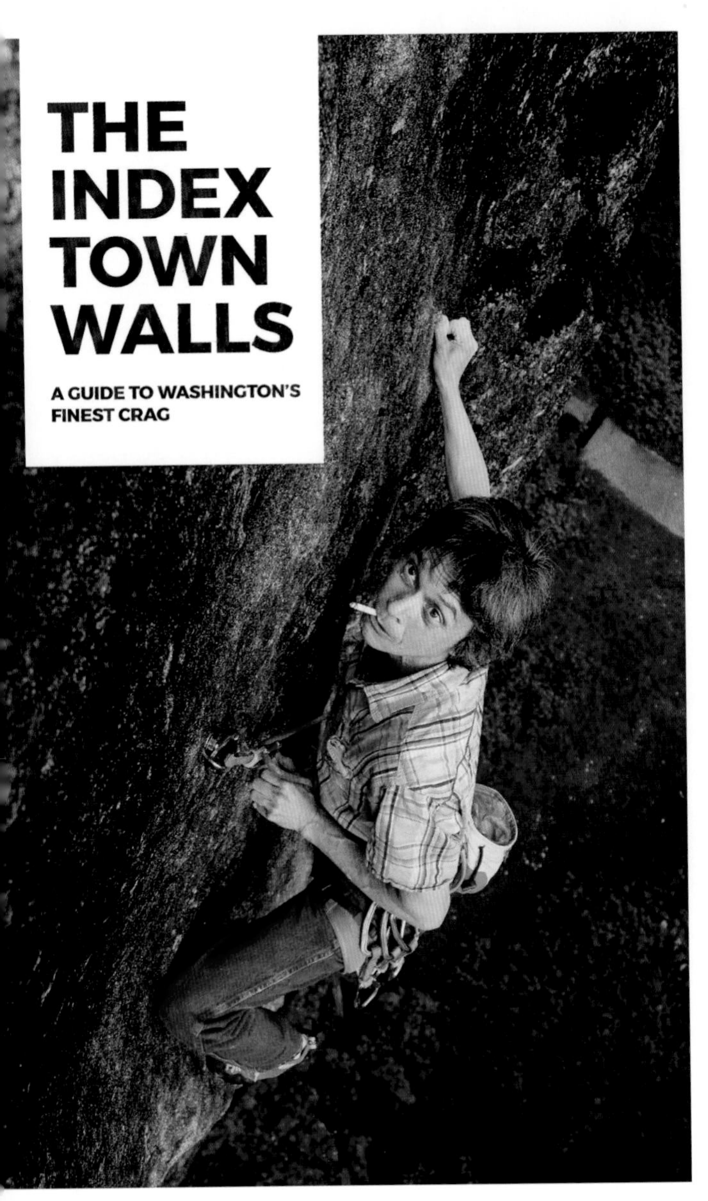
THE INDEX TOWN WALLS
A GUIDE TO WASHINGTON'S FINEST CRAG

In a world where climbing has become increasingly commercialized (we know, we know, the irony of saying so in a new guidebook does not escape us), Index remains a shining beacon of hope for the subversive counter-culture that the sport once was. Its less-flashy, less-sexy, less-hipster vibe is part of what makes the place special. It was with this in mind that we wanted to put out a limited release book with a uniquely "Index" cover... something that really caught the feeling of the place as it truly is: a locals-only inside joke that most people simply won't get, and some might find downright repellent.

Hence, the Mike Massey cover. For those of you who frequent Index, you've likely seen him floating Wham (5.11c) in The Country countless times, only to return to the ground, casually light up a smoke (Marlboro Light Menthol, to be specific), and embark on an enduro belay for whatever poor soul tries to follow in his graceful footsteps. Massey is true blue Index—a dyed in the wool local who has been climbing there for decades. We appreciate him letting Matty capture this incredible moment for the camera.

The other cover image—Stamati
Anagnostou on a flash attempt
of Bobcat Cringe—really speaks
for itself. Everything about BC is
superlative: best finger crack in
Washington, best pitch at Lookout Point, and one of the finest
5.12b (may be soft for the grade)
at Index. The colors are right, the
ocus is (as it should be) on the
stone itself, and Stamati's hair is
awesome. What more could you
want in a cover shot? Even the
name—Bobcat Cringe—invokes
he unique and peculiar Index
rope of the "Bobcat", which
learly played an important role
n the evolving mythology and
reation story of Index Climb-
ng for early Indexans such as
on Nelson, Greg Olsen, Darryl
Cramer, and Terry Lien.

We hope you enjoy BOTH covers!
f you can't find the one you want
n stores, try Sharp End directly
online at stores.sharpendbooks.
om. They may still have what
ou're looking for!

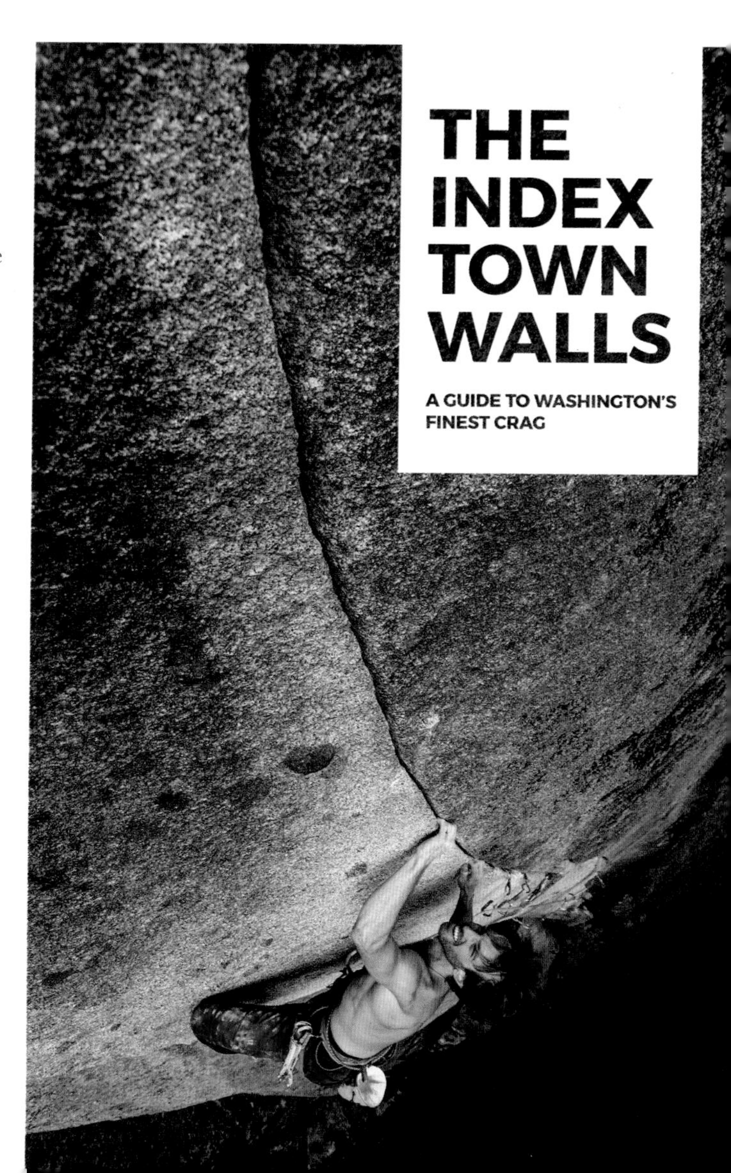
THE INDEX TOWN WALLS
A GUIDE TO WASHINGTON'S FINEST CRAG

Jenny Abegg approaching light speed on The Starfish Enterprise. | Photo by Scott Rinckenberger

MATTY VAN BIENE

Matty is a student of Nature. He enjoys the forests, the rivers, and the mountains. He appreciates all beings and wishes everyone could experience something similar to the freedom and joy that climbing the upper wall gives to him.

CHRIS KALMAN

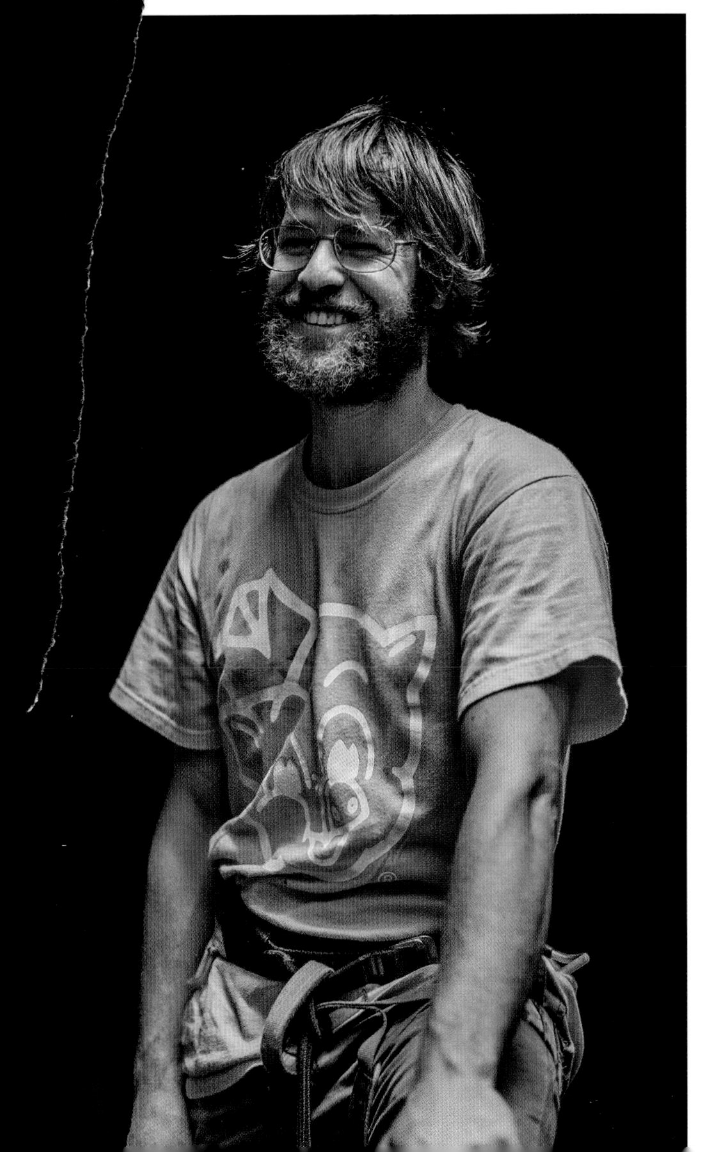

Chris Kalman is a writer and climber who used to live in the Pacific Northwest, and misses it every day. He is well-known for telling unsuspecting strangers from all corners of the globe about how Index is the best crag not just on the planet, but in the universe. His writing has appeared in Alpinist, Climbing, and Rock and Ice magazines, and online at Adventure Journal and other media outlets. You can see more examples of Chris' work at www.chriskalman.com.

ATTACK OF
By Jessica Campbell